# Landscapes of the Psyche

## Sandplay in Jungian Analysis

**Paolo Aite**

English Translation by Robert W. Mann

**IPOC**
**www.ipocpress.com**

IPOC di Pietro Condemi
3, Via Maddalena
I - 20122 Milano
Ph.: +39-0236569954
Fax.: +39-0236569954
ipoc@ipocpress.com

Original title: *Paesaggi della psiche Il gioco della sabbia nell'analisi junghiana*
First edition: July 2002
Publisher: Bollati Boringhieri Editore Turin Italy

Translated by Robert W. Mann
The moral rights of the translator has been asserted

Printed in the United States and the United Kingdom on acid-free paper

ISBN: 978-88-95145-13-6

Front cover: A sand-scene (part)

**PLEASE NOTE: This book contains only the text portion of the complete work. Photographs of the sandplay scenes described herein are available in paperback format (ISBN 978-88-95145-12-9), which may be ordered separately from your bookseller or internet book shop. Alternatively, a mini-CD containing the images (ISBN 978-88-95145-15-0) is available from www.ipocpress.com**

*For Livia, my companion in life and in study*

# Contents

# Introduction

*A man sets out to draw the world. As the years go by, he fills a space with images of provinces, kingdoms, mountains, bays, ships, islands, fish, houses, instruments, stars, horses and people. Just before he dies, he discovers that his patient labyrinth of lines traces the image of his face.* J.L.Borges (1960, p. 71, 73)

Building small worlds out of sand, natural elements, houses, humans and animals in miniature, is a way children spontaneously deal with their emotions while playing. The new approach that informs the following pages is the result of thirty years of experience in using sandplay in the analysis of adults, as well.

The "landscapes of the psyche," the sand scenes created by the men and women I've worked with in analysis over the years, made it possible for me to see how the psyche operates from a different point of view. The successes and failures we meet with in the setbacks and encounters in life have uncovered a field of enormous possibilities both for therapy and research.

Dreams have always caught man's attention, because through them we perceive the mysterious world we call the psyche. Playing, as a way of dreaming through physical objects, is essential to the growing process. So why not apply this possibility of communicating with the psyche to adults, as well?

Hidden in the dreams, the fantasies and representations of sandplay, in which our emotions are "staged" as images, is a secret, an unexpected potentiality. In their work analysts see how sometimes, with the appearance of representations that go to make up the dream world, fantasies or play, a force is set into motion that can radically change the life of an individual and open new horizons in his way of thinking.

Man has always distinguished between "little" and "big" dreams. Some dreams and fantasies tend to compensate frustration, but in the end they lead the individual to lose contact with the changing world. Other dreams, instead, are so powerful they leave a mark that lasts a lifetime. Likewise, fantasies appear in which a body of still indistinct perceptions and emotions is suddenly organized anew. This particular imagery can open up new paths.

The history of human "progress" itself shows that the highest achievements of scientific and artistic thought were first expressed in the images, in the dreams or fantasies of creative minds.

### *First Questions*

What determines this transformational power? Can it be called upon to treat the psyche? The representation it gives birth to seems, in fact, to speak of the mysterious depths from which it emerges: it "stages" and organizes in the presence of consciousness an indistinct, sometimes violent movement in those psychic forces which we call emotions or feelings.

Is the visibility obtained through fantastic representation a message that paves the way to knowledge? How does it affect the seething and unconscious melting-pot that threatens consciousness? Can the resulting form alter the individual's usual responses?

Questions that interact and cross-refer; but the analyst also wonders "how," "where" and "when" the transformational power of the representation can be brought about.

In this way, a new, largely unexplored horizon opens up. Our answers are still incomplete, barely sketched, though analytic research has, from the start, covered the ground in which dreams take shape. More than a hundred years after the publication of *The Interpretation of Dreams* by Sigmund Freud, whom everyone admits was the first to enable us to enter this world at once so near-at-hand and so different and difficult to understand, the problem looms larger than ever.

## *The Jungian Approach*

The territory we have entered, the territory of dreams and fantasies, is constantly active, not unlike organic metabolism. In this intense, never-ending activity, going on day and night, emotions change into feelings, sentiments and thinking which alter our relationship to the world.[1] Emotion, construed as energy in motion rooted in corporeal experience, only gradually becomes a representation on the stage of our inner theater.[2]

According to Jung, it is in this change that the transformational mystery of the symbolic process is concealed.

My point of view is that emotions are considered libidinal pressures that tend to integrate into representations, where perception and emotion, the real world and imagination meet, modifying the individual's ability to respond. In the beginning, the feelings, which are already the result of this integration, produce previsual sensations, ultimately reaching, in a more advanced phase of visibility, the perception of "things" seen in one's inner theater or "staged" in the process of playing.

[1] I differentiate here between the terms "emotion," "feeling" and "sentiment." By *emotion* I mean libidinal energy rooted in corporeal experience and as yet lacking form on a conscious level. *Feeling* indicates a more evolved organization of this same energy, which takes on a recognizable form, one that can be used for adaptation. *Sentiment*, which is the highest level of the same process available to the ego, the level of a rational faculty that includes, modifies and gives direction to our ability to respond to the environment. This differentiation of terms shows how emotion is already a certain way of reading the world, of behaving towards things, which can evolve into sentiment. Not a physiological disorder, therefore, but an organized attitude that makes it possible to escape something which at the moment is otherwise unbearable. In Chapter XI I go into this differentiation in the light of Jung's theory of feeling-toned complexes.

[2] Mental representation is here construed as the unconscious organizational structure of psychic life. It's a cliché, as we shall also see in Chapter IV, to lump the concepts of representation, imagination and image together with "vision," ignoring the fact that it is merely a preliminary organization of experience, a disposition to "see" something which only at a certain moment can gain access to visibility. On the vicissitudes of the concept of mental representation, which with different inflexions runs through the entire body of analytic research, see Bordi (1998, p, 27).

The assumption that is central to these pages is that the attained imaginal visibility of a feeling is a crucial step towards the possibility of handling those forces at work in the unconscious, interfering with set balances. Therefore the imaginal experience met with in dreams and daydreams, as in the sandplay described here, represents a higher level in a process which is remote in origin. This process is comparable to a new symbolic integration of the initial energy, which modifies the responses of consciousness.

The primary matrix of this "working" of the psyche, of this metabolism of emotions, is found in corporeal experience. Under the stimulus of emotions, a process takes place which, from the earliest stages of life, organizes sensations into perceptions. Analytic research shows that body experience is where imagination is first staged, where emotional life begins to take shape.[3] In an early stage, the integration of visibility still needs space and concrete objects for organizing experience. I consider sandplay a return to that level of representation: a way of evoking, or better, provoking, the transition to the visibility of active emotions in the analytic field, but which the shared speech does not yet reveal. Only subsequently, thanks to a process of transposition, do those emotions reach the level of words, both in verbal exchange and in the act of interpretation.

## *The Potentialities of Play Activities*

Using sandplay in analyzing adults is the result of a lengthy process of analytic thinking. The body, long considered a mere carrier of "acting-out" or discharges of desire, has for analysts become more and more the place where the elaboration of primary fantasies takes place.

Among physical activities, playing seems to be the one laden with the greatest imaginal experience, and considered therefore a privileged channel for reaching the emotional world of children. Play, in the way it confronts deep emotions, has often been used as a metaphor of analytic work with adults, but never actually used with adults in the way outlined in these pages.

[3] I'm thinking mostly of Winnicott (1971), Anzieu (1989), Sami Ali (1974) and Gaddini (1982).

Intellectual conquests often take place by stages: using play in analyzing adults, as a way of distinguishing and elaborating emotions, was the last step in a long process. The sandplay approach, in fact, excites great interest but also great deal of uncertainties. It is considered one of many imaginative techniques for translating into images the emotional tension which words are unable to express, but of dubious application in the analytic field.[4]

We know, in fact, that the corporeal immediacy of experience can bring about an activation of interpersonal emotions and impede conscious elaboration, which is the main purpose of all analytic work. So to suggest using sandplay in analysis, and what's more with adults, understandably raises many questions.

In considering pathological disorders, I have always shared the common impression that in people who suffer, there is an overloading of images. So why should more images, in addition to the ones that already overburden the individual, be stimulated by play?

Italo Calvino (1988, p. 91) asked the question:

> Will the power of evoking images in absence continue to develop in a human race constantly flooded by a deluge of prefabricated images?

Words that suggest an important difference. As is frequently observed, before the explosion of a clear psychic disorder, the individual manifests recurring and recognizable attitudes which are the expression of widely-shared "prefabricated images." Mass communication, with its deep ability of persuasion, can create needs and generate predisposed responses. The power that must be saved, mentioned by Calvino, is the power of invention and planning, which in

[4] I'm referring to the various imaginative techniques used today in "art therapy," such as drawing, dance therapy, in which the corporeal symbolization of emotions and feelings is used for attaining psychic knowledge and transformation. A comparative examination of these different approaches has not yet been made for understanding the terms, the risks, as well as the advantages, of each, and to study their possible use in the analytic field.

the period of growth finds its primary and most natural expression in the act of playing.

"Images in absence" come to children while playing with material objects, which then develops into collective games. The fantasies active in their playing represent experiences, and in them the individual's possible responses to frequently aggressive and overwhelming emotions, are first structured. Psychic disorders find the terrain most favorable for their development when they make us lose our ability to create images in response to our need to adapt. Preformed responses, mediated by the environment, may not suffice and in some cases are self-destructive.

Images springing from our first contacts with reality shape our possible response to that impact, in their potentialities and limits. They contain, in their structure, the tensions of that encounter, but also the mot personal aspect of our nature and our evolutionary capacities. In this respect, it is of vital importance to reawaken our particular responses, those hidden "in absence." Generally speaking, suffering forces us to look for them by overcoming our mental inertia. In pathological disorders, there is a nucleus that is not yet differentiated which, in certain emotional situations, violently demands a shape. This occurs in the symptoms afflicting us and in the dreams we keep at a safe distance because they often contain the vital force we have denied and which still bears the mark of our initial responses.

Sandplay offered me a way for getting in touch with and getting others to touch that disturbing nucleus and for making it visible in the act of playing. A way, therefore, of giving new possibilities of expression to those emotions which go to make up the prime center of experience which has been left outside the capacity to represent them.

I might say that, thanks to this experience, I have had the good fortune to open another small window onto the mystery of the psyche and its transformations. It was, first of all, a way of gaining a new perspective on the emotional dynamics of the analytic relationship. With time, I realized that, from this point of view, I could review, explore and in some instances modify my relationship with the analytic theory referred to above, so as to find my bearings and carry on my everyday work.

### *The Structure of the Book*

An architect friend once told me: "If you want to see all the details of a view from your house look through a small window. A large opening will let you see the near and immediate surroundings, but will not let you make out the details, even those furthest away."

This book seeks to describe the horizon which the window of sandplay allowed me to observe, but I think it is of the utmost importance to tell the reader at once, right from Chapter I, about my point of view towards the "psyche" as phenomenon and my encounter with sandplay. When trying to understand and treat the psyche by psychic means, it becomes more necessary than ever to constantly question our attitude towards, and our comprehension of, the phenomenon we are experiencing. An exciting and difficult task, always to be improved upon, which forces us to update our theory as our experience changes. I propose, therefore, an overall view of "what" first struck me, and of "how" I changed my approach towards the landscape which the psyche gradually allowed me to observe in thirty years of analytic work.

In Chapter II, I introduce the reader into the particular experience of sandplay, by describing the analyst's consulting-room, a sort of laboratory where, aside from the chair and the couch, there are other areas and other instruments, such as the sand tray and the bookshelf of miniatures and figures. Sandplay involves a different way of sharing, a different way of understanding and attempting to modify emotions and feelings present and active in the analyst-patient relationship. The real risk is to consider the experience just one of the many techniques for setting the imagination into motion. Each of the described instruments, as well as the way the analysts uses them, must be seen in terms of the theoretical narrative structure of analysis, brought to light over the last hundred years, however various the points of view.

In the next chapter, in order to carry the reader into the “landscape of the psyche,” I describe a series of play scenes that arose in the analysis of a patient over a period of one month. It was, for me, a momentous experience, making me realize the power of communication and transformation in sandplay.

In the Chapters IV and V, I investigate the underlying theory of what I presented and experienced firsthand. I begin by considering the use of imagination in analysis, ultimately arriving at that specific form of imagination which is playing with objects. A brief survey of the history of analytic thought, through the contributions of Freud and Jung, Melanie Klein and Winnicott. I especially pursue that line of thought which with great difficulty opened a path through the wall of resistance against accepting play activities as a way of gaining access to the unconscious. Playing with objects in analyzing adults was a gradual achievement which, in my opinion, is of epistemological importance because it offers new possibilities, in both analytic therapy and research.

The physical concreteness of sandplay discloses a range of feelings and gives form to drives that elude the communicative capacity of words. An unexpected field of investigation thus opens up for studying the psyche and its pathological forms and for exploring the theory which guides out approach in the analytic field. The representations produced by play under the particular the psychic field conditions. I have tried to give an account of, may give rise to a symbolic integration which brings about an energic change of feelings experienced in the analyst-patient relationship.

In Chapters VI and VII, I go more deeply into the analytic area and try to describe some particular clinical moments. Sandplay gave me an approach to the psychic act performed by the analyst when he or she tries to perceive and empathetically respond to what happens in encountering the other. Whether the interpersonal communication is verbal, or play activities predominate, analytical listening on the part of the analyst gradually turns into building a representation of the feelings shared in the relationship: the attention given to the imaginal visibility of what appears in the field is similar to a “sand-scene” which, as I listen, I construct in my own inner theater.

In Chapter VII, I show that the two levels of communication, words and play, are two aspects of a single phenomenon. This two-fold perspective offers more effective channels for communicating and understanding what is happening in the analytical field. Shared speech is often ruled by defense mechanisms, especially in the early stages of analysis. Play activities, instead, can stimulate a freer narrative, one more closely reflecting the contents of underlying feelings. I stress this aspect in Chapter VIII, by describing some preliminary interviews to consider the possibility of analysis. In the initial stage, playing as a way of self-expression makes a strong impression.

In Chapter IX, I introduce a young man's play scene as it takes place in space and time. An opportunity for examining Jung's view of the unconscious and for understanding when and how symbolic events materialize in the analytical field.

Proof that a scene is successful, in other words that the symbolic activity has caused some changes, can be found only in the manifest modifications of the analyst-patient relationship, marked by variations in the verbal tone of the conversation, sudden memories, dreams subsequent to the play activities, just as by the echoes of the feelings encountered in the relationship, in transference and countertransference.

In Chapter X, I try to describe the building of a scene and the shared emotional reactions, to show what happens in the analytical field by using sandplay in particularly intense moments.

In Chapters XI and XII, we come to the heart of the book. I believe that sandplay represents an important contribution to the study of the mysterious relationships between perception and emotion in the creation of symbolic representations. The feeling-toned complex is for me fundamental, useful in exploring this topic and essential for updating the theory of Jungian analytical technique. Watching the play scene take shape is like observing a metabolism of feelings, in which various levels of integration are distinguishable in the relationship between the ego complex and repressed or split complexes.

In Chapter XIII, the self-image of the player and his relationship to the narrative structure of his personal story comes to light in the detailed description of a first sand scene reviewed years later with the player himself. Jointly reviewing with the players the whole series of sand scenes after a certain period of time was for me a formative experience of fundamental importance.

In Chapter XIV, I describe my experience which, undertaken at the request of some of my patients, has now become a possibility available to anyone interested. It is at present, a well-established formative practice in the Analytical Laboratory of Images (LAI), an association of Jungian analysts belonging to the International Society of Analytic Psychology, who use this approach in their analytical work with children and adults. Discovering what happened long before between oneself and one's play scenes alters one's view of the symbolic event and makes it possible to discern the independency of the symbolic process. A feeling of surprise is the reward of moments like that.

In Chapters XV and XVI, I attempt to show how and when play activities and words can modify feelings in the analytical field. Play-gestures and verbal gestures, the first in the space of the scene, the other in the temporal sequence of dialogue, offer a perspective of the psychic field condition that can activate a spontaneous process of self-healing. The act of interpreting which alters the relationship to feelings is to be found, as a psychic action, both in the construction of the scenes and of the words. These different moments, apparently so dissimilar, proceed through the same steps of a single symbolic process of integration.

By studying the how and when of play gestures I have learned to understand the nature and timing of verbal interpretation. I make a distinction between words that convey the metaphors produced in play, indicating the shared emotional situations in the analytical situation, and words that construct, put together the fragments gathered during the various stages of analysis, and eventually succeed in telling an individual story.

Chapter XVII deals with the hidden, but active "staging" of the vital process that transforms the relationship to feelings. I describe the series of scenes by a woman as a way of viewing the concept of Self, which Jung considered the organizing center of psychic development. The process, observed both on the level of play and words during the analytical work and reexamined together years later with the patient, reveals the complexity of the phenomenon. This two-fold perspective enables us to single out the first impersonal level of representation, its subsequent evolution into personal forms, up to the tranpersonal resonance of the process we have shared. Years ago, during analysis, we grasped only part of what had happened.

The book ends by focusing on the features that differentiate sandplay from other methods where the body is the vehicle of the relationship to feelings. I believe that by understanding these differences new possibilities of research open up.

Finally, several lines of further research are suggested. Play scenes provide a narrative structure that helps stress the dynamics of the feelings to be found in the analytical field. With the metaphors they suggest, compared to what the analyst experiences, it is possible to get another point of view of the vicissitudes of the transference and countertransference. The organization of representation in sandplay sheds light on the differences between psychopathological cases that demand further investigation. To conclude, new horizons open up for understanding psychoses, and one senses that sandplay, precisely because of the physical level it works on, can help us see more deeply into the mysterious relationship between mind and body.

# I A First Overview

*Theories are to be avoided, except as mere auxiliaries. As soon as a dogma is made of them, it is evident that an inner doubt is being stifled.* C.G. Jung (1945) par. 198

Between what we say we do and what we happen to experience in analysis, there is always room for the question. When we set out to understand and treat the psyche by psychic means, it is of fundamental importance, I feel, to question ourselves about the changes induced in us over years of clinical experience, the attempt to make our participation more and more conscious, to ask ourselves first of all about "how" we stand in relationship to the psychic phenomenon. The question about what we happen to experience in sharing with the other comes as a surprise. This is a feeling we must never forget if we want to improve upon and further investigate the theory instead of remaining imprisoned defensively in previous explanations.

I met the Jungian analyst, Dora Kalff,[5] and sandplay in 1968. The meeting took place in Zollikon, near Zurich, in her aristocratic old home, brimming with history and events. I noticed immediately in her study the trays of sand and a multitude of small objects arranged on shelves: stones, moss, shells, houses, human figures from all over the world, domestic and wild animals, along with typical fairy-tale figures such as dwarfs and fairies, all in miniature.

[5] In the 1960s Dora Kalff was the first to introduce sandplay into the sphere of analytic psychology. She worked with small children and subsequently with adults. Her book, *Sandspiel,* was published in 1966.

The representations I saw projected were play scenes built not only by children but by adults, as well. Some of them were parents who, having brought their children in for treatment, also tried their hand at expressing themselves that way; others instead had already adopted that means of communication in their psychotherapy.

I particularly remember a young man's sequence of sand-scenes, created over several months of consultation. As Dora Kalff remarked, the deepest level of sharing in that psychotherapy took place not so much through words as through the means offered by that particular way of playing. The young man used both the plastic possibilities of sand and the objects available. I was surprised that an adult could give himself up so completely to a game, like a small child. Up until then I never thought that playing with physical objects could reach a level of expression complex and well-constructed enough to bring about unexpected and meaningful representations of the subject's intrapsychic world. A first question came immediately to mind.

Would regression, induced by play situations, open new paths for communicating deep emotions? I thought that in many cases, particularly in adults, physical activities produce a liberating discharge, delaying or even preventing the passage to the verbal symbolization of the emotions and feelings present in the relationship. At that time I was still convinced that actions in the analytic field always produced an emotional discharge, and hence prevented or restricted the ability to understand present feelings. Using space and time in the construction of real scenes seemed, instead, to offer a deeper perspective, one possessed of highly meaningful implications.

In the enthusiasm of the moment, what I saw struck me as totally new and revolutionary, but I thought that the expressive capacity I observed was certainly due to Kalff's faith in sandplay and to the warmth of her particular personality. Even so, certain basic questions remained unanswered: was that form of communication a new way for getting to know the psyche? Could it be used, together with words, in analyzing adults?

The images offered by the sand-scenes carried out later by Dora Kalff's patient seemed to recount a well-constructed story. The scenes summoned up a dreamlike emotional atmosphere. What emerged was a sense of allusiveness, as if their meaning was on the verge of being understood, opening the mind to a series of hypotheses. The shapes induced a meditating, or rather a circular mental attitude. At the same time, in the temporal sequence of the scenes represented recurring motifs could be detected, as if they were characteristic nodal points of one particular personality. In addition to the meditating attitude induced by the individual scenes, there was a consistent consequentiality: in the recurrence of situations, characters and shapes the player's search for an ever greater clarity of expression could be seen, an attempt to find an imagery that corresponded more and more clearly to the narrative structure of his individual experience. The temporal succession of the play scenes clearly indicated the outlines of a story that seemed to be just waiting to be translated into shared speech. These representations need to be perceived in detail, in order to be identified and translated into words. As I saw them, they were associations strictly connected to the life of their author, and at the same time metaphors for communicating a difficult content, one maybe not yet possible to express in words.

For the first time, images and words, till then considered contrasting modes of expression, seemed to me close together. While observing the sandplay scenes the primary impression was of a structurally complex world, like a language to be decoded and restored to normal verbal communication. Those shapes "spoke of" their author and bore his individual imprint, like a specific handwriting.

More questions came to mind: was this a means for entering that mysterious space where emotions become representations? Could it be a way of overcoming the often defensive limits of shared speech?

At that moment I indulged in the pleasure of being surprised and of the flow of those pressing questions. I remembered what Rilke had to say in a letter of 1903 to a young poet (Rilke, 1928/1993, p. 34-35):

> ... I want to beg you, as much as I can, dear sir, to be patient toward all that is unsolved in your heart and to try to love the *questions themselves* like locked rooms and like books that are written in a very foreign tongue. Do not now seek the answers, which cannot be given you because you would not be able to live them. And the point is, to live everything. *Live* the questions now.

As a first reaction I felt the need to go see Kalff in Zurich for a while and experience sandplay directly. A fundamental moment for beginning to understand and for thinking about using the same method in analysis. Still today, so many years later, I think back on those encounters and remember with joy my own sand scenes.

Despite the direct experience of sandplay there still lurked in me an ambivalent attitude towards all that was new. Deciding to use sandplay in analysis, which I had been practicing for years with adults, was by no means immediate. I resorted to every sort of excuse not to begin. Introducing this method into my normal analytic work struck me as problematic. I wondered if adults would be able to play by using concrete physical objects. It was a question of getting people to "play," people who with words already possessed a valid instrument, often polished and honed by use.

Verbal language conveys experience by giving it a name, drawing upon established experience and memories, even if it often takes already well-trodden paths. Playing uses perception at the interests of imagination, takes place in the present, in the "here and now" of the analytic session. Certainly two possible paths of communication, or perhaps from an energic point of view, two opposite fronts, one of which might have hampered the other. I was still convinced that physical actions almost always served to discharge emotional tensions and would take away the ability of putting into words the emotional and feeling-toned contents of the analytic field. This is what I had been taught and what I continued to feel was true, though the opposition between words and play, between verbalization and playing was far from being proved.

This new resource which I had just experimented continued to intrigue me. Would the meaningfulness of the scenes, like dreams caught in the bud, tend to fulfill a wish of mine, instead of opening a path to understanding? Would the fascinating sandplay serve to protect me perhaps from the doubts which might arise in the presence of psychic conflicts? Would the urge to first build some sand scenes on my own and then use the method with patients, conceal a hidden lack of faith in the analytic work I had so far carried out with success?

Uncertainty gained substance in these and other questions. The last doubt to appear was that adults, unlike children, might refuse that unusual analytic possibility or use it only to create a path of escape and merely as a vent for unresolved conflicting tension. In that way I defended myself against the desire to explore that possibility I was at the same time drawn to.

When I decided to suggest it, my patients talked about it and accepted it more readily than I expected. Some of them entered the new experience immediately; others approached it warily and with less frequency. I realized with ever-greater clarity that when patients used sandplay, a new point of view opened up on the emotional texture that activated of our relationship.

It was for me very important to start considering sandplay as a level of communication to be combined with shared speech. Patients could use that means of expression whenever and however they pleased. Playing did not replace words, but offered a new level of communication, a sort of story summed up in images viewed as a metaphoric expression of emotions and feelings present in the analytic relationship and till then only partly expressed by shared speech.

Words are often incapable of holding the tension of a deep emotion and of transforming it into a communicable feeling. These are the moments when gestures and facial expressions increase in intensity, in expressive force. The act of playing seemed to be more and more capable of conveying and giving representational form to those emotions which are usually discharged on a physical level, such as the tone of words more than their contents. When I finally decided to introduce concrete play into analytic practice, it was precisely in difficult situations that I began to gather the first fruits. Sandplay revealed its potential when words were distant, conventional, repetitive, or in any case incapable of containing intense and violent emotions. I can state categorically that the two levels of communication, play that creates scenes and words, in their mutual connections and differences, for the first time offered a more complete perspective for understanding the varied and complex emotional states present in the analytic field.[6]

Another aspect eventually came to the fore. I realized with surprise that sandplay could also produce a striking change in the shared emotions and feelings of the relationship. The process of symbolization, activated by sandplay during a session, produced emotional variations in the patient and in me, even in the absence of palpable reasons or reasons that could be traced back to the verbal communication in progress.

Later I realized that a distinction should be made between moments in which "valid" play scenes appeared and others in which the building of scenes seemed almost automatic and had no influence whatever on the relationship. Scenes of the first kind modified the perception of feelings, gave way to memories, triggered dreams, the others induced tedium and stagnation. In these latter scenes, it was easy to detect tokens of the player's emotional problems, which froze both the verbal communication and the playing imagination into repetition. In order to figure out the reasons for these differences, greater attention needed to be paid to the interpersonal relationship, to the emotional motives affecting the two different situations. I realized, for example, that the keenest and most effective scenes took shape in the very first sessions when both parties, moved by eagerness and apprehension, possessed a higher emotional temperature, or when after identifying and describing the defenses, I could perceive and share a deep core of suffering in the player. It was no longer enough for me to emphasize the restraint, the shared silence, the analyst's ability to assure the free unfolding of the imaginal process, as I had learned from Kalff, but I wanted to understand what it was that determined the release of a symbolic process capable of modifying feelings. The idea that other emotional elements played an essential role became more and more imperative.

[6] In my first article about sandplay (Aite, 1970, p. 273) I still shared Dora Kalff's point of view. With time my attitude changed precisely by taking into account the relationship and resonances between verbal communication and play.

The emotional crucible in which a transformational symbolic process is set off, is determined by complex, still unknown emotional elements. The never finally decided question in this fundamental matter helped me reappraise the role of the relationship and the constant interchange between images and words, as a way of understanding the emotions that determined the imaginal event which modifies the analytic field. Shared words can open the way to representation, or block it. Likewise, play scenes can release words of a new emotional tone, sudden memories, or bring forth dreams that had gone unnoticed. Sandplay often offers the possibility of a new elaboration, but it can also become a simple stopgap, almost as a way of overcoming a moment of embarrassment.

The relationship between words and play scenes began to become a border zone teeming with possibilities for research. For me it seemed easier to grasp the psychic phenomenon in the bud, both when it tended to preserve the positions gained by consciousness and when new integrative possibilities emerged in the analytic relationship.

With time I started noticing more and more that the scenes offered metaphors useful for understanding the active feelings in the relationship. Sandplay channeled part of the "unsayable" and made it easier to contact and understand. The two levels of expression sometimes followed a parallel course for a long time, before succeeding in joining forces as different aspects of a single communicative narrative structure.

I will, of course, come back to these fundamental issues. For the moment, I would just like to stress that the mental attitude which sandplay was creating in me implied the simultaneous presence of an intrapsychic and a relational perspective. The first, best expressed by imaginal thinking, took shape in the play scenes, as well as in dreams, the other, contained in verbal thinking, was marked more deeply by evidence of the defenses necessary for confronting archaic emotions.

The intrapsychic-imaginal perspective can be described by the spatial metaphor of "verticality," in that it brings to play scenes an emotional depth inherent in a still pre-representational phase. The interpersonal-verbal perspective, which I would call "horizontal," clearly brings into the field the possible level of the relationship between the ego and the active emotions in the analytic relationship.

Introducing sandplay certainly widened the range of my analytical listening and opened a new path of communication, but it also put me in touch with moments of transformation on the level of both images and words. I could catch more distinctly the echo of those sudden emotional changes that take both parties in the analytic relationship by surprise and lend a different pace to the ongoing emotional phenomenon.

The two sides of the symbolic process, the representative side found in play scenes as well as in dreams and spontaneous fantasies, and the verbal side, seemed to me more and more like two levers of an instrument geared to getting a stronger hold on events as they happen.

The mental attitude described here seemed to tally with the way of understanding the psyche which Jung called "antinomic" (1935a, par. 1):

> Contradictions in a department of science merely indicate that its subject displays characteristics which at present can be grasped only by means of antinomies – witness the wave theory and the corpuscular theory of light. Now the psyche is infinitely more complicated than light; hence a great number of antinomies is required to describe the nature of the psyche satisfactorily.

In other words, sandplay in analysis offered an antinomic perspective of the psychic phenomenon: words and images, in their complex relationships, in the mutual activations and inhibitions of the transformational symbolic process, gave the therapist greater possibilities of perceiving and participating.

I became convinced that in psychotherapy sandplay and words corresponded to the two different kinds of thinking strictly related to Jung's research. Verbal and imaginal thinking (Jung, 1912/1952, par. 4) are two ways of transforming the ego's encounter-clash with emerging feelings, and of stimulating reflection. Two stages, two levels of the symbolic process, each governed by different rules that aim at integrating a new relationship to feelings. In confronting emotions, these two kinds of thinking, antinomic in their course of formation, but also linked, like the corpuscular and the undulatory theories of light mentioned by Jung, are constantly at work. Two antithetical ways of perceiving the same emotional phenomenon, which always remains however beyond the reach of both the possible reflections, one formed through images and the other through words.[7]

In this way, I adopted, or tried to adopt, an attitude capable of grasping, in myself and the other, these two levels of symbolization. The first level, implemented by the perception of the materials used in the scene, took place by means of isolated metaphorical images which gradually formed a representation, with a circular development in confronting emotions. The second level tended to objectify experience in a linear fashion, through language. The feelings called forth were reflected in the play scene, but were also present in the feeling-toned atmosphere of the relationship, in the involuntary gesticulations, in the facial expressions and in the tone of the words well before their contents. The difficulty was keeping the attention focused on these two levels, one antinomic to the other in that the feeling projected in the relationship and discerned at first only in each other's facial expression, often tended to provoke on both sides sometimes almost unbearable defense reactions. The play scene and the emotional relationship between the player and me were a sort of double mirror reflecting our present emotions.

I became personally aware of the difficulty of maintaining this way of perceiving the two levels of symbolization. I could see that the defenses I set into motion could swing back and forth between the two extremes. An initial attitude firmly concentrated on the play activity, rather than on the words of the player, prevented me from understanding what I began to see on the interpersonal level. Carried to an extreme, this attitude could lead me to give exaggerated importance to the representation, as if what appeared in the play scene was always revealing and of high symbolic value, even without the necessary translation in terms of the "here and now" of its appearance in the analytic field. In some clinical situations, to be sure, the symbolic integration through images by itself led to considerable alterations in the field. The event shed light on the

[7] On the antinomic approach to psychic phenomena, see also Aversa (1995) and Trevi (1999).

transpersonal aspect of that change, governed by archetypal determinants, but the question still remained as to the emotional factors present in the interpersonal field that encouraged it.[8] Emphasis on the imagination sometimes concealed a defense on my part, a placing of myself at the center as the "go-between of the mystery," instead of asking myself what had happened.

An inflation everyone risks in the process of confronting deeply involving emotions, which however if not accepted can have a harmful effect on the therapy. Gaining access to the transpersonal dimension of the symbolic event can only come about by paying the strictest attention to the "when," "how," and "why" of a given phenomenon, in an attempt to connect and understand, through the play images and words, the emotional event that involved us with the other.

Attention paid exclusively to the form of images and not to the field of their appearance reveals a tendency to translate the forms appearing in the play scene, in a conventional and literal way. Considering only the images, without taking into account the interpersonal field and the verbal symbolization, induces a kind of repetitiveness in practice and arid doubts about what is taking place in the analytic field.

I began to realize that my defenses against the shared emotional event led me to give an exaggerated importance to the representations created by the patient, and a stereotype symbolic reading of them. The persistence of this attitude, which emphasizes what goes on between the player and his or her game, results in an underestimation of the interpersonal aspect of the symbolic images appearing in the play scene, as well as of the involuntary words accompanying them.

To be sure, words can only approximate transpersonal experience but, by circling it, like the *circumambulatio* described by alchemists, they tend to express in always different ways what is contained in the sphere of the mysterious and the sacred. In my own experience as well, when still today I happen to remember certain sand-scenes I made over thirty years ago, I always discover

[8] In Chapter III, while describing the scene sequence of a woman to which I gave no verbal interpretation, I will try to understand the factors in the field that encouraged the unfolding of the transformational symbolic process.

new connections, new ways of indicating and recognizing the meaningfulness of those images in relation to my personal history. The surprise comes from realizing that those representations already contained in their structure, at the time only partly perceived, elements which emerged gradually over the years. In this never fully completed process of approaching the transpersonal nucleus I feel that the determining factor lies in an attitude which, by aiming at words, seeks to reach the conceptual narrative structure still only potentially implicit in the first images to appear in the trays.

In my opinion, emotions, at first uncontrolled and physically embodied, reach the dimension of shared feelings through mental representation. Only after a long elaborating process can expression in shared speech be reached, that is a new level of integration. Referring to the transformative sense of this transition, Jung remarked (1928/1931; par. 739, par. 738):

> Analytical psychology seeks to break through these walls by digging up again the fantasy-images of the unconscious which our rationalism has rejected.

> Nevertheless, it would be a misunderstanding to suppose that the fantasy-images of the unconscious can be used directly, like a revelation. They are only the raw material, which, in order to acquire a meaning, has first to be translated into the language of the present.

This translation into the language of the time demands paying attention to symbolic images on both levels, the intrapsychic and interpersonal, the imaginal and verbal ones.

The resonance of both participants in the symbolic process thus became more and more important for knowledge of the psychic event. Scene-building and verbal communication provided a two-fold perspective of the psychic phenomenon we both shared. In fact, after careful analysis, the spatiotemporal structure of sandplay and its figurations offered me ever-new metaphors for approaching, for understanding the exchange of identifications and projections going on between us. I gradually learned to extract from those images the words most suited to indicate and interpret the shared experience. The sandplay scenes thus turned out to be an unexpected source for understanding the transference and countertransference dynamics active in the analytic field.

An antinomic attitude, aimed at interrelating the two symbolic levels of play and of words, was not always easy to maintain. When I emphasized the "imaginal," "intropsychic," or "vertical" element of the psychic phenomenon most of all, I lost sight of the role of words, which in the interpersonal emotional field sometimes aid and sometimes prevent its unfolding. But if, instead, I placed the accent primarily on the "interpersonal," "horizontal" dimension of the relationship, the loss of shared silence and sometimes the excessive use of words provoked in me a defensive tendency to lock the emotions prematurely into a verbal-conceptual cage, invading the other with my interpretations. Attributing verbal significance should instead be sought through trial and error, and then only gradually. It must not come too soon, and even less be linked to what has already been said; each time it asks for the most suitable translation of the experienced moment. Truly new words, the ones that do the transforming, are rooted in images and need a long incubation period before acquiring the clarity and the operational capacity of the new concepts.[9]

In this perspective, words and images, viewed as different levels of a single symbolic process, are both carriers of transformational possibilities, differentiated according to the analytic field they take place in. Effective communication, the narratives rooted in the basic structure of a personal story, resides in gestures no less than in words, but releases a different amount of transformational energy on the two different levels. In a certain relational context, the emergence of representations, in dreams or in sandplay, can already on its own alter the energic field and release new capacities for consciousness.

For me the verbal translation of what is first represented in sandplay, but not yet put into words, has more and more become the cornerstone of psychological transformation, that is, when the maximum of transforming energy is made available to consciousness.

[9] I return to this subject in Chapter XVI, when I discuss the interpretation of sand scenes.

# III The Consulting-room as Laboratory: Origins and Characteristics of Sandplay

*Alchemy lost its vital substance when some of the alchemists abandoned the laboratorium for the oratorium, there to befuddle themselves with an ever more nebulous mysticism, while others converted the oratorium into a laboratorium and discovered chemistry. We feel sorry for the former and admire the latter, but no one asks about the fate of the psyche, which thereafter vanished from sight for several hundred years.* C.G. Jung (1945/1954) par. 482

With the return to the concrete act of playing, using sand and material objects in the space and time of a scene, a new path is charted for understanding the emotional dynamics on the analytic field.

In recent years, with the increasingly widespread application of this method to a broad range of psychic pathologies, in both the private and public sphere, the great expressive and transformational potential of sandplay has emerged. What I sustain here is that the sensitive-sensorial corporeal level activated by sandplay succeeds in giving metaphorical and shareable form to emotions and feelings that still cannot be represented on the stage of our inner theater and therefore remain outside the expressive possibilities of words.

In referring to sandplay I prefer the term *method* instead of *technique*. The important thing is to retain the idea of *another way* of stimulating the expression of emotions, feelings and sentiments which, while determining our attitudes and understanding, fail to reach the threshold of shared speech. *Technique*, in its common acceptance, gives the idea of a series of well-defined actions for attaining a preestablished goal. In a world dominated more and more by technology and with a growing need for meaningfulness, using concrete lay for doing research about the psyche is still far from being a well-known practice.[10]

[10] See Galimberti (1999).

# 1 Past History

Sandplay stems from World Technique which, starting in 1925, Margaret Lowenfeld (1939) introduced into her London clinic while she was looking for a psychological instrument capable of representing directly the world of children.

She also introduced an important innovation, that of combining toys and a tray of sand. The limited size of the container, the sand and the objects, by working together, seemed to back each other up, ultimately endowing the resulting scenes with a wealth of indications and possible interpretations.

It was the children themselves who with their preferences during the game showed how useful this association was: they preferred to build their scenes by arranging the objects *inside* the sand tray. With that well-defined container, with a material as malleable and indestructible as sand, they found solutions better suited to their emotional needs. With this apparently simple change, the playing field became a place where communication between the child and his representation was easier to read.

Theoretically, Margaret Lowenfeld's considerations not only of the expressive, communicative and cathartic importance of playing, but also of the therapeutic value of the scenes the children build, are still valid. Reflected in these scenes is a form of immediate and fluent thinking, even if still preverbal, which Lowenfeld (1939, p. 71) regards as the representative and fruit of a "protosystem of consciousness." Children feel and build their world, though yet unable to use the cognitive structure of thinking typical of the "conscious neosystem," which develops only in a later stage of life.

Lowenfeld maintains that the expression of emotions in play scenes help the child pass from "experienced consciousness" to the "reflected consciousness" of verbal thinking, with distinct changes in the anxiety and the symptomatology accompanying it.

The expressive effectiveness of this method gave rise to much later research. The first studies, undertaken mostly for diagnostic purposes, created a standardization in order to obtain useful solutions in the study of various psychopathological cases. Bolgar and Fisher (1940) with the "Little World Test,"

Arthus (1947) with the "Village Test," revised by Mabille (1950), Charlotte Bühler (Bühler and Kelley, 1941) with the "World Test," Mucchielli (1960) with the "Imaginary Village Test," followed in the footsteps of this English pioneer:[11]

> Jungian analyst Dora Kalff, who attended Lowenfeld's Institute of Child Psychology in London for two years, clung more closely to the original method. She was the first to understand its transformational and communicative potential and to integrate it into a Jungian theoretical framework.

World-play in the field of analysis was first called sandplay by Kalff. The name itself stressed the usefulness of the association of sand-objects-limited space in handling the deepest emotions. In the above attempts at standardizing the method as a test, it was precisely the sand had been eliminated.

In 1962 Dora Kalff first communicated her findings during the Second Analytical Psychology Congress, and in 1966 she wrote her book, *Sandspiel*, in which, after a short theoretical introduction, she presented the case histories of several children and young people she had treated with this method. With a view to consolidating her concept of healing through sandplay, she founded in 1985 the International Society of Sandplay Therapy.

Over the last thirty years, sandplay has exceeded the limit which long restricted it to the therapy of children and entered with full rights into the analysis of adults, in both the private and public practice. Using it exclusively with adults, as I have during these years of research, led to new discoveries and gradually changed my attitude towards what I had learned from Kalff. With clinical experience, my theoretical approach, outlined above and which will be examined more thoroughly in the following chapters, began to take a different tack. In 1998, together with the analysts I had worked with over the last twenty years, I founded the Analytical Laboratory of Images (LAI). It is worth point-

[11] On the history of these various tests and the accompanying theories, see Mucchielli (1960).

ing out, I believe, the differences in the way sandplay is used in the analytic field, precisely in the interest of an open debate on its potentialities and limits.[12]

## 2 Play Scenes in the Consulting Room

The analyst who uses sandplay must arrange his consulting room in such way that both the verbal level and the play level can become a part of the sharing process. As I pointed out in the last chapter, it is of the greatest importance to maintain a relationship between the interpersonal and the intrapsychic view of the phenomenon taking place. The transition from playing to words and vice versa provides valuable proof of the emotional event. The structure of the play scene and the verbal communication are two different ways of reflecting on what has been experienced in the analytic relationship; two antinomic perspectives of a symbolic process aimed at representing the feelings active in the analytic field.

According to a procedure that has evolved over the years, I ask patients to do a sandplay only once in the meetings preceding the actual analytic work. After that, using the game or not is left up to them. In my consulting room patients working with me can choose three different positions: facing armchairs, a couch where the patient can always see me, and lastly the playing area slightly off to one side to assure the player's privacy and concentration. What I present to the person beginning analysis is a well laid-out environment, where seeing

[12] To distinguish the viewpoints of the members of the International Society of Sandplay Therapy, see Kalff (1966, 1984), Ammann (1991) and among the Italians, Garzonio (1989, p. 29; 1994, p. 123; 1997), Mancini Carducci (1989, p. 99; 1997), Mazzarella (1994, p. 133; 1997), Montecchi (1989, p. 145; 1997b), Marinucci (1989; p. 139;1997), Navone (1984; 1989, p. 63; 1997). Different approaches to sandplay in the analytic field on behalf of the members of the Analytical Laboratory of Images (LAI), described and examined in the present volume, emerge in many other articles: Aite (1989c, p. 7), Aite and Crozzoli (1992, p. 609), Bona Pompei (1997; p, 148), Castellana (1994, p, 97), Codignola (1994, p. 89); Crozzoli (1989, p.83; 1994, p. 63); Donfrancesco (1994, p. 51); Fersurella (1997, p. 152); Màdera (1994, p. 181; 1998); Porseo (1997, p. 156); Tarantini (1989, p. 117; 1994, p. 81; 1996).

and being seen, both in the building of scenes and in the eventual movements around the room, play a fundamental role. My purpose is to bring about the transition from the verbal to the preverbal register and vice versa, but at the same time to let patients experiment three different ways of entering into the relationship. The range of possibilities in their use of space offers further points of reference for distinguishing the emotional dynamics present in the relationship. Moving around from one place to the other, according to what is being experienced, always says something about the relationship of the patient to the emerging feeling in the analytic field, whereas a repetitive and unchanging use of the space can indicate an emotional resistance that one should try to understand.

For anyone starting to play, a rectangular zinc tray, cm. 57x72x7, with a blue floor and containing sand is available. The dimensions of the tray are still the ones Lowenfeld suggested, a playing field of agreeable proportions based on the rules of the golden section: the shorter side of the rectangle corresponds to the golden section of the diagonal. One wonders whether Lowenfeld's choice might not create in the player a tendency to unite the various parts into a single harmonious whole. Future research might seek to find out whether a change in the dimensions influences the organization of the whole. What differences, if any, would appear in scenes created in spaces of different sizes?

The boundaries of the tray and the relation of the figures to the background, that is the proportion between the objects and the play area, act as regulating factors, which facilitate the use of space at the service of the underlying emotions. Each object in the emerging three-dimensional scene is above all an experience which has been given concrete expression. What we place near or far, to the right or to the left, on top or beneath, suggests an immediacy of experience not unlike what we meet with in dreams.

The sand tray is the scene, let us say the screen, where the representation takes shape. It is the player opening up to the psychological happening, becoming present to himself and the world, but also questioning the event as it occurs.[13] From another point of view, the playing field can be said to be a place

[13] "Presence" is to be understood in a phenomenological sense. See Galimberti (1983) p. 139.

where tactile and proprioceptive sensations, accompanied by the player's watching, becomes physical perception at the service of the imagination. Typical of sandplay is the activation of a relationship between the player's hands and eyes for creating a *mise-en-scène* where the active emotions and feelings of the moment are condensed into concrete forms. In this way, adults can relive experiences they had during the period of growth, whose constituent element is the encounter-clash between the perception of limits that derive from the concrete relationship to the sand and to the objects used, and that multidimensional space in perpetual motion known as the psyche.[14]

## 3 Using Space for Expressing and Understanding the Psyche

I believe that using and studying sandplay in analysis can provide useful information for understanding the relationship between emotions and the subjective experience of space.

The symbolic expressiveness of space can be seen most clearly in our dreams. The places, the chosen perspectives, the real and imaginary constructions in oneiric space reveal, in a precise, clear-cut way, the narrative structure of the underlying emotions and feelings. More than the story told, which immediately catches our attention, it is the scenography of the dream's representation that makes specific reference to the dreamer. Precisely because of the concrete scenes it brings about, sandplay gives prominence to this "naturally intelligent" way of giving shape to the emotions that invade us and the feelings we experience.

When players build a landscape, the blue floor of the sand tray is not only a device meant to imitate water as compared to land. While organizing a scene,

[14] In Chapter XVIII, I will go into the particular symbolic corporeal experience activated by sandplay. The materiality of the sand, of the objects and the play space offers the feelings taking place in the analytic relationship endless possibilities of expression. The spatiotemporal emergence of the scene is, in my opinion, a more legible and comprehensible text than other symbolic experiences that use the body as their vehicle, art therapy or dance therapy, for example.

they discover in that color, the color of both water and sky, the secret of another dimension.

I believe the color blue speaks of remoteness. With that color on the floor of the sand tray not only is it possible to give greater clarity to the shapes modeled in the sand, but also to stage that "beyondness" we all feel when we contemplate the sky and sea.

Both the individual and collective dimension of feelings transpires in the way space is used, in dreams and in playing. We have long known that a "spatialization" of feelings exists in which the same recurring aspects appear in different individuals. Dreams and imagination, by staging the narrative structure of the feelings that influence or determine consciousness, use space as a signifier of the emotional experience. On top, beneath, right, left, near and far tinge feelings with meanings that have a collective, archetypal value, to be found with the same features in different individuals.[15]

In the sixties, Mucchielli, in reporting his research carried out with the "Imaginary Village Test," remarked (Mucchielli, 1960, pp.223, Author's translation.):

> The regions of the imaginative universe, which suddenly flood the tray after the subject has "inhabited" it oneirically, possess particular and specific feeling-tones: when the subject starts thinking about the most appropriate place to put a thematically-tinged and meaningful figurative element, he tends to unite the element's feeling-tone and the remembrance of the region of imaginative space that correspond to the said feeling-tone

An observation which emphasizes the expressive meaningfulness of space, though from another point of view the author was primarily interested in proving the validity of the test.

[15] The construction and use of architectonic space seem to offer significant indications of the relationship between psyche and space or between experienced feelings and the forms around us. On the differences referable to male and female identity and the use of space, see Coppola Pignatelli (1982) pp. 83-97.

Analytic research has constantly referred to space in order to represent and understand the psyche. We cannot conceive of the psyche and its dynamics without introducing the parameters of space and time, which are the constituent elements of our consciousness. Our very awareness of being in the world is closely linked to the experience of space. Also in analysis what presumably is happening not only in the patient's mind, but also in the analyst's, and in their relationship, are understood and described in spatial terms.[16]

Freud (1938, p. 300), in one of his last miscellaneous notes, wrote:

> Space may be the projection of the extension of the psychical apparatus. No other derivation is probable. Instead of Kant's *a priori* determinants of our psychical apparatus: psyche is extended, knows nothing about it.

In Freud's last short and enigmatic phrase I read the need of the psyche to express itself in the space-time of consciousness in order to discover its extension, to be able to reflect upon itself.

With time, the attention of researchers began to shift more and more distinctly away from the psychosexual conflicts of the Oedipus nucleus of neuroses, in the end integrating them into a broader perspective of the problems connected with the differentiation between self and objects, between self and the other. In this new perspective, psychic pathology is considered one of the stages in the gradual and painful detachment of the individual from an initial matrix.

In fact, this view of psychological development stresses the dynamics of the process of differentiation between self and the other, with the resulting emotions and feelings. The "outer side" of this process corresponds to the individual's evolution from total dependence to an ever increasing autonomy with respect to others.

As a matter of fact, the spatial dimension enters into these new operative concepts and becomes central to understanding the evolutionary history of individuals (Resnik, 1994). On the intrapsychic level, the visualization of feel-

[16] Regarding this, see Chianese (1998) who stresses what happens between analyst and patient in terms of space and not only of interaction.

ings in the representation still gives prominence to the spatial dimension. The capacity to represent emotions confined to a psychic level that have never before attained symbolization, whether imaginal or verbal, uses space as its vehicle of expression.

Analytic thinking over the years has created many metapsychological concepts in which the theme of psychic space is returned to on various levels. Suffice it to remember Winnicott's "intermediate space," considered an imaginary place where the intrapsychic and intersubjective worlds influence and change each other. The process of differentiating the individual found in the concepts of "transitional space" and "potential space" that Winnicott elaborated in his research, instruments useful for understanding the transformations and failures in the integration of feelings, both in the period of growth and in later stages of life, when a change necessarily becomes inevitable.[17]

Clinical theory becomes an instrument that is easier to use when it offers spatial metaphors of the analytic relationship. I am thinking also the concepts of "psychic field" or "bipersonal field" (Baranger and Baranger, 1990), or of relations as a space of alchemical transformation (Jung, 1946).[18]

## 4 Using Sand and Its Expressive Resources

Sand can respond to the most delicate touch as well as the most violent blow and always leave a trace, without being destroyed; of the remaining imprint, when dry, to the more or less firm modeling, when wet, so that even highly complex shapes can emerge. It resists and survives all mistreatment. Each patient uses sand differently: some patients immediately sink their hands into it and let it trickle, gently or vigorously, until a sign conveying meaning is pur-

[17] I will return to and go more deeply into these concepts, which highlight the spatial dimension, in Chapters IV and V, concerning the imagination and the sandplay experience.
[18] For me the most important authors on this subject are Jung, Spitz, Winnicott, Mahler, Klein, Kohut, Fairbairn, Bick, Fordham and Bion. For more recent research in Italian, see also Gaddini (1982), Matte Blanco (1975) and Chianese (1998).

sued until the barely suggested form is completed. A sort of coming and going between the player and the sandy surface, which assumes the dialogical pace of a direct encounter with emotional states, whether conscious, vaguely prescient or subconscious, and even unconscious. Other patients won't touch the sand, as if they were afraid of it. In these cases, the player leaves the surface of the playing field intact, placing on it the objects he goes about choosing. In this way, he seems to be defending himself and keeping his distance from the material, as if it aroused emotional states that cannot yet be absorbed. The use of sand, its manipulation, brings to the scene the most archaic level of the relationship to emerging emotions. This is, in fact, the stage that precedes the separation of the object from the background and prepares it to become visible.

Because of its amorphous nature, sand nicely represents the indistinctness that precedes the intuition of a form. The disorientation of consciousness, which is still unable to see, is reflected in the apparent evenness of the sand, like a desert waste. In verbal analysis, it is the equivalent of the silences full of expectation that appear in certain fruitful moments in the sharing process. It is certainly no accident that the first involuntary association many people make with the empty playing field is the desert: the place which is usually associated with solitude, with the loss of direction, with the dangers of an unknown, uncontrollable world, but at the same time also alludes to the opening of another dimension of being. These are archetypal experiences which mythology reserved for anyone who confronts the desert before the possible revelation of the new.

I believe that in the presence of that unbroken stretch of sand, still void of objects, almost as if were waiting for some gesture to change it, the player's experience can be called the *presence of absence,* an image-phrase borrowed from the poet, Attilio Bertolucci (1990): "Absence, keener presence," he says with regard to an experience we have all had in our lifetime.

The typical characteristics of sand, its malleability in responding to manipulations of any kind along with its indestructible resistance to any sort of violence, make it possible to understand another aspect of this material which contains the history of the world. The appeal sand has for children and adults, aside from the reassurance it gives with regard to individual destructibility, may have deep roots in an archetypal substratum: the earth, which is an integral part of our experience of being in the world.

Earth in the sense of *humus*, of "mother nature," is closely connected to the stability, to the persistence of our always feeling the same despite the passing of time, but also to the return to earth at the end of the life cycle. Sand especially, in its very constitution, bears the mark of an evolution and a transformation that is the result of contact with, and the endless action of, the sea, which in mythology is considered the primary source of life. Sand reveals a wide range of expression when by adding water the player can try to create a different consistency that enables the construction of various shapes. Handling the sand represents the most archaic level of relating to emotions and, energically speaking, can also be very intense for the player. Adding pigments further increases the expressive resources of sand, also because different shades of color can be found that correspond to the feelings perceived at that particular moment. The analyst, aware of what might happen on these primary levels of experience, knows that contact with the tactile, proprioceptive, sometimes olfactory and visual sensations of sand, can bring about a direct relationship to deep emotional charges, with obvious resonance in the individual and in the analytic relationship.[19]

"Slime is the dust of water, as ash is the dust of fire" remarked Gaston Bachelard, who saw clearly the meaning of our relationship to natural elements (Bachelard, 1943/1997, p. 92, Author's translation):

> In order to dream deeply, you must dream with matter... The modeler comes closer than anybody else to intimate dreams, vegetating dreams.

[19] In Chapter VII, I try to describe and understand, from an energic and symbolic point of view, the moment when the patient establishes contact with sandplay. The above-mentioned archetypal characteristics show the importance of the unconscious charges at work. In Chapter XVIII, I reconsider the corporeal symbolic process activated by sandplay and its energic influences on the analytical field.

Typical characteristic of sandplay is that it stages the way both the material and the objects are used. We know that as children develop, handling materials precedes using objects. In creating a scene it is possible to distinguish, in the use of sand, a primary relationship with the emotional charge as well as the moment of defining feelings represented by the use of objects. Emotions still indistinct, rooted at a physical level, can find the possibility of being expressed along with shapes and objects that indicate a definite relationship between self and the primary emotional charge.

## 5 Using Objects for Relating to Feelings

When a patient decides to leave the chair or the couch and build a sandplay scene, what one sees is the direct confrontation with the emotions and feelings present in the analytic field. Using space, sand and objects stages what, in my opinion, establishes an authentic contact with the unconscious or subconscious determinants active at that moment. In the period of growth, handling and using materials and objects are the first way of dealing with feelings. Recognizing, as an entity in itself, what changes and sometimes deeply upsets an individual's balance, begins through the concrete act of playing.[20]

Winnicott (1971, p.120) went deeply into the relationship with feelings brought about through the use of objects:

> The thing that there is between relating and use is the subject's placing of the object outside the area of the subject's omnipotent control; that is, the subjects's perception of the object as an external phenomenon, not as a projective entity; in fact recognition of it as an entity in its own right.

[20] Winnicott was the first to throw light on the complexity of the emotional event connected with the use of objects in transitional space. See Winnicott (1971).

These words very clearly refer to the radical transformation from an "omnipotent control" of feelings to the recognition of its power and independence that the use of objects conveys and testifies to. What is taking place is (*ibid.,* p.120):

> in fact recognition of it as an entity in its own right. This change (from relating to usage) means that the subject destroys the object (...) "object survives destruction by the subject." But there may or may not be survival.

The drama of the moment is stressed. It is what happens when the relationship to an emotion is such that the person experiencing it is transformed. Winnicott's insight is useful for assessing a fundamental step in the development of consciousness at the moment when, as he remarks, children succeed in leaving the omnipotent illusion behind in order to experience the disillusion creatively and evolve by recognizing the existence of the other.

At every stage of life the urge to create a new relationship with an overwhelming emotion, one capable of transformational consciousness, passes through the same moment of evolution. Contact with the destructiveness of loss and the possibility of overcoming it are a constant rule in the transformation of consciousness, which sandplay reproposes also in visual terms: this moment is revealed by the way the player uses the material at hand. Taking adults back to the creative regression of playing with objects offers a new perspective on the transformational event.[21] Virginia Wolff (1950) describes the moment when emotions appear through things:

> You can't write directly about the soul. Looked at, it vanishes; but look at the ceiling, look (...) at the lowest beasts in the zoo (...) and the soul slips in.

In my consulting room, natural materials are available for building scenes, such as stones, pigments, plants and shells; miniature figures of everything we find in the world: trees, houses, wild and domestic animals, men and women in various facets of life. The objects, set on shelves near the sand tray, are very

[21] Crozzoli (2001) pp. 318-332.

stimulating and can create in the viewer countless associations. Players, coming into contact with them, feel the "urge" to find something that reflects them.

The presence of objects pertaining to the mineral, vegetable and animal world, including humans, to the forms of everyday human life and to those created by imagination, is a special feature of sandplay, whose expressive possibilities have yet to be systematically assessed.

The way forms from the inorganic, vegetable, animal and human world or abstract geometrical figures are chosen in constructing scenes in space and time, intimates the relationship between consciousness and the emerging contents. Experience over these years confirms my opinion that the choice of each object's expressive level, just as the way it is placed in the space of the scene, reveals different levels of integration of emerging feelings and at the same time shows what the functions of the ego are set going in that moment: from sensation to intuition, from feeling to conscious and differentiated thinking.[22]

The objects chosen little by little may summon up past emotional experiences, bring about unexpected memories or suggest associations of ideas apparently unrelated to what is happening. In the perceptual structure that characterizes objects, there are signs of places and situations that recall the past, but also the intuition of emotional contents never before expressed in words. So what happens is the equivalent of a spontaneous free association.

[22] See *Mitobiografia* by Ernst Bernhard (1969) pp. 67-89. The book offers valuable clues for investigating the theme of the functions – sensation, intuition, feeling and thinking – brought to light by Jung in relation to emotions. The author offers an evolutionary view of the confrontation with emotions: from sensations to thinking. The idea of function is, in fact, associated with the idea of successive integration: "In a preorganic stage, we must imagine sensation as the sole function, which contains, so to speak, the other three, operating embryonically under its authority. Its intuiting, feeling and thinking came about through 'form,' for example through symmetry, the numerical relations through quantity" (*ibid.*, p.70). Sandplay describes a phenomenon that can be considered also from this point of view. In confronting feelings, the player starts from primary sensations linked to the concreteness of an object in order to integrate successive and more and more differentiated levels: from sensation to intuition as perceptual functions, from feeling to thinking as evaluative functions. This is a field of research yet to be investigated. I wonder whether in this way new paths might not be opened for understanding the relationship between individual typology and psychopathological cases or the specific choice of organs in somatic diseases. I return to this subject in Chapter XVIII.

When open-minded adults grasp the meaning of this work, not only do they quickly adjust to sandplay, but are, I would say, quite intensely "taken" by it. Watching the way the player uses objects, placing them in the space of the scene, makes it possible to define certain moments in the relationship to underlying emotions. I am impressed by how players usually start off from what is familiar before undergoing a sudden change. The sand very frequently recalls the idea of sea or desert, and the player's first actions are the result of this association, up to the moment when am unexpected association takes place. I remember a young woman who, after placing some sea objects, such as shells or pebbles, started digging and buried a little pot in the sand, changing the tone and pace of her conversation and revealing an important memory of her personal history. The antinomic perspective of the psychic phenomenon, outlined in the previous chapter, is also confirmed by these actions, as if the emotional content had found a corresponding perception in that little pot. In the linear flow of the early stages of building, "free association" suddenly intervenes, bringing to the surface feelings not yet expressed and a corresponding recollection.

I would like to mention some typical moments I believe are always to be found in the transition from an indistinct, archaic emotion to a recognizable feeling of consciousness. Jung (1921, par. 486) called an early aspect "empathy" *(Einfühlung)*:

> Empathy is therefore a kind of perceptive process characterized by the fact that, through feeling, some essential psychic content is projected into the object, so that the object is assimilated to the subject and coalesces with him to such an extent that he feels himself, as it were, I the object (...) He does not, however, feel himself projected into the object; rather, the "empathized" object appears animated to him, as though it were speaking to him of its own accord.

Contents that are syntonic for the player and carry basic aspects of his personal history, are projected onto the chosen object and placed in the field. Other emotional contents that are felt to be different from self, sometimes even alarming, suddenly appear and fall into the same pattern.

Another aspect of the emotional relationship induced by the use of objects is what Jung called "abstraction." That is, an attitude which does not go towards the object, but moves away from it, to create a distance and circumscribe it into a recognizable organization (*ibid.*, par. 490):

> Empathy presupposes that the object is, as it were, empty and seeks to imbue it with life. Abstraction, on the other hand, presupposes that the object is alive and active, and seeks to withdraw from its influence

The need to express, staged by the act of playing, marks off the active emotions of the moment and links carried with it a quite unexpected feeling she felt to be invasive, something with which she refused to be identified. From this point of view, the choice of objects, like the way they are placed in space and the relationship between them, takes on a most interesting significance.

Objects chosen through "empathy" recount basic elements of a story which the player recognizes as his own, whereas those chosen by "abstraction" are charged with the imaginary and indicate something the player feels to be working against him. Sometimes they are representations borrowed from fairy tales and myths, at others, the abstraction is obtained by means of geometrical figures which at once circumscribe and indicate emotions that go beyond everyday experience and transcend the individual. This way the "different from self" is represented, but also kept at bay, both through the forms chosen and through the use of space.

So the terms "empathy" and "abstraction" describe the way the player gets in touch with an object and uses it. Jung's notes of 1921 highlight the vicissitudes of the ongoing emotional exchange between the ego and feelings through objects. In my opinion, they already bear the seed of the concepts which Winnicott, in another way, would resume and further explore in 1951 with his theory of transitional phenomena, and in 1969 by indicating the use of objects a highly intense field of emotional experience where subject and object are differentiated and come into being.[23] Aside from people of genius who intuit them, vivid concepts reappear in the work of various researchers, differing in time, changing and deepening their meaning. Along this same path, full of possibilities yet to be explored, sandplay can, in my opinion, offer a great abundance of new evidence.

## 6 Notes on Miniature Objects

I think sandplay makes it possible to understand the role miniature objects play both in the psychological development of children and in human cultural experience. They are the concrete representation of Winnicott's transitional objects.[24] Properly speaking, they belong neither to the internal nor to the external subjective sphere, but to that space of illusion, or potential space, where both playing and human cultural experience in all stages of life, are located. Their presence not only as a childhood stock-in-trade, but also in ancient mystery cults and burial ceremonies, points to a basic need: miniature objects, widespread on various levels of experience, seem to express the active presence of, but also the human need for, an intermediate area, a third area, for establishing contact with emotions we cannot otherwise contain. Miniature objects, therefore, stand for what is incomprehensible or too big in the life of the individual, children or adults. The reduced dimensions, by making them easier to handle, facilitates the possibility of confronting obscure emotional contents, maybe their "use." An object charged with deep emotions, hence endowed with unconscious power, has the special advantage of making it easier to contact and control experience. As is also the case in the rites of sympathetic magic, where miniature objects play an important part. Through objects, emotions that are

[23] Both works can be found in Winnicott (1971). Jung's theory of feeling-toned complexes offers a theoretical grid helpful in understanding the complexity of the emotional event created by the relationship to objects and by their use.

[24] I return to the subject of Winnicott's transitional space in Chapter V. Regarding miniature objects, see Agamben (1977).

even overwhelming in life enter the subject's world and become a psychic experience capable of changing events and the subjects themselves.

## 7 From Inanimate Objects to Personification

The variety of objects, characteristic of sandplay, provides a wide range of expressive levels. To organize our emotional experience and assure the distance necessary for assimilating it, we have always made use of materials, inanimate objects, but also of the inclination to personify. As happens every night in our dreams, but also by day, a process is constantly active through which the soul, in order to understand the emotions running through it, invents characters and events. In dreams or fantasies figures move about whose faces are familiar because they are taken from personal history, or unfamiliar but still meaningful.

Mythical gods, like the characters in our fairy-tales, are the fruit of this same inclination. It a way of constructing an experience which, by giving a face to emotions, makes it possible to contact them, experience them, perceive their independence and lastly to establish a relationship to them.[25] The psyche's

[25] James Hillman (1978) discusses the question. He does not agree with the term "personification" and prefers speaking of "personifying": "Personifying is a way of being in the world and *experiencing the world as a psychological field*, where persons are given with events, so that events are experiences that touch us, move us, appeal to us". The terms animism, anthropomorphism, and personification presume, he remarks, that thinking "makes soul [whereas] personifying recognizes soul [as] existing prior to reflection." (p. 13). I believe that when entering that mysterious breeding-ground where the transformation of emotions into representative visions takes place, one always runs the risk of losing either the psyche's spontaneous formative activity or the function of the ego complex, which is connected to the body and is basically unconscious, though at its center it attains the highest integration: the integration of consciousness. The characters that appear in dreams or in the sand scenes are the fruit of this encounter. It is for me important to stress the levels of this confrontation. Dream scenes are as significant as the characters in them, and express in space (as in the structure of the play scenes) a level of relationship between the ego complex and emotions no less significant than the figures moving about in them. By placing undue emphasis on the characters there is a risk of losing the structure of the whole. I agree with Jung and Hillman in believing that the unconscious proceeds independently towards an integration not effected by consciousness, but the mysterious character that animates dreams

inclination to personify the more integrated levels of the relationship between the ego complex and emotions is facilitated by sandplay. The presence of "characters" taken from the real world, or purely imaginary, encourages, aside from the different use of space, the distinguishing of the various levels of relationship with underlying emotions. Any character that appears on the scene indicates, in my opinion, a feeling on the verge of becoming shared speech. In the next chapter about one of my patients, we shall see how a deep emotional problem runs through the whole process of integration. From an initial "two-dimensional" expression of a still unspeakable emotion she eventually moved on to the "three-dimensionality" of a human figure and its evolution though different shapes corresponding more and more closely to the narrative structure of her personal story. The sequence of scenes showed a process of differentiation from a confused red spot to the emerging head of a wild animal and finally to a human figure. This transition to a more and more distinct personification may be seen as a metabolic process of assimilation of a deep emotion: from a drive dynamic experienced on a physical level, the emotion becomes shareable feeling first through images and only subsequently through words. When in the sequence of successive scenes an emotion, at first silenced and expressed in an amorphous and impersonal fashion, takes on a personalized form, its verbal expression in the analytic field also seems to be facilitated. The feelings moving in the analytic space appear to be not only more "speakable," but also more recognizable. The narrative structure of the feelings experienced in the relationship, the transference and countertransference, find images that help understand the psychic event. The elaboration of a different relationship between the ego complex and still unsayable emotions hence transpires from the successively emerging forms. The personification that appears in the play scene not only releases new possibilities of verbal expression, but also captures in images an emotional dynamic already active in the analytic relationship. As if an emo-

is the highest achievement of a dialectic between two equally significant moments. For this reason I continue using the term personification because what interests me is the "making" of the above encounter and its levels. As to the fundamental meaning of personification I really don't know what to say.

tion, at first indistinct and chaotic, needed the face of the other, of a human figure, in order to define itself.

Dreams, like playing, stage this inclination to personify. From my experience, I am convinced that the more expression through play conveys the inclination to personify, the more the analytic field breaks free of the emotional dynamics we call transference and countertransference. In other words, the analyst who puzzles also over the interpersonal meaning of a play scene can at a certain point discover the similarity between a character that has appeared on the scene and an emotional invasion of personally experienced feelings. Sandplaying improves the analyst's capacity to assimilate the feelings that have contaminated him, just as it channels for the patient the dynamic which, in order to emerge, needed the face of the analyst, through the mechanisms of projection and identification that are always active in the metabolism of emotions.[26] From shapeless matter up to the different levels of representation that objects encourage, the analyst witnesses the beginning of what seems more and more clearly a story told in images.

[26] Gaburri (1992, p. 351) places emphasis on how the analyst unconsciously tends to personify free emotions in the analytic field, split parts that lead him to act upon or reject the experience. They are to be seen as the emotional forerunners of a countertransferential feeling yet to be recognized. The analyst's *rêveries* are the key to this fundamental transition. The analyst who uses sandplay in the analytic field enlarges his listening band: from the verbal to the preverbal by means of another possibility. Aside from words and silence, he extends his perception to include the impact the act of playing and the scene taking shape has on him. His personal *rêverie* of the emotions active in the field is enhanced and discovers new incentives in dealing with the patient's *rêverie* that sandplay brings about.

# Anna's Story

*It is on stage that the unity of thought, gesture and action is constructed.*
A. Artaud (1938, p. 22)

For me, the sequence of scenes created by a patient has always seemed to be a story told in images. From one play scene to the next, even over a period of months, recurring shapes and characters would appear that were unique to that particular person. Viewing a series of scenes as a chain of events makes it possible to experience and follow a subject's personal narrative structure step by step.

It is as if the images in the first scene, particularly important like first dreams, be-came more and more explicit and the relationship between the individual parts evolved into a story. The sequence of scenes suggests the idea of an authentic metabolism of emotions. So what we see is the distillation of interconnected shapes which more and more sharply define the underlying fabric of emotions.

Of the many sequences I have watched during my thirty years of work and reviewed for purposes of study or at the request of patients, I decided to choose the one by Anna for mostly sentimental reasons. Hers was, in fact, the first sequence in which, concentrated into a period of one month, I was able to discover, though at first only intuitively, the consistency of this development through images. As often happens at the beginning of any experience somebody appears on your path who succeeds in opening your eyes: Anna was one of those persons.

Her intelligence and sensitivity were as deep as her suffering that prevailed at the time, which often quite literally invaded the analytic field. Through play she could exploit her manual and verbal skills, thanks to which I was able to reach a deeper understanding of sandplay's expressive potentiality.

The analytic relationship had, for some time, come to a standstill and turned repetitious and this left us both feeling helpless. Her words as well as mine failed to touch the deep uneasiness we both experienced. The emotions present in the field transpired from the tone of her exclamations, at times ironic or violent, as well as in the emotional tedium of her repetitious subject matter and behavior. Only sandplay succeeded in triggering a symbolic process that put her in touch with deep emotions.

Another sentimental reason involved the intensity of the feelings we experienced in that situation, both of helplessness and of surprise. In addition to the difficulties we shared in those days we were for the first time astonished by a remarkable change in Anna. I saw that change distinctly on a clinical level but at the moment was unable to construct a satisfactory explanation, much less an interpretation that could explain what was going on in her and between us. From the helplessness we felt at that moment I learned a great deal about the emotional conditions which activated a transforming symbolic process that affects the clinical situation.

At that moment, my participation was intense, though lacking clarity. I sensed a meaning in that sequence, and the only thing I tried to do was to keep a careful eye on what happened both during her playing and verbally. The prevailing element in the therapeutic field was Anna's despair, along with my total incapacity to understand the emotional dynamics she was experiencing and which encumbered us.

There are times when the psychic suffering is so deep and so foreign to normal experience that neither of us can find the right words for communicating it. At such moments, even silence, apparently easier to understand, is a problem for her: under certain circumstances it can accentuate the alien and disconcerting presence of an inexpressible emotion.

This is a situation in which sandplay can make it possible to contact the emotions present in the field, and lead to the transformation in the attitude of consciousness. My belief in this new means which I had experimented in my encounter with Dora Kalff, and the despair I shared in my relationship with Anna, were, I feel, decisive in creating the possibility of representing and transforming our shared experience. Our interest in the new instrument of communication and our active attention, as well, helped stimulate and carry to a level of representation the underlying emotional narrative structure of her suffering.

These are some of the emotional elements present in the field which certainly activated the capacity to represent and symbolize the deep emotional situation which, hidden until then, had caused Anna to go on repeating herself, both in her behavior and in her language.

The "alchemical vessel" metaphor, dear to Jung, seems particularly appropriate to me for describing the emotional dynamics at work in the analytic field, consisting of the complex interlacing of projections and identifications active in the relationship. And this choice is not simply an affectation, a way of "taking over" Jung's interest in alchemist literature. The image of the vessel in which different chemical elements react, aside from placing emphasis on the space it holds, also suggests the idea of a "distillation" of organized and recognizable forms, such as feelings, out of a magmatic chaos of emotions.

In *Psychology and Alchemy* (Jung, 1944), that controversial and complex book, which at times I found confusing, there are, I believe, many observations and images useful for giving visual shape to the emotional elements present in the analytic relationship and until now formulated in largely mechanistic terms. My purpose is to go beyond formulations of this kind, which, to be sure, facilitate understanding but which are often repetitive and ridden with jargon, in order to explore, through the visual metaphors drawn from sandplay, the emotional substratum that affects the analytic present. Using alchemical terminology, we might ask what it was at that moment that transformed the analytic relationship into a *rotundum* or a *vas mirabilis* and aroused such a meaningful process of symbolic representations of Anna's deep experience and of what was shared in our relationship.

From the experience of this all-involving process, I began to realize how important the transition to visibility was in the psychic economy, that is the moment, perceptible to consciousness, of the mental act which produces the representation. Using play materials solicits and stimulates this transition, whose secret is that it offers consciousness a first possibility for confronting, however partially, the emerging emotion, and therefore produces an intrapsychic and relational change that is clinically verifiable.

Going back over my notes of Anna's sequence of scenes, I recall the emotional atmosphere between us. For over a year, I had to deal with her recurring fits of depression. Her words, ringing with violent rage, were the exact counterpart of her passive behavior towards the people she loved, her husband in particular. Violence colored her repetitious conversation which would wander off into irrelevant descriptions, while it tended to provoke passiveness or helpless anger in me, as well. The strain and mental dullness which, together with Anna, I experienced in the relationship and in a certain sense endured in my perception of the countertransference, coincided with the uneasiness and the sense of loss described by alchemists before the v*era imaginatio* emerged. Jung writes (*ibid.* par. 360):

> The anonymous author of the *Rosarium* says in another place that the work must be performed "with the true and not with the fantastic imagination," and again that the stone is found "when the search lies heavy on the searcher."

In presenting the sequence of scenes I have preferred giving, as far as possible, a careful description of every single aspect. I realize that the reader may find this tedious, but it is the only way of dealing with the complexity of the narrative structure I wish to bring out in each single representation.

## 1 First Scene: "The Monster That Soaks Up Energy"

The first time Anna goes up to the empty tray of sand, she looks inhibited, uncertain, and speaks to me in an aggressive tone of voice. Why should she be playing games when the whole world is collapsing around her! She empties a whole carafe full of water into the tray almost as a way of showing total refusal. Only one small part of the sand remains dry. Then she sprinkles some red pigment onto the wet surface.

Using color as a first choice seems to give Anna second thoughts, to slow her down. Evidently something in her responds to that watery red substance resembling blood. As if an emotion she feels to be menacing had found a foothold in the color red. This is confirmed by the way her actions slow down, as if she were pausing to consider that watery spot of sand.

Anna goes back to the shelf and takes four stones and more thoughtfully places them in the upper left corner of the field which she has just splashed with water and color. Taking some small black pieces, she very carefully outlines a form vaguely suggested by the red stain (Fig. 1, Images). "It's a beast," she suddenly says, to my surprise, "a beast that soaks up nearly everything."

Her involuntary words underlined the moment when an invasive emotion, perceived as different-from-self, first takes on an image. She has started to play!

After outlining the red stain, the "beast," as she called it, she takes a stick and draws a line around the piece of dry sand on the right side of the tray. The sinuous shape that emerges looks like some sort of plant, but Anna says nothing. She then chooses some gold-colored pieces and, showing unexpected patience, arranges them almost forming horns on the shapeless head of the animal which I too begin to make out. The last thing she does is to take a fifth stone like the others and place it in the upper right hand corner with a single gold piece beneath it, as if to pick up and connect again the opposites of gold and black already present in the violent head.

From the sequence of the scene, two distinct stages can be seen. In the first, when Anna pours water into the tray, she seems to be expressing through gestures the same aggressive impulse that informs her words. She is clearly not looking for results, but acting out a discharge of emotional tension. The flooding of the tray coincides with, one might say, the psychological condition she is experiencing: the falling water would seem to be the infuriated expression of an as yet undefined feeling that she lacks substance, like a fluid, a shapeless something falling to the ground.

Her significant choice of the color red makes it possible to see what the next step would be: a representation will begin to appear. The shape gradually emerges now and Anna has to figure out how to complete it. The stones and black pieces are carefully chosen and placed specifically in order to give an outline to what is still only vaguely distinguishable from the background. Representation is first given to what she feels to be foreign, violent, different-from-self, whereas she seems to be alluding to a feeling of her own precariousness in that part of the tray that has remained dry, which she marks off with a furrow. The sequence strikes me as a process of extraction, which from a still formless level culminates in the recognition and definition of the form as an animal head. Her exclamation confirms this: "It's a beast that soaks up nearly everything." I see this as the personalized metaphor of an experience which, like a hemorrhage, leads to a loss of vital force. Up until then, Anna's only way of responding to that incommunicable sensation was by wavering between anger and passive resignation. I would say that her involuntary words are a resonance to the ongoing symbolic event; they express the perception of the symbolic moment. The exclamation stresses the recognition of a corresponding form and, to her own surprise, gives a momentary meaning to an inexpressible feeling.

In the relationship, something can start changing. The representation enables a distancing useful for beginning to relate to the emotional involvement that closely touches us both. The form appearing on the scene resonates in the analyst's listening, aside from the patient's direct remarks.

In our work, there is always the risk of clinging to the first definition of contents that emerge on the level of fantasies, dreams or play. The important thing is to always ask what emotional effect a certain content has on us, what it tends to make us do and say unconsciously.

I immediately associated the animal with the golden horns that soaks up energy with the uterus. A year before beginning analysis, Anna had an operation on her ovarian tubes and remained sterile. My association was connected with a feeling of loss, and was possibly not unrelated to that blood, to that presence which soaks up energy. The validity of an analyst's free association is or is not confirmed with time and in the way the process develops, so he keeps it to himself as part of the phenomenon of deep sharing. Ascribing meaning can be a living metaphor that reflects an emotion present in the field, that shapes the contents of the patient, as well as of the analyst or of both.

When that violent animal head appeared in the sand scene, a different atmosphere grew up between us. In this reconstruction, I remember the interest I took in that appearance, as the tension created by the anger and resignation which for some time had been ever-present in our sessions, faded away.

The finished scene, the whole appearance of it, shows an obvious bipolarity though still only slightly differentiated. Out of the empty tray of sand, from the initial chaos of the violent flooding of water and color, the modeling activity of consciousness extracted two figures: the dominating animal figure on the left and the narrow plant-like figure on the right. The careful outlining with black pieces, which comes after the division into two parts, confirms the predominance of the "beast," but at the same time, choosing a precious element like gold, brings out an unexpected value. Another highly significant polarity is the way the space is organized: the displacement of the scene to the left ("sinistra") as the expression of an unconscious content, which is at once frightening and "sinister" for consciousness, but also precious.

The spatial arrangement of the images is structurally significant. In dreams, as well, what is unfamiliar and troubling is very often placed on the left, whereas on the right appear the contents nearer to consciousness, easier to understand and to assimilate into what is already known. In this perspective, the plant-like spot of dry sand may be the emerging expression of perceptions of self in the face of the brute force of an emotion.

The last gold piece placed under the black stone in the upper right-hand corner would seem to indicate a possibility of synthesis. The gold looks as it if had been drawn out of the "blackness," out of the darkness that consciousness passes through, like the quintessence, as the alchemist would say, that can spring from the dialectic of opposites. A form, therefore, which, by joining opposites, gives the idea of a symbol. But this can be proved only by what happens in later sand scenes, and above all by the transformation of the emotional dynamics in the analytic field.

The analyst's comments on the individual scenes are to be considered his *rêverie*. It is important to seek a thread of association that connects the different moments and aspects of a scene to the deep feeling shared in the analytic field. What in the end reflects most closely the psychic event experienced in analysis is the sequence of the scenes, which taken as a whole express the increasingly clear organization of an unfolding symbolic process which for both of us has transformed the relationship to emotions.

Through the sandplay images the first metaphors emerge, or rather the first interpretations by images, which show that Anna has established a contact between herself and the deep emotional charges present in her life, as well as in the analytic relationship. Her initial choices (water, stones, color) reveal a primary level of expression through materials, but a distinct image suddenly takes shape in that chaotic jumble: the head of a violent animal. Enriched by years of sharing with Anna in analysis, I can begin to associate the forms appearing in the play scene with some key elements of her personal story.

The "beast that soaks up energy," which Anna often felt identified with in her invasive attacks of anger or which she endured passively, almost provoking it in others, we later on connected with the moments of catastrophic disruption in her life. Her father's sudden death in Africa, when Anna was a little girl, first brought on a serious state of stupefying depression which it took her several months to get over. It then reappeared time and again, for no apparent reason, suggesting some sort of cyclothymic disorder.

During the war, after risking death in the collapse of her house, she started suddenly losing consciousness, with convulsions or absences. Both the recurring fits of depression and the epileptic seizures she suffered as a girl were certainly closely connected with explosive emotional situations. When she began analysis, generalized convulsive attacks (with positive electro-encephalogram), though kept under control with medicines, would appear every four or five months, while violent shifts of mood were more frequent.

"I'm tied up in a sack and my mother bangs me on the head with a stone," is the way Anna, from our very first meetings, described the aura that preceded her convulsive attacks. The story of this difficult relationship, of central importance to her life, appears in the representation preceding the outbreak of convulsions. This is an important fact because it brings back the main theme of this first scene, as well.

The head stands out as the chief figure. It is a special way of expressing a feeling of utter loss where only a small part of the self, the piece of dry sand, escapes the flood and, I might say, the loss of blood, the color red, that suddenly invades her mental space.

## 2 Second Scene "The Monster and the Woman Who Isn't"

Anna comes back two days after creating her first play scene and without a word starts working with the sand. Her interest in the new means shows that her experience of the previous session has had an effect. On the right side, she digs an oval hole down to the blue floor of the tray. With lichens, moss, stones and a shell a face begins to emerge. "It's a woman," she states briefly in a low voice. Working with intense concentration, she creates a form on the left side: the body of a fish with an outsized human head (Fig. 2, Images). "It's a monster, a male," she says, intent in her work. The two halves of the scene, at first separated, are joined together by a little tunnel which is invisible in the photograph.

There is moderation, pace and precision in Anna's gestures. Finally, she digs out another oval in the fish's tale and in the upper left-hand corner adds a stone which seems to give weight to the figures on that side. As in the previous scene, the disconcerting intensity of expression on the left side of the scene reappears. As a final move, she places two boats on the face of the "woman who isn't." She looks satisfied and unusually more relaxed.

As in the first scene, what is striking here is the bipolarity of the representation. The woman's face on the right side, made out of stones, moss and a shell, suggests an image reflected in water. The myth of Narcissus, ever present in analytic thought, comes immediately to mind, but it also recalls the ability to ponder the image of self as the beginning of a differentiation.

The predominantly plant-like character of the woman's face has, as its consistency, the empty floor of the tray. The moss outlines something that still isn't, like the line marking off the dry sand devoid of objects in the first scene. It would seem to express the same main theme, to represent its development towards the level of personification.

Even before analysis, Anna has always had a remarkable gift for recovery. She would resprout and reflower like a plant even after very painful situations. Her strength was a depth of feeling and a constant desire to understand, despite everything. The shell in the place of the woman's mouth reminds me of her talent for using words, for writing, in trying to deal with her emotions at difficult moments, until succeeding years later in writing poetry. Aside from her seizures, her profundity, represented by the face which looks like it is made out of water in the scene, was translated into a capacity for listening and relating to others. When she was unwell the other side of this aspect would reappear, in being the woman who isn't who in a state of complete passivity and "fluidity" in the hands of her loved ones.

The figure on the left, the fish with a man's head, picks up the theme already present in the previous scene and links it to monstrosity: "half animal, half man," like the fantasies that illustrate alchemists' texts or fairy-tales.

In life, as in analysis, Anna sometimes acted this part, all brain, but brimming with irrationality: in those moments, she was ruled by an invasive animus.[27] Her speech was pungent, critical, incapable of listening. If this represents one animus aspect, it has the place it merits in the scene; it has become a pathway into the deepest level of the unconscious, a go-between in her relationship to it.

In this scene, the two aspects of the psychic polarity take on the connotation of "male" and "female." The tunnel between the two halves indicates a possible relationship, on both an intrapsychic and interpersonal level, between what was separate in the previous scene.

Anna's last move, placing two boats on the woman's water-face would seem to indicate a way of crossing it, of getting to know it.

This short sequence shows us the birth of a representation. After reaching in her playing the level where visual images emerge, what was first experienced, but unseen, changes it relationship to the ego complex. That Anna was more tranquil offers proof of this transformation. Her change of mood can be seen as the transition from the condition of being related to a yet undifferentiated emotion to the possibility of symbolization. Contact with materials succeeded in activating a symbolic process and hence an elaboration so far impossible through words.

As of the first impulsive inundation we witnessed the emergence of an active image emerge, which was drawn forth thanks to Anna's careful outlining. This is the moment when the unconscious and consciousness confront each other, or rather the moment when the emotional nucleus, still at an archaic level, encounters the modeling activity of consciousness. Observe, moreover, how in the first scene, the "monster" was two-dimensional, barely sketched on the surface, whereas now it has acquired the three-dimensionality of the man-fish. As if the different-from-self had become more and more explicit and also taken on significant consistency, whereas the similar-to-self, first the light line

[27] In the terminology inaugurated by Jung, "Animus" and "Anima" represent the functions of relating to the unconscious: the personification "Anima" in men and "Animus" in women.

around the piece of dry sand and now the woman's face, stressed emptiness and inconsistency as an inmost experience of self.

Two opposites meet and a process of symbolic representation by images begins, leading to a first attempt at synthesis. From that moment, the emotional field of the relationship has also changed. In the evolution from the shapeless monster to the man-fish, from the barely outlined plant-form to the woman who isn't we see a symbolic activity emerge that corresponds to a change of energy in the field of the relationship.

I have spoken a great deal about Anna's choices but little about her use of space, which in sandplay has great expressive potentialities. Note, for example, the diagonal arrangement of the imagery, and remember that diagonals are to be considered the result of two right-angle lines: the tension between contraries here finds expression not only in the tunnel connecting them but possibly also in the spatial arrangement itself. The moment a symbol is created, opposite forces come into agreement. Anna goes beyond her old position and unwittingly discovers a new adjustment of libidinal energy. In the sequence of representations that appeared in the scene, I was able to assist the manifestation of a symbolic process at first hand.

## 3 Third Scene: "The African Witch-doctor"

Anna is so taken with sandplay that she herself is surprised. The atmosphere of the relationship has completely changed. Words no longer convey the violent reactions still present during the making of the first scene a week earlier. It is as if sandplay had absorbed all her energy and interest. Conversation with me is limited to a few comments about what is happening in the play scene. An unusual silence reigns between us, a sort of peaceful and relaxed concentration.

Anna immediately begins by piling up wet sand in the middle of the tray, and carefully forms the head and shoulders of a human figure which fills almost the whole space (Fig, 3, Images). "It's an African witch-doctor," she says, as she emphasizes the features of the face with shells, madrepore, moss, lichens and stones.

She then concentrates on the right side, where she carefully adorns the figure of a bird sitting on the witch-doctor's shoulder with blue, green and gold pieces. "It's a peacock," she says, adding after a pause, "Like a baby eating the bogeyman." This remark takes me by surprise like a sudden, acute and striking act of interpretation, even though I do not understand it yet. For the first time, she creates a real landscape in the background: a house, flowering plants, and two boats on a beach to the left. Anna's last move is to make a necklace out of colored beads, which she says are precious, and put it around the neck of the "witch-doctor."

The two opposites are still there, but inserted into an everyday world. Archaic and irrational elements still prevail, both in relation to the background and in the disproportionate dimensions. Beside the primitive witch-doctor and the peacock, a bird which in mythology is identified with Venus, room is made for everyday life for the first time. The witch-doctor is powerful, demoniacal, and seems to superimpose reality; like the man-fish in the last scene, he is characterized by sea elements. Though its size and the description itself of "African witch-doctor" are laden with the imaginary, the figure seems more closely related to the human world than the previous monster.

The magnificence and solidity of the workmanship seem to have nothing in common with the emptiness of the woman's face in the previous scene. What Anna calls it is revealing: a "witch-doctor," therefore a being in touch with chthonic forces, at once a destroyer and a healer, like the great unconscious. The witch-doctor again leads to the representation of an emotional content that has already appeared. It seems, in fact, to be the new metaphor of the shapeless monster in the first scene and the man-fish in the second, so it is a figurative expression which reaches a new level of personification, one easier to contact, that lies nearer to consciousness.

The name "African" helps to make things clearer. Africa was where Anna's father caught the contagious disease that shortly led to his death, the first real catastrophe in her life. As emerges from her case history, for over a week Anna remained in a state of complete indifference to her surroundings, denying the evidence of the facts. Africa was, for her, a place of loss, of death, but many years later also the source of deep cultural interest and job opportunities.

It is very important in sandplay to note the moment when involuntary verbal commentary begins. Her phrase referring to the peacock: "It's like a baby eating the bogeyman," still puzzles me and gives pause. She had certainly "assimilated" the unsettling contents represented by the "witch-doctor" but why a peacock-baby?

This free association on Anna's part offered the possibility for further amplifications. In alchemy, the peacock appears as a sun symbol representing the synthesis of colors. Conflicting emotions reach their first synthesis, I might say, in its representation. For alchemists, elements formerly separated in the "massa confusa" are carried to a new unity that organizes them. Also in Christian iconography, for some scholars the peacock, like the phoenix, is a symbol of resurrection, resurrection in the sense of a radical change of direction that alters our view of the world.

Then as now, the peacock strikes me as an outgrowth of the woman's face in the last scene, and also bears the same colors. This metaphor, which replaces the empty space, lays stress on the mysterious and disconcerting creativity of the feminine side, which generates something new out of apparently nothing. From my point of view, the "pea-cock-baby eating the bogeyman" association alludes to subsequent levels of integration of consciousness with respect to the unconscious.[28]

In its earliest stages, the process of integration is given the simplest graphic expression: from the boundary lines in the first scene to the reflected image that begins to emerge in the second, we now reach the animal level. It would be most interesting to follow in the path laid out by Jung and discover the recurrence of certain forms of ex-pression, like those I have just mentioned, picking up some of the notions of the "pea-cock" figure and the way human imagination has used

[28] In Chapter XI, I go into the subject of the levels of integration of consciousness which the expressive capacities of sandplay bring out.

it over the years. Peacocks are associated with babies probably in the sense that they represent a still partial level of consciousness, one certainly more integrated, however, than the woman with the empty face in the previous scene.

It would seem that for each new assimilation of deep emotions, those remaining or those which have become unconscious, consciousness shows the stages of our evolution during growth in progressive order. From personification on a still animal level, the peacock, Anna would reach, in a subsequent stage, the human figure that is only anticipated in that session by her verbal comment. Her remark, however enigmatic and paradoxical, surfacing like an impulsive interpretation, foreshadows an as yet unattained verbal level and therefore a new possibility of relating to the underlying content.

## 4 Fourth Scene: "The Monster Is Attacked"

Anna returns four days later, saying she needs to go on working with the sand. As she starts playing, she tells me a dream she has had:

> I had to cross the sea to Africa to take away a dead body and bury it. I know it is a man though I can't see it because he's covered with rags. The whole trip would take place in one day.

We don't talk about the dream, even though it contains the idea of death in Africa, one so important to Anna, who lost her father there. She is busy creating her scene. I sense that seeking contact with the sand and adding water to get the right consistency have something to do with the subject of her dream, laying to earth an emotional content charged with death.

Anna first made something resembling a face in the middle, punching in the eyes and putting a stone in the mouth. The figure immediately has a deep emotional effect on me, gives me a sense of something gruesome and rotting. The silence between us is very intense and would last for the whole session. I notice her concentration and effort as, next to the immobility of that head, she creates two dynamic forms which in the end she would call "crocodiles." The hour has passed in silence and the scene is unfinished. She asks me to save it until the next day (Fig. 4, Images).

In this scene sequence the head is still predominant. For me too, it is charged with a feeling of death that had never appeared so distinctly before. But what is now clearly expressed was already implicit in the preceding scenes.

The playing would seem to be a continuation of the dream and create a metaphor which corresponds to the burial that is to take place. The converging of dream work and sandplay indicates that a fundamental thematic nucleus, until then only relatively identified, is approaching a new possibility of expression: the presence in the dream and in the sand of a single nucleus of meaning, here the elaboration of an old, but still deeply-felt loss, indicates a fully-reached maturation. A process of symbolization has been set into motion which, in the dream and in the sand, tends to pass from the representative level to the verbal level, though as yet without attaining it. In fact, Anna is not yet able to put into words what she succeeds in saying with her hands, just as in the dream she fails to recognize by sight the identity of the dead body. It is covered with rags, probably old defenses now fallen into disuse, and cannot be reached by the differentiation of a lucid consciousness that has shared speech freely at its disposal.

The dynamic circular arrangement of the crocodiles reminds me of the *uroborus*, the snake-dragon that eats its tail and in alchemy signifies the *opus circulare*: the *uroborus* in fact represents the mysterious circulation of chemical elements in the hermetic vessel during distillation. Another association regards the *circumambulatio*, the typical way many ritual dances move around a center to assimilate the contact with the divine and surrender to it, reaching new levels of consciousness.[29] Assimilation attacks the head in the form of crocodiles. The peacock in the last scene was probably the first attempt to es-

[29] See the tradition of the tarantists in Southern Italy, described by De Martino, or of the dervishes in the Middle East.

tablish contact with the "bogeyman" that appeared in Anna's comment, and which here is imbued with the intensity of total loss. The two crocodiles represent the energy that seeks to metabolize a mortal dread that is always active in the unconscious.

In ancient Egypt, crocodiles were considered the great initiators. They frequently appear in tombs and, according to scholars, represent the journey into the hereafter. It is a crocodile which at midnight, at the dawning of a new day, reconstructs and regenerates the creatures it has devoured. Also in Anna's dream a sea crossing has to be made in a single day. It is a question of laying to mother earth a deep emotion which had so far never reached the level of visual imagery. It is as if to say that Anna, ever since the death of her father, were dealing with the anguish of the complex active in her unconscious. At that moment, instead of repeating it in symptoms she succeeds in bringing it to representation.

The next day, as she looks at the scene I had saved for her (an unusual thing for me to do, which shows my emotional resonance at the moment, though I was only partly aware of it), she is nervous, tense, aggressive, as she never has been since the first scene. "Do you believe in what I'm doing, might I not be playing a silly game? If you weren't here I'd smash the whole thing."

She starts with some moss which she tucks into the cracks of the head and says: "There's an infantile block around this big head." Then she places more plants in the background and finally some spikes of wheat with some animals among them, a couple of hippopotami and rhinoceri and two race horses. She takes some water, adds red coloring and pours it all out on the head in the middle.

"It has to collapse," she says to herself with conviction. She adds a crocodile and a dog crawling out of the eye sockets and two monkeys and a squirrel on the forehead. She looks around and finding the right color, paints a pelican blue and places it among the spikes of wheat at the top. Then she adds some stones, a piece of wood on the left side and, as a last move, six astronauts landing from a space ship. One of them is photographing the big head with its red stain (Fig. 4A, Images).

After the relief she felt in previous sessions, Anna again finds herself dealing with an emotion from the distant past, "an infantile block," as she herself remarks. It is something that must be resolved once and for all, but which still makes its oppressive presence felt. Her words, in their harsh, ironic tone, reveal the deep uneasiness that contact instills in her.

The process of assimilation, noticed in the previous scenes, evolves. Separate parts continue to be seen, as if they were gradually distilled from the whole, and human figures appear for the first time: the astronauts. This latter choice is significant because it is as if Anna had contacted a different dimension, one unknown or yet only obscurely familiar, of her experience of self. The relationship between her and this deep emotional nucleus, which bears a characteristic mark of her story and her psychic disorder, is changing. For me, the photographer is the representative of the lucid integrated consciousness that differentiates and uses the representation of an emotion without being subject to it any longer.

The use of miniature human figures in the scene shows a new level of integration in Anna's relationship to her emotions, one that is, I would say, closer to spoken language. Something becomes sayable and is extracted from the previous indistinct emotional material. The incomplete and encumbering presence of the African witch-doctor who ruled the world was different: here it is the human world which, with its technology, approaches the mystery in order to discover an aspect of it.

Every sand scene, like every dream, has infinite levels of expression and is never completely understood. I consider it of great importance to bear clearly in mind the criterion of interpretation we intend following. From my point of view, the levels of expression in the representation must be singled out before identifying their contents.

The "monster" in the first scene is two-dimensional, made of nothing but sand and color, the "man-fish" and "African witch-doctor" are already shown in relief: three-dimensionality is present if only for parts of the body. With the use of objects full figures appear, the astronauts and the photographer in the last scene.

First inanimate objects, then animals and lastly human figures can thus be seen as more and more integrated levels, as consecutive steps in a single expressive process. So it is the sequence of the various shapes that indicate more and more clearly the contents we are beginning to discern. This view of the so-called "vertical" perspective, from the less integrated to the more evolved, must always be combined with the "horizontal" perspective, where the single attributes of an object and a shape that has appeared have an importance that must be extracted, a meaning that can be amplified, as I did, for example, with crocodiles. The amplification of individual shapes on the basis of historical and cultural knowledge is necessary in order to provide a new hold on understanding. Even so, should this becomes the only key of interpretation, it would risk lapsing into a sort of generalized literariness which would leave out of consideration the personal and relational context in which the significant shapes appear.

It should also be remembered that, when the time comes to interpret a scene in detail (as happens only in reviews and not while the scenes are being made, except for pointing out limited similarities between the metaphors of sandplay and the feeling present in the relationship and in the life of the player),[30] it is important for each of these figures to be reexamined against the background of the patient's personal history and of the emotional vicissitudes shared in analysis. Theoretically, every choice clarified by amplification could be added to this mosaic and increasingly embellish it in a process of excavation that never completely comes to an end.

Amplification can now help us approach at least two of Anna's choices: the monkey on the forehead of the gruesome head in the center and the blue pelican at the top of the tray. Iconographically, they are both recurring images that have been used to express certain emotions, and amplification can make them easier to understand.

[30] As to the whens and hows of interpreting play scenes, see also Chapter XVI.

In his comments on the 16th dream described in *Psychology and Alchemy*, Jung (1944, par. 169) observes with regard to the monkey:

> Now he is to be "reconstructed," and this can only mean that the anthropoid – man as an archaic fact – is to be put together again.

And then goes on to add (par. 175):

> The gibbon belongs to the anthropoids and, on account of its kinship with man, is an appropriate symbol for that part of the psyche which goes down into the subhuman. Further, we have seen from the cynocephalus or dog-headed baboon associated with Thoth-Hermes, the highest among the apes known to the Egyptians, that its godlike affinities make it an equally appropriate symbol for that part of the unconscious which transcends the conscious level.

These remarks serve only to explain one way of exploring the meaning by setting every single choice into a mythical framework. It is significant that precisely at the moment of the destructuring of the old world, with its burden of a long conflictive history, the choice should fall on a monkey as if to indicate a possible reconstruction out of the archaic depths of the human world. These metaphorical suggestions borrowed from myths help give a broader scope to individual events, but at the same time show an archaic level of thinking, full of new metaphors for understanding personal experience.

One senses that behind each choice there is an overdetermination connected with the player's history, but also with the very structure of the psyche, with the typical, or archetypal, human dimension. These amplifications, also related to the transference and counter-transference activated in the analytic relationship, open up a perspective of the experiences of both participants. So the monkey on the forehead of that rotting head could represent the possibility of renewal after Anna's contact with loss and the experience of destructiveness deeply felt by her and shared in analysis.

At the top of the scene we have the blue pelican. The odd color raises an issue no less intriguing than the mythical bird itself. Anna chooses blue as a free association referring to the deepness of a world that is different from land, but which, like the sea, can be crossed. In Christian iconography, the pelican is the symbol of Christ in the two-fold aspect of sacrifice and rebirth: the theme of the above quotation returns with a different meaning. It appears as a content that has risen from the depths, and in the scene assumes the significance of a new center of energy whose radiating forces are represented by the animals running off to the right.

The expressive power of Anna's scenes so far must not make us lose sight of the verbal response to the symbolic event activated by sandplay. It is the other aspect of the phenomenon, the changing expression of her involuntary remarks, that must be kept in mind. Anna's first exclamation when she recognizes the "monster that soaks up energy" (first scene) is followed by the thoughtful silence that accompanies the construction of her second scene. Her quiet comment, muttered under her breath, about the "woman who isn't" seems to concern only herself, a soliloquy.

The tone changes when she speaks about the "African witch-doctor." The words not only give a name: "... it's a witch-doctor... it's a peacock," but also indicate something happening, an interpretation, I might say: "... like a baby eating the bogeyman." The last scene, completed in two installments, begins with her telling me a dream. The same dramatic tone seems to color both the dream and the play scene. The attention given to the two symbolic levels of play and words, with all their differences and similarities, stresses even more the transformational event we have observed.

As I mentioned in the last chapter, words would seem to break free from defensive repetitions and take on new tones and contents as the shapes are gradually "personified." From the shapeless spot of water and color to the part-object head of the monster, from the imposing and invasive figure of the witch-doctor, all the way to the astronauts in the last scene. They indicate the transformation of emotions in progress which the scene brings out as a progressive definition of human forms, and which seem to have an immediate effect on the capacity to verbalize. From then on, in the following scenes, conversation and play activities would flow more freely in the analytic field.

## 5 Fifth Scene “Split Objects Appear in the Field”

I must confess that for a long time this scene annoyed me. I tended to forget it. Even the usual notes I take at the end of every session were, compared to former ones, shorter and more limited. Now, some time later, I can try to understand this countertransferential reaction.

From my notes, more than from my memory, I can put together the sequence of Anna’s choices and only two things she said. The first thing she built on the empty floor of the tray was an owl crowned with leaves and with sharp eyes, particularly significant because they were made out of flashbulbs I used for taking photographs. Then to the left the shape of a fish emerged with sticks in it. The owl and the fish are whole figures, whereas the two breasts in the foreground are clearly incomplete (Fig. 5, Images), which would seem to suggest the intensely felt loss of the whole. An element all the more striking because it is set against an inhabited world to the right, full of vegetation and with domestic animals, an image that engenders a sense of tranquility and containment. On the one hand, nourishing mother earth, on the other, rising out of the blue floor, those impersonal breasts that have nothing to do with the rest.

“A fish has become a bird,” Anna said enigmatically, referring perhaps to the change of imagery that occurs while she is in the process of making the owl. She spoke as if she had experienced the sudden onset of an active fantasy that had appeared despite her initial intentions.

“I’d like the other fish to become a boat,” she added putting in the sticks, after which she finished the session without a word. She looked calmer but the main thing I felt was a tendency to dismiss the whole thing.

The sharp sight of the owl that sees in the dark, with its flashbulb eyes, recalls the analyst's routine practice of photographing scenes after every session. The sharp sight of them both, the analyst's in particular, can become persecutory in the analytic field. The history of psychoanalysis proves it with the brilliant invention of the typical analytical setting.

But there are always two sides to every question! Taking pictures of an image is also a sign of the attention and memory the analyst carefully preserves and then at the right moment restores to the patient through interpretation or the photographs he gives him at the end of the analysis, possibly after the revision or in any case upon request. I think the owl also brings to the scene the persecutory character of a deep emotion that threatens old defenses. Klein's concept of projective identification is very useful for understanding what was happening between Anna and me. That persecutory object caught, in the form of an owl, a play of projections and counterprojections which invaded the analytic field and which for a long time bewildered and troubled us. Sandplay, by rendering visible those invasive charges of feeling, gave relief to the patient and at the same time made me aware of the personal emotional counterresponses which I would probably rather not see. The same consideration applies, perhaps even more intensely, to the representation of breasts, which touches the foundations of our psychic experience.

The objects in the scene bring out Anna's uninhibited emotions and change them into negotiable feelings, difficult as they are to control. Her sharp, intuitional lucidity was sometimes a problem for her because it led her to take unthought-of risks. When she contained it by writing, succeeding in giving it a shape, she would feel better. In this scene, she has succeeded in the same intention, though at a more archaic preverbal level and therefore one more incisive for both of us. The owl that hoots and sees at night suggests this aspect, which Anna found difficult to contain, also because of an old wound, that has caused a fundamental need for restraint and nourishment, represented by the breasts in the foreground, to be partial, split and disconcerting. It is significant that these part-objects took shape only after the previous scene, in which the nucleus of death represented by the head, had dissolved and astronauts could land in that world apart. Only later did I realize how nicely these objects represented my emotional counter-reactions, as well. In fact, in the analytic field, I tended at times to become impulsively over-protective and maternal, at others inquisitorial and maybe persecutory, like that strange owl. The dissolution of the infantile block of the "big head," had allowed the split fragments of a complex experience I had undergone without realizing it, to appear in the play scene.

## 6 Sixth Scene: "Waiting for the Birth"

Anna returns four days later: she looks calmer and more serene than she has ever been since beginning the scene-building process. It is as if in the last session she had left her persecutory part-objects in me. My countertransferential disturbance proved it. She tells me a dream:

> I was sleeping with my head on the stomach of X [a man she trusted]. I had a sense of well-being and that his stomach was hugely capacious and cozy.

She begins by digging three circular holes in the sand all the way down to the blue floor of the tray. She circles the first hole on the left with spikes of wheat and adds some houses, moss and two boats; she lines the second hole with pieces of coral and in the third hole creates something she calls "a cradle" out of a piece of white Pongo. She stops and presses the seal of the signet ring she is wearing into the Pongo. "It's the one thing of my father's I have left," she remarks. Then she arranges flowers and cows around the cradle. She asks: "Do you see that the pools are the eyes and the cradle the mouth of a face?" She takes some blue stones and makes eyebrows on the face; at the top of the scene she adds the same piece of wood that was near the astronauts in the fourth scene and fastens a "Christmas star" on it, as if to confirm the dominating idea of birth. In the end she makes a path out of pebbles that winds up from right to left all the way to the star. An old man, a young man carrying a torch and a woman walk along the path (Fig. 6, Images).

I am immediately struck by the uniform and peaceful character of this scene compared to the previous one, for me almost unbearable, with its split forms charged with the imaginary.

A birth is now announced. The cradle, impressed with the seal of her father's signet ring, is rich in meaning. Thinking back over Anna's story, in which that sudden death had left a feeling of unbearable grief, its emotional charge repressed and therefore never elaborated, that seal of identification seemed to fill a void. The oldest nucleus of her trouble, which always reappeared with the male figures in her life, has opened up to the announcement of the new. The "face" is no longer the head fraught with a sense of death and decay in the next to the last scene, but a friendly landscape like the stomach of the positive father figure that welcomes her in the dream, allowing her to relax. Again, the thematic convergence of the dream and the sand scene shows that the emotional nucleus of that story has reached a new level and is probably about to undergo a change.

The color red, that appeared in the first scene, as invasive and agonizing as a hemorrhage, is condensed here into the coral. This too is a transformation charged with meaning: from a feeling of mortal loss to the discovery of a value.

My free associations with Anna's metaphors could be further amplified. What matters however is the sequence of transformations, by no means accidental, of a signifier like the color red.

## 7 Seventh Scene: "The Birth: An Earthquake"

Three weeks have gone by since the first scene and four days remain before the last. Anna feels better, has resumed her normal activities, both at home and elsewhere.

She goes immediately over to the tray, as if she were following a train of thought all her own, without a word of explanation. She piles up some sand in the middle of the field and sticks three stones in it: a white one in the middle, a black one just above it and a gray one below. Pointing to the white stone, she immediately remarks: "It's the skull of a primitive man, it's coming out of a monkey skin. It's a birth, the arms and legs are still inside".

Then digging all the way to the blue floor of the tray, she creates an encircling hole in the shape of a vase. She places three more stones on the right side and with daubs of blue paint turns them into the heads of a sheep, a fish and a rabbit, from top to bottom as she herself specifies:

> The animals are waiting for the man as the monkey skin sinks into the depths. The man has everything to do, it's a beginning: his companions are primitive.

Then she places some houses, trees and vehicles on the left side and, knocking them all over, says:

> The birth of the man doesn't happen without seriously damaging certain structures, everything is topsy-turvy as if there had been an explosion, an earthquake.

She goes back to work on the right-hand side and adding some white and blue tesserae, says: "It's a spring of pure water that flows into the deep water of the vase". To finish, she places on the original island a crocodile and a hippopotamus who are in the process of leaving (Fig. 7, Images).

The quiet expectation of the last scene no longer exists: here the birth is taking place as a great upheaval. The scene becomes strongly realistic in tone, with that emerging primitive human skull. The white, black and gray stones seem to point up the fact that the new contains its opposites and also seems to mediate them: mix black and white together and you get gray. I am struck by the reference to the monkey skin which recalls the animal she placed on the rotting head of the fourth scene. In my comment, I quoted Jung (1944, par. 169):

> The anthropoid – man as an archaic event – is to be put together again.

What is now represented confirms that context. Beneath that first form, the new man emerges: this is the real upheaval. When a new possibility of consciousness emerges, it always does so through the loss of the previous world.

Anna speaks in mythical terms, with an over-emphasis which to my conscience proves almost irritating, but she moves through the archetypal moments we all experience whenever the themes of birth and death prevail. Everything happens in the vase where the water is very deep. There is an echo here of such alchemical themes as *aqua permanens*, which for medieval scientists was the figurative expression of the vital factor that dissolves, but also synthesizes, their contents.

The whole scene is dominated by the act of birth. As in myths, the animals are spectators and helpers. The meaning may lie in the fact that renewal, when it is authentic, can only emerge from the instinctive bedrock of our animal structure. The vitality of the birth is also confirmed by that spring of pure water as the bearer of life. The scene also lends something rhetorical also to my comments, as happens when the basic psychic structures which Jung called archetypal, are activated. My feeling of irritation over that contact, even now long afterwards, offers indirect proof that Anna had gone very deep.

## 8 Eighth Scene: "The Dragon: Only the Little Girl Sees and Talks to It"

Two days later Anna starts building a strange animal out of moss, leaves and wood in the middle of the scene. She digs a canal around it to isolate it from the surrounding world. "It's a dragon," she says, "it's invisible to everybody except the little girl who talks to it." All around it she adds some houses, human figures and trees and to the right side of the scene a little girl in front a church with a large black stone towering over it. The eyes of the dragon are made out of flashbulbs (Figs. 8 and 8a, Images).

To be sure, that dragon has been around a long time, unseen, in the reciprocal play of projections and identifications. It was present and exerted its influence without my realizing it. Those flash-bulb eyes remind me that, in certain moments, as I took notes and photographs, I was also defending myself against invasive emotions that were hard to control because I still barely understood them. It was my unconscious way of fending off that troubling presence, perhaps just because I was unable to identify it, as happens for the people in the scene who live in the surrounding world.

Anna now makes it clear that the little girl in her is precisely what makes it possible for her to make the dragon visible and talk to it. This is the result of a month-long process.

In this context, it is the little girl that represents Anna's self-image. The dragon is the last representation of the "different-from-self," the forms of which we followed as they unfolded, starting with the animal that soaks up energy. The similar-to-self part took shape gradually: from the barely recognizable figure that survived the flooding (first scene), to the "woman who isn't" (second scene), to the peacock (third scene) down to collective personifications, like the astronauts (fourth scene) or the people in landscapes that resemble the conscious world. It is the first time Anna recognizes herself in a female personification, even though a little girl. She is the protagonist of the scene: she sees what others don't see and converses sympathetically with her solitary "monster." This is what happens when an analysis is successful.

What made a person different and caused years of suffering, is finally recognized, seen and confronted in a dialogue that will last a lifetime and which, in the end, for better or worse, represents his or her individual uniqueness. In the first impact with emotions the distance of an adequate defense is always necessary. Only later, as was the case with Anna, can one enter into a relationship that transcends the previous situation. What seems certain to me is that the scene describes, on the one hand, a more stable relationship to reality, till then never represented in such detail, on the other, the discovery of a dialogue with the unconscious.

## 9 Ninth Scene: "Balance Restored"

Two days later, Anna returns to the play area and starts digging two symmetrical holes in the sand at the top of the tray. In the left hole, she places a heavy stone, in the right an ancient long-handled drinking cup. Further down, between the two holes, she piles up a round heap of sand and places a pinecone on top. With the greatest care, she builds a tunnel between the two round holes and digs two more small symmetrical circles adding a red stone in the middle. With great concentration, she takes some gold tesserae and makes eyes in the large stone on the left: the result is a face with a twisted expression. "it's an African Jupiter!"

In the drinking cup to the right, she makes a woman's face out of wet sand and carefully places around it a diadem of gold tesserae. She devotes her last moves to the pinecone in the foreground: she adds some blue and white tesserae and branches of red coral and at the top a penguin. She sprinkles the cone with gold dust and lastly inserts four spikes of wheat at right angles, asking: "Which way's north?" as if it were a compass.

> I thought of a man and woman united by this red stone; maybe it represents God the father. I see the pine cone as their son: it's a sundial pointing in the four directions of space (Fig. 9, Images).

What immediately draws my attention is the last thing she added to the scene, the carefully decorated pine cone: a sundial, according to Anna, but also a point of reference in space with the spikes of wheat indicating the cardinal points. Time and space, categories of consciousness, find a center of reference. This round mandala-like shape, a sundial, marks the position of the sun and therefore gives the time; it is also the side of the tray nearest to Anna, which helps her find her bearings in space. After a long process lasting thirty days, Anna has finally established a relationship with the representation of a center which, for the time being, seems to steady her. It is a moment of integration which, in the symmetry of the scene, seems to conciliate still intensely conflicting emotions. The woman's face, now present inside the cup, and that primitive, bestial "African Jupiter," are the protagonists.

Each scene examined so far is to be considered a step in a process of assimilating deep emotions, up to this important finding. That it is a particularly harmonious moment for Anna is proved not only by her sense of well-being but also by a dream she told me at the end of the session:

> I bought a comfortable house overlooking the sea. Before me in the sunlight is a blue bay; on the opposite side I discover a landscape with old ruins. I am very pleased.

Space and time in the dream too! Later, in the chapter devoted to the emerging narrative structure of the Self in play scenes, I will return, on a theoretical level, to this central moment in the metabolism of feelings, so clearly represented by Anna's scene.[31] For the moment I would like to discuss the overall structure of the scene.

What is immediately striking is the symmetry of the representation. All the parts turn on the center described above, the bestial "African Jupiter" with its gold eyes, and the cup containing the decorated female face, it too very carefully composed. The woman's face, now consistent and recognizable, takes me back to the woman's face made of water in the second scene that was set against the man-fish monster. At that time, all the weight was on the left side of the scene, where the monster was, now there seems to be a greater balance. The personalization limited to faces only, both of the woman and of "Jupiter," indicates in my opinion a still partial integration of the emotions. In the strange abstract image inserted between the two faces, impossible to see in the photograph, unfortunately, special care was given to joining the two parts. It is a mask-like form consisting of two round holes and a red stone, which Anna calls "God the father." For the ancient Greeks, Jupiter was also the father. Here the attribute "African" plays up its primitive, perhaps bestial aspect. The

[31] Dora Kalff has pointed out these moments of psychic integration, calling them "manifestations of Self." On this subject, also see Chapter XVII.

father, in the archetypal sense, holds together the opposites of life and death, of good and evil. We know that Anna's story was marked by the violent loss of her father in Africa.

The scene takes perpetually conflicting parts of her story, condenses them in unexpected ways and makes them coherent. It shows a point that has been reached, and it is important that this happened at precisely that moment, at the end of the process I have described. The balance sought in the symmetry of representation seems to point to a need that Anna had always felt: a fullness of life, a center capable of giving meaning. It was a me-experience which she seemed to have attained in adolescence and which she lost after her father's death and with the appearance of her epileptic seizures.

I have tried to describe the sequence of Anna's scenes with the greatest possible care, because they made me realize, as few others did, the meaning of sandplay. An "epoch-making" experience for me, one that represents the moment when I took the new path which still today I follow with interest. I am grateful to Anna because she introduced me to the world of images and made me realize its transforming power.

Anna had experienced loss and succeeded in depicting it in a series of shared representations. While the process was taking place I was still very much unaware, but for me it was important to retrace, reexplore and reexamine it time and again and realize there is always something new to discover, still today after all these years.

I believe that in the course of analysis Anna found her balance, even if only part of what she succeeded in telling me in play scenes became words and therefore energy at her disposal for a lifetime.

# IV Imagination in Analysis: Prospects for Research

*Every psychic process is an image and an "imagining," otherwise no consciousness could exist and the occurrence would lack phenomenality.* C.G. Jung (1939) par. 889

To understand sandplay more thoroughly and attempt to see its potentialities and its limitations in therapy, as well as in research, we must discuss imagination, of which sandplay is the particular expression.

In the history of thought, the act of imagining has had its ups and downs. It is still an open question and it would be very instructive to retrace the constant fluctuations, between underestimation and overestimation, which imagination has come up against.

In the present chapter I will limit myself to indicating some problematic issues raised by the research of Freud and Jung, in order to get a picture of their different approaches to the question. This will make it easier to see how the use of sandplay in the analysis of adults is a natural offshoot of some of Jung's theoretical premises.

## 1 Imagination as a Complex Phenomenon: Uncertain Definition of Terms

In everyday use, the words "image" and "imagination" or "fantasy" refer to the psychic experience of forms taking shape in our inner theater. What becomes visible in our mind is possessed of a special character, and cannot be traced to the outside world as it appears to our senses, nor to the experience in which we recognize ourselves as subjects. It has rightly been called the "intermediate" between us and the world.[32]

In the history of analytic thinking the use of different terms – representation, image, fantasy, phantasm – to indicate that experience, proves the at once complex and slippery character of what we are trying to name.[33] It is also significant that in everyday use the word "imagination" indicates both the scene that appears and the psychic activity that shapes it. The act and its product are contained in the same word. But also among adepts the words "image" and "fantasy" suffer from the same uncertainty. In fact, they apply both to visibility as an introspective experience of representing, to the "thing" that becomes visible in our inner theater, and to a greater inclination to experiment, which results in, and organizes into, a consistent whole, a multitude of perceptual and not only visual stimuli.

Only under certain conditions in the psychic field may images, viewed as the organization of emotional experience in visible forms, such as in dreams and fantasies, may reach this level of inner perception and thus appear as forms that stand out against the background. But they are already an active psychic presence before becoming visible in the inner theater. The word image or "fantasy" is also used to indicate the simple readiness to experiment which, unseen, directs and informs the actions, the behavior, the gestures and feelings of every individual.

It is a matter, therefore, of two different moments in the psychic economy and it is significant that no word has yet been found to distinguish them. Integration on the level of visibility is reached, in fact, only at a certain point of the imaginal experience. My thesis here is that when subjects integrate their emotions into a visual form, they are able to handle their relationship with them in a different way. It is as if to say that already on its own the attained visibility trans-

[32] It is to Winnicott that we owe the most far-reaching conjectures about intermediate space, also called "transitional" and "potential" according to the meaning it is given, in which images take shape. On this subject, see Chapter V.
[33] In the present text, I often use the words "fantasy" and "image" as synonyms, a residue of the problems of terminology under discussion.

forms the relationship between consciousness and subconscious or unconscious feelings.

## 2 Initial Research: Freud Points the Way

Depth psychology found its field of investigation by occupying that intermediate territory between the inner and the outer world, the within and the without, where the imagination takes shape.

Over a hundred years ago, with the foreseeing clarity of creative men, Nietzsche wrote (1879):

> Direct observation is not nearly sufficient for us to know ourselves: we require history, for the past continues to flow within us in a hundred waves.

This poetic image foretells the path which not long after depth psychology would follow in the attempt to understand psychic suffering. Characters, places, basic patterns of our history emerge spontaneously in dreams and daydreams. Freud was the first to venture into the place where the "hundred waves" of our history are formed, that place, between the real and the mysterious around us, where representations begin.

Science, in an attempt to explain psychic suffering, had up until then focused its attention on that "immediate observation of oneself" which could be attained by studying the functions of consciousness. This viewpoint tended to identify the psyche itself with consciousness, and failed to see that imagination was a useful pathway to knowledge. For Freud, instead, the psychic activity which gives form and movement to what occurs in our inner world, no longer seemed accidental, but was sustained rather by a narrative structure, like a story with a hidden meaning. What emerges in dreams and fantasies are stories in which events and figures are significantly linked together. But what goes to form that narrative structure?

For Freud the unifying theme was to be found in the history of the individual himself: an event or a particular moment in his life could have been experienced as overwhelming, or downright traumatic, in a certain stage of his growth. Even if banished from consciousness, repressed, and hence apparently forgotten in the unconscious, the "trauma" could go on producing effects on an emotional plane: a hidden presence which seemed to govern the patient's life, like the scenes of his dreams or fantasies, almost as if it were a basic narrative structure.

Subsequently, the stories, the memories themselves recounted by the patient, at first thought to be based on real events, were also considered imaginary by Freud. Those "memories" were perceptions by images of deep largely unconscious feelings, which governed the life of the individual and at the same time determined the particular nature of his suffering. So imaginal activity became the way for approaching and understanding the determinants of the psychic conflict.

To find meaning in that submerged world which triggers psychic suffering, Freud resorted to a borderline concept: wishes. Wishes appear on the scene of imagination as obscure figures, dynamic elements lacking reflection, which seek to release their tension in immediate gratification. The goal they aspire to is like a mirage, something people have already experienced in life and want to return to when they end up in the wasteland of privation. Often the accumulation of wishes is too explosive, and becomes destructive for the established order of a familiar and enduring relationship with reality by which consciousness is reassured. So wishes appear on the scene in disguise, garbed in attire more acceptable to consciousness, anything to achieve their purpose.

From this point of view, the human drama, the drama of consciousness, lies in this constant struggle between wishes that seek fulfillment and reality which opposes them. So the task of the analyst is to divest wishes of their disguises and help consciousness establish a new relationship with them. Only in this way can an attempt be made to mitigate the explosiveness of that accumulation buried beyond the confines of time in the unconscious: otherwise, out of these obscure, unseen depths, wishes will continue to operate, governing life and touching off disorders, both physical and psychic.

So far, the "hundred waves" of history that Nietzsche referred to, still reflect the emotional presence of each of our particular past. After further research, it became more and more obvious that the traumas around which patients built their stories, their very lives, as well as their dreams and fantasies, would reappear in different situations in accordance with recognizable models.

Though the "Oedipus complex" appears in Freud's writings only in 1910, already during his self-analysis he had recognized a model whose presence was felt in everybody's life. The mythical Greek king Oedipus had deeply interested him for years, precisely because he embodied that restraint we are all familiar with by having felt its presence during our formative years.

The psychic world was being depicted more and more as a reality with a consistency of its own, an organizational and formative capacity of its own with regard to the life of the individual. Loving, desiring the parent of the opposite sex, the veto and punishment for the infringement, were for Freud an active and constricting presence. The Oedipus model appeared in every story and seemed to transcend individual experience, a model that rose from the depths, structuring the life of individuals and their conflicts, presenting itself in the theater of the imagination.

This organizational "working" of the psyche emerged more and more in Freud's research. So the "primal fantasies," arranged into scenes connected with the triangular Oedipus situation, the primal scene, castration, seduction, appeared as universal ways for representing the most significant moments of individual development in coping with the enigma of sexuality. As of that moment, what could not be found in the history of the individual was traced back, as well, to the history of the species.

The independent existence of a narrative structure that shapes experience and cannot be traced back to the contingent events in the history of the individual was in any case always linked to an outlook whose realization dated back to the clash with reality. So, according to Freud, the formative activity of the psyche, which revealed the action of the Oedipus complex, with its related phantasms, appeared on the scene of the imagination: models at work in us in the dramatic confrontation between wish and reality.

In this theoretical framework the images that appear are fundamentally an attempt at mediation. Masquerading becomes necessary, so that at least part of the tension of wishing finds fulfillment in the clash between opposite tendencies. In this perspective, images are not in themselves trustworthy, but are to be held up against the light in order to discover their secret. Whether they appear on the scene of dreams or of fantasies, they represent an attempt to reestablish a balance between wishes that demand fulfillment and reality which prevents it. The representation mediates the tension, but essentially covers up a failing.

Freud remarks (1899, p. 279) a propos of the importance of this appearing, in one of the most pregnant and significant chapters of *The Interpretation of Dreams*:

> Dreams are brief, meagre and laconic in comparison with the range and wealth of the dream-thoughts.

And later (*ibid*. p. 308):

> Dream-displacement and dream-condensation are the two governing factors to whose activity we may in essence ascribe the form assumed by dreams (...) The consequence of the displacement is that the dream-content no longer resembles the core of the dream-thoughts and that the dream gives no more than a distortion of the dream-wish which exists in the unconscious.

Dreams, the visual manifestation of them that remain in the mind, likewise with fantasies, are not trustworthy in their manifest dimension.

Rereading a text so fundamental to the history of analytic thought as the sixth chapter of *The Interpretation of Dreams*, devoted to "dream-work", enables us to examine a point of view of imagination, of the significance to be ascribed to this "working" of the psyche that leads to the visibility of images. Certain passages strike me as being particularly useful for understanding Freud's viewpoint. If, in fact, an idea takes on substantial form in the logical connections, consistent with the fundamental conscious approach, it also lets some of its layers, even if only hinted at, transpire between the lines. In the free rereading of Freud's text I propose here, I consider his spontaneous metaphors to be not so much a rhetorical device for catching the readers' attention, as intuitions of a further complexity, not yet brought to light by close thinking.

We may observe, for example, how Freud describes the action of condensation and displacement, viewed as the two mechanisms that govern the transformational activities that lead from dream-thoughts to manifest contents, to emerging images. As he says (*ibid.* p. 312; italics added):

> When the whole mass of these dream-thoughts is brought under the pressure of the dream-work, and its elements are turned about, broken into fragments and jammed together – *almost like pack-ice* – the question arises of what happens to the logical connections which have hitherto formed its framework. What representation do dreams provide for "if," "because," "just as," "although," "either–or," and all the other conjunctions without which we cannot understand sentences or speeches? In the first resort our answer must be that dreams have no means at their disposal for representing these logical relations between the dream-thoughts. For the most part dreams disregard all these conjunctions, and it is only the substantive content of the dream-thoughts that they take over and manipulate. The restoration of the connections which the dream-work has destroyed is a task which has to be performed by the interpretative process.

From these words it would appear that the dream-work, moved by the need to create a connection with the underlying wish, was led to break the dream-thoughts into fragments, to simplify them in order to attain its purpose. Freud reasserted once again (1900, p. 660):

> The modes of expression open to a dream may therefore be qualified as meagre by comparison with those of our intellectual speech.

In the above quotation, my attention is caught by the use of such an unusual metaphor as "pack-ice," only partly qualified by "almost like." In the imagery used by Freud what stands out is the dynamic intensity of elements "turned about, broken into fragments and jammed together." The sense of destruction of the preexistent unity "pack-ice" is accompanied in the reader by the sensation of a change of condition: something solid tends to liquefy. If in Freud the concept of fragmentation prevailed to indicate the effect of the dream-work, why did he use precisely the metaphor of ice?

What his words seem to express is the insight that in the transition effected by dream-work there is a mobilization in progress, a change of condition, of what up to the moment the images appears remained unitary, but also immobile and cold as ice. The metaphor therefore seem particularly appropriate for indicating the transition of an emotional content from the unconscious condition, where it repeats itself always remaining unchanged, to the obtainment of the level of representation in the relationship with consciousness.

So a new presence is mobilized on the scene of the imagination, showing what was previously experienced in a fixed, never-changing condition. In this way, a different perspective seems to appear, a change of state, from solid to liquid, of a deep feeling with respect to consciousness. With the use of the metaphor, "pack-ice," Freud seems to have caught sight of an approach that was different from the one that prevailed in his research. The basic idea of his theoretical structure is in fact the primary antagonism between drives and reality, between unconscious and conscious, and fragmentation is the result of the breaking of existing connections. The insight of a sort of liquefaction as a change in the structural relationships between conscious and unconscious has yet to be worked out theoretically, though, as I see it, the metaphor of "pack-ice" points in that direction. In imagination and dreams, similar to the molecules in the solid and liquid conditions of Freud's metaphor, there is a clear evidence of the relationship between feelings, with which consciousness defends itself, and emotions connected with the impulsions that invade it.[34] As we

[34] Jervis (1989, p. 166) observes: "Freud himself, for that matter, was not necessarily rigid in his view of drives. In his writings the drive model is set forth, consistent with the style of most of his work, as much as a figure of speech as well as in the way of a 'technical' explanation on the model of the exact sciences. In fact, Freudian drives are to a large extent an image." I share this opinion, though the need to turn psychoanalysis into an exact science for years prevented re-

shall see, this approach, not yet fully expressed here, will gain consistency in Jung's thinking, in which the relationship between the ego and drives is no longer only antagonistic.

## 3 The Jungian Approach

For Jung, the "working" of the psyche that appears in imagination is certainly a way of adapting to the environment and of surviving, but also reveals, under favorable conditions in the psychic field, a capacity to "create" and conceive new approaches.

From this point of view, the unconscious takes on a more complex connotation: its actions are not only determined by the vicissitudes of individual stories, but bear the marks of a never-ending mythopoeia aiming at integration, which entails transforming and destructive dynamics in both the single individual and the group. So the unconscious is no longer identifiable only with what is repressed, but also allow a collective, archetypal structure to be seen. This "working" of the psyche expresses itself in the collective activities of humanity, in its past and present myths, but also in the ways emotions and feelings are "staged" by the single individual's ability to represent.[35]

We have seen how Freud, by stressing more and more the formative activities of the psyche, had resorted to mythical thought, to the drama of Oedipus, which is a classical expression of that thinking. Freud pointed out that during child development confronting the enigma of sexuality determines a recognizable psychic activity in which one figure appears repeatedly in different people:

searchers from discovering the moments in which dream-images or fantasies express the relationship to unconscious determinants and implement them with the utmost precision. In the present text, I try to describe how sandplay helped me see clearly when and how an interpersonal field is created where these effective symbolic forms take shape. Regarding this, see Chapters VII and IX.

[35] This "working" of the psyche is already present, even if in an exclusively energic perspective, in Freud's very concept of "unconscious mental representation."

the mythical figure of Oedipus. However varied the individual contents, this figure comes through as a typical way of giving form to experience and of regulating its responses: a complex which Freud calls "core" to specify its propulsive and formative centrality in individual experience. From his point of view, the "working" of the psyche, which, because of its universality, cannot be traced back to merely individual events, remained even so a reproducing, a repeating of what had possibly actually occurred in the history of mankind.

The enigma of emerging sexuality, with the entailing torment of emotions, is certainly central to our development, but in Jung's view every human age has its unanswered moments, which force us to cope with other enigmas: the moments in which other forms emerge that organize the unfolding of the representation and "stage" the ongoing emotional experience. Oedipus is the model that gives form to the encounter with the enigma of sexuality, but every age, every significant and conflictual stage of life, raises new questions, hence offers new possibilities of answers on the part of the psyche.

So Jung offers a perspective in which human drama no longer stems from the irremediable conflict between wishes that demand fulfillment and a reality that opposes them, that is by the insuperable discrepancy between two irreconcilable forces. The man that Jung proposes experiences a constant yearning to carry out a mental representation whose form is drawn from the invading drive. But every form obtained is only temporary, because it is consumed in the progressive accumulation and enrichment of experience, and now and forever reverts to the void as a further impulse towards new configurations.

In the fantasies imposed from within, typical of psychic suffering, as in those which are the fruit of long and tedious expectations, the at once creative and "destructive" "working" of the psyche appears. In fact, the new synthesis which active fantasies can bring about often fails, and the tragedy of psychopathological disorders invades the life of the individual. It might be said that from this point of view mental pathological disorders are the failure of the aptitude for representation which alone guarantees the development from the somatic to the psychic.

Creating and destroying are always closely connected. Losing power is a negative experience of the psyche, one that engenders anxiety, but it is also the archetypal condition for transformation (Aite, 1998). By singling out the factors in the analytic field that are useful for facilitating the encounter-clash with emotions and for preserving the organizational forces of the ego complex, we can understand "how," "when," and "where" the unifying, hence transformational function of "active fantasies" can be brought about.

The imagery that appears is, in Jung's words, a Janus: it indicates the past, what is behind us, but also what lies before us, in the future; it is the materialization, in a given individual's specific historical situation, of a psychic condition which, though linked to the past, already contains in itself the blueprint, the germs of the future. Consciousness perceives in the active fantasies thus obtained the creativity of the psyche, which combines past and future, what has already taken form and what is still expressed only allusively through metaphor. Jung remarks (1921, par. 78):

> The psyche creates reality every day. The only expression I can use for this activity is *fantasy.*

What is brought out in this perspective, is a complex "working" of the psyche, which is the expression of a spontaneous symbolic process, a constantly becoming "metabolism of emotions" which, among possible responses, selects the ones most suited to the impact with life. The psyche, whose scene of action is in the imagination, proceeds by gradually distinguishing and reuniting the constituent elements of this emotional complexity in different ways (*ibid.* par. 72).

> Imagination is the reproductive or creative activity of the mind in general. It is not a special faculty since it can come into play in all the basic forms of psychic activity, whether thinking, feeling, sensation or intuition.

What does Jung mean by denying imagination the state of a special faculty? Personally, I believe that what he wishes to stress is its character as a psychic activity in a broad sense, to oppose the tendency to identify it with the visibility of a form. A process that begins long ago can reach the possibility of vision in our inner theater only gradually. At a certain point, the working of the psyche, which is imagination, integrates only the level of visibility.

It would be useful, I believe, to think about the widening of perspective suggested by Jung, when he defines imagination as the reproductive or creative activity of the mind. "Sensation" is only one way, along with the others, the mental activity identified with imagination is expressed. But does sensation mean the proprioceptive sense of touch, or the perceiving of the sense organs, such as seeing and hearing? They are, in fact, two very different moments: the former is organized early on in our development and does not yet distinguish forms that stand out against the background. The latter presumes a relationship between a subject and an object, and is reached at a later stage of our evolution.

It is significant that in the original text Jung uses the verb *empfinden*, which indicates a not yet fully differentiated sensation. The type of sensation characteristic of the sense organs is expressed in German with the verb *wahrnehmen*. It is hard to make this distinction in other languages. But confusing the two distinct levels of "sensation" is no small matter.

In *Memories, Dreams, Recollections* there is a phrase of Jung's which makes us see the importance, in the psychic economy, of the transition from having sensations (*empfinden*) to perceiving that the level of the differentiation between self and outside-of-self (*wahrnehmen*) has been reached. In this transition we begin to understand the meaning of imaginal activity, conceived as a level that has been reached, which transforms our relationship to the world (Jung, 1961, par. 712):

> To the extent that I managed to translate the emotions into images – that is to say, to find the images which were concealed in the emotions – I was inwardly calmed and reassured. Had I left those images hidden in the emotions, I might have been torn to pieces by them (...) As a result of my experiment I learned how helpful it could be, from the therapeutic point of view, to find the particular images which lie behind emotions.

Accordingly, the ability to give visual or auditory form, to place the typical sensations of the sense organs on the scene of the imagination, appears as a successfully attained level of integration. It is the result of a process, an apex, in the relationship between consciousness and underlying emotions. Consciousness lends the perceptual and mnemonic wealth of its experience to what is pressing in the unconscious: when it reaches the level of sensorial forms, it integrates a level of clarity and distinctness never before attained. The distinction between self and outside-of-self, between consciousness and emotion, has been reached, and at this point changes the subject's ability to respond. What transpires from what Jung says above is the change and energy gained by the ego complex.[36]

It is useful to point out that implicit in the effort to "find the particular images which lie behind emotions" is a particular mental attitude, an attitude assumed towards the psyche, a style of relating to oneself and to patients in therapeutic work. In my opinion, the nodal point at the basis of the Jungian analytic approach lies precisely in this aspect.

## 4 Confronting Fantasies

Jung makes a distinction between "passive" and "active" fantasies, depending on the way they appear and the way they act. In *Psychological Types*, he remarks (1921, par. 712):

> We can distinguish between *active* and *passive* fantasy. *Active* fantasies are the product of *intuition*, i.e. they are evoked by an *attitude* directed to the perception of unconscious contents, as a result of which the *libido* immediately invests all the elements emerging from the unconscious and, by association with parallel material, brings them into clear focus in visual form. *Passive* fantasies appear in

[36] In my reading of Jung the ego is to be seen as a particular feeling-toned complex related to the perception of the body, to the corporeal framework. Consciousness is only part of this complex, expresses its aptitude for relating to, and changing, the other complexes. Also see Chapter XI.

> visual form at the outset, neither preceded nor accompanied by intuitive expectation, the attitude of the subject being wholly passive.

The criterion of passiveness or activeness would seem to apply only to subjects who experience the phenomenon, to their conscious approach to the perception of emerging imaginal forms. Jung's observation invites closer investigation because "the attitude directed to the perception of unconscious contents (...) by association with parallel material" lays emphasis, in my opinion, on the field where the encounter between emerging fantasies and perception takes place. Fantasies are active when the individual establishes a relationship to the response his actions produce in the field, whether it be connected to the use of objects or materials, as in sandplay, or is intrapsychic and based on the association of corresponding perceptions. The determining factor would seem to be the field where this encounter-clash takes shape, because the above activeness is closely related to the feeling-tone, in both an intrasubjective and interpersonal sense, whereas the response perceived in the field is as important as the emerging feeling that takes shape in fantasies. Jung goes on to say (*ibid.* par. 713):

> Active fantasies, on the other hand, owe their existence not so much to this unconscious process as to a conscious propensity to assimilate hints or fragments of lightly-toned unconscious complexes and, by associating them with parallel elements, to elaborate them in clearly visual form. It is not necessarily a question of a dissociated psychic state, but rather of a positive participation of consciousness.

Again the accent is placed on consciousness rather than on the facilitating psychic field, which with further research has taken on ever-greater importance.

Years later, in his study of alchemical texts, Jung found further support of his 1921 observations. In *Psychology and Alchemy* (1944, par. 219) he pointed out that the old alchemists had grasped the difference between *vera imaginatio* and *imaginatio phantastica*, in other words between active and passive fantasies or images:

> *Imaginatio* is an active evocation of (inner) images, *secundum naturum,* an authentic feat of thought or ideation, which does not spin aimless and groundless fantasies "into the blue" – does not, that is to say, just play with its objects, but tries to grasp the inner facts and portray in images true to their nature.

His research now aimed at distinguishing the conditions in the psychic field where new forms capable of modifying the emotional situation and enabling a different organization of experience, could emerge in the theater of the imagination. The distinction suggested by Jung has important implications in terms of clinical theory. The task of the analyst is to succeed in creating an interpersonal field which aids the integration of "active" images or fantasies.

After 1935 Jung devoted increasingly more time to studying imagination, thanks to his encounter with alchemical works. In the autobiographical text dictated to his pupil, Aniela Jaffé (Jung, 1961), as in the above quotations, one catches sight of a basic preliminary element needed for summoning up active fantasies: contact with the loss of confidence and of the loved object, with the resulting feeling of destructiveness, is one of the structuring and consistently recurring moments capable of giving rise to the imaginal act and the representation which carry out a unifying and organizational function in the relationship between conscious and unconscious (Aite, 1998).

In a psychic field which permits both containment and abandon, the organizational capacity of the ego complex, with regard to the deep emotions that can overwhelm the individual, appears only under the prodding of necessity. Subjectively, it is the moment of psychic suffering, when responses capable of assessing what is being experienced are lacking, the moment when the doors open to imagination, to the possibility of understanding through active fantasies. Everyone knows that this moment is reached by degrees. First we deny the dissatisfaction and increase our activity, then the anger we feel towards others and ourselves explodes, in the end, nothing remains but emptiness and isolation. The power of psychic dynamism can devastate our life. According to Jung, the forms that appear through imagination offer consciousness both the elements useful for establishing a relationship with the ongoing emotional dynamics and the possibility of containing, of understanding them. Imagination makes it possible to realize what is in question and what its possibilities.

The activity of consciousness in the experience of active images, as Jung brought out, is actually not the first cause but the consequence of the event. The relationship that enables emotional containment and at the same time copes with the loss of certitudes and the resulting disorientation is the field where active or transforming images can take shape.

The scene that is depicted and the characters in it are not cover-ups for something unacceptable, but the most suitable way for the ego complex, at that specific moment, to represent something which it does not yet fully know. Thus in the crisis, there is the possibility of a radical renewal, and the images that appear provide a field of investigation which, on a clinical level, makes both diagnosis and prognosis possible.

Images or active fantasies hence seem to spring from a state of necessity: a field of emotional tensions that demand new responses for adaptation appears to be decisive for their appearance. Jung's outlook cannot be understood if emphasis is not laid on the feeling of emptiness, of the lack of responses, which precedes and determines the forming of an active image.

In the presence of a pressing unsolved problem, of an overpowering mental state that is impossible to express in words, the imaginal activity can offer an opportunity or a new perspective in the form of an intuition, of a still indistinct perception. Upon reaching the level of visibility, active fantasies become the capacity for symbolization and the birth of new ideas, which can subsequently reach the level of words and concepts. But it is here, in the void, that creativity can emerge, that thinking in images which we find in poets, painters, researchers, and in all of us in certain situations.

The high-profile examples I have just given must not let us forget that the imaginal moment stressed by Jung is an experience we all share. In the analytic field, contact with loss and emptiness is a necessity, not only for the patient but also for the analyst. The latter learns from experience how important it is, for listening to and understanding the other, to personally sustain the desperate feeling that comes when what is known is abandoned.

The experience of loss can trigger its transformational actions also in situations that are apparently less dramatic, but which depict the same transition. Faced with the empty tray of sand, the patient as well experiences the moment when the usual referential parameters of consciousness are lost and, by necessity, surrender to the perception of the "here and now."

The new imaginal synthesis, the active fantasy, appears in the psychic field whose essential elements I have described. I believe, however, that we must learn to understand many other elements. At present, we can only make out the catalyzing function of the experiencing of difficulties, from the sense of insufficiency and futility to the fear of not making it and of loneliness, which we cross, like a trackless desert, with great suffering. The apparent absurdity and incomprehensibility of what appears in the theater of imagination brings on a feeling of insufferableness, anger, futility, fear, before we succeed in discovering that in it a different perspective presents itself. In Jung's remarks there is above all the suggestion that the images which appear be taken for what they are, reacting to them as if they were real (Jung, 1955/1956, par. 753):

> You yourself must enter into the process with your personal reactions, just as if you were one of the fantasy figures or rather, as if the drama being enacted before your eyes were real. It is a psychic fact that this fantasy is happening and it is as you – as a psychic entity – are real. If this crucial operation is not carried out, all the changes are left to the flow of images, and you yourself will remain unchanged

This advice, apparently so simple, is hard to put into practice. It means most of all relinquishing the supremacy of consciousness and the defenses procured with such effort. It is losing the identity we recognize as our own, in order to abandon ourselves to the perception of the event. The perspective changes completely and the usual, egocentric view is replaced by the independence of that appearing implemented by the imagination. Present in the form itself of the images is a synthesis between what we are now and the unconscious determinants that propel our lives.

Fantasies are passive when they disconnect from existent reality and use previously formed representations in service to the defenses. The "flights of fancy" of everyday speech express, in fact, a need for control, an attempt to escape omnipotently both the outside reality and the inner emotional reality.

Among the passive fantasies, special attention should be given to those introjected by the environment, also useful at first for adaptation, but which can eventually inhibit individual development. Collective consciousness has always been based on a network of shared images or fantasies, which last for a certain period of time and then fall into disuse, no longer able to meet the new demands. They often condition and guide our wishes unconsciously, also making us incapable of coming up with individual responses to the pressing issues of life. They are unconscious representations that leave their mark unnoticed and sometimes cause the disorientation of consciousness, more and more dominated by models shared by many and further and further removed from their true roots.

Fantastic images induced by the encounter-clash with the environment are like introjected islands of experience, which Jung called "feeling-toned complexes." Considering their presence and actions as passive fantasies, he remarks (1921, par. 713):

> It is probable that passive fantasies always have their origin in an unconscious process that is antithetical to consciousness, but invested with approximately the same amount of energy as the conscious attitude, and therefore capable of breaking through the latter's resistance.

In this way Jung suggested that the images introjected during our personal stories were active complex-cores, capable of conditioning our life beyond conscious control.[37]

[37] In Chapter XI, I examine more closely the theoretical issue of feeling-toned complexes and their relationship to the ego complex.

# 5 A Proposal for Further Research

In view of the perspective advanced by Jung, it is easy to see how sandplay was a consequence of his intuitions. It is, in fact, a special method for bringing about that inclination for representation where feelings are "staged". It is an attempt to create a field in which the "libido immediately invests all the elements emerging from the unconscious and, by association with parallel material, brings them into clear focus in visual forms" (Jung, 1921, par. 712).

Active fantasies, as we have seen, appear in a psychic field where the sensation of personal limitations predominates and control has turned out to be impossible. This is what happens when adult players are faced with the unusualness of the play situation. When players succeed in entering into the spirit of sandplay, under the pressure of emotions, they abandon themselves to the perception of the present and to listening to the reverberations of the spontaneous imaginal activity.[38]

As it occurs, the phenomenon can take the person experiencing it by surprise, opening new pathways for his thinking and his ability to perform. The relationship between the feeling-tone in the psychic field and the conscious attitude that allows the perception of emerging contents in the form of fantasies, prepares the way for a matter of fundamental importance for a theory of analytic technique which is aware of the factors that determined this attitude. In my opinion, sandplay fosters this condition of the field and lends itself therefore to a further investigation of the question.

The concrete act of playing, as applied to adults, enables the complexity of the relationships between the inception of the representation and its perception to be studied more closely at hand. In these years, I have realized how in the spatio-temporal framework of the perceptions caused by the sandplay materials, emotions find the form in which to express themselves. From this experience, I have also realized how the visibility of the scene under construction in

[38] In Chapter VII, I examine this moment in which fantasies and the perception of reality enter into confrontation.

space and time, gradually takes shape in the acts of choosing and placing induced by the emerging emotions. The use of sand and objects corresponds both to the temporary situation of consciousness and to emerging subconscious or unconscious pressures. The transformation of emotions into feelings occurs precisely by discovering the perceptual form that most closely corresponds to its deep structure. And the distinctly perceived representation changes the relationship between the ego and the emotions. One might say that what up to this moment was disconcerting, at times even capable of overwhelming consciousness, also in virtue of its indefinite character, takes on a preliminary form and becomes recognizable. Emotions, no longer free and indefinite, are yoked to a form, turning into feelings.

The purpose is to succeed in discovering when and how the energic intensity of the feelings that change and involve both the analyst and the patient appears in the analytic relationship. This is what I began to explain in the previous chapter, and will further examine by presenting other case histories involving sandplay. In this way a new level of experience is attained which offers patients a possibility of acting and reflecting. This transformational process is like a laboratory that is always active on a subliminal level. The dreams or fantasies that take over consciousness, like the scenes created in sandplay, are the products of this essential process in individual adaptation.

It may be asserted that sandplay facilitates the emotional condition suited to getting this spontaneous attitude of the psyche to emerge. The concrete stimulus of the sand and the objects chosen and placed in the field follows the same course. The objects, their particular material and their arrangement in space, correspond to the possible encounter between emotions and the conscious attitude of the moment. Bachelard, speaking of imagination, also referred to this psychic act (1943/1997, p. 79):

> It was considered the ability to form images but it is instead the ability to deform the images offered by perception, to free us of immediate images: it is above all the ability to change images.

In Jung, condensation and displacement, already formulated by Freud, take on a different perspective. The change in the immediate perceptual images, implemented by imagination, bear witness to a specific choice, precisely because it is indicative of an integration between consciousness and the emerging emotion. The perceptual material that the ego complex can draw upon to give form to the imaginal activity originates in our experience of life. Forming a part of that experience are both the perceptions which were once conscious then forgotten, and the subliminal perceptions which have never reached the level of awareness.

## Ways and Levels of Imagining

Playing with materials and objects, activated by sandplay, is the first and oldest theater of imagination. Through the physical relationship to the surrounding world and the handling of objects, children begin to "shape" their experiences and confront their emotions. This phase in which objects are necessary for imagining is followed, at a later age, by another phase in which the introspective possibility of visions and dialogue with imaginary figures is involuntarily brought about. The elaboration of experience through imaginal acts reaches a verbal level only at a further stage of development, and only then can it begin to exclude objects. It is the phase in which the experience of "active imagination" appears physiologically. To evoke the transformational power of the active fantasies he himself experienced, Jung devised a method of confronting feelings which he called "active imagination."[39]

Jung, however, did not stress the difference between imagining through the use of objects and concrete space and imagining provoked by introspective concentration. In accordance with the thesis sustained here, there are, instead,

[39] For further discussion of this question, I recommend the works of von Franz (1958, 1979, 1999), Hannah (1953, 1981), Fordham (1956, 1967), Hillman (1978), De Luca Comandini (1991).

two integrative and energic levels of relationship with images which should be distinguished, because of the various possibilities of their being used in clinical situations. I believe that when feelings are deep, still confined to the somatic level, using objects offers greater possibilities: transforming deep and inexpressible emotions into representations can then also come about in subjects who would not be likely to adapt to the concentration and introspection needed for active imagination. In fact, this experience requires an already much more integrated level of relationship to feelings, that corresponds to a relative stability of the ego complex. Even in complex psychopathological situations, the transformational potentiality of active fantasies seems to be more attainable with the return to the concreteness of materials and objects.

Anyone who uses sandplay in analysis knows that a involuntary shifting between playing and active imagination takes place. Parts of the scene can become active fantasies in the patient's inner theater at particular moments of life. Subsequent concentration on these images, as is the case with active imagination, changes them in ways that are extremely significant for understanding the feelings at stake. Some patients succeed in getting personally involved in those fantasies, witnessing surprising changes in aspects that suddenly appear, such as vivid memories or active fantasies.

We must now take a closer look at play activities as a way of stimulating imagination. I think that the field of investigation this method offers will also allow active imagination, as a way of confronting the unconscious, to be more widely regained on a clinical level than is presently the case among Jungian analysts.

# V Playing As a Way of Confronting the Unconscious: In Research and in Analytic Practice

*In a utilitarian world, interwoven with the closely-knit web of significant connections, in a practical universe where everything is given a function and a value in use and exchange, the entry of the clown blows a hole in the web and makes a breach in the stifling fullness of accepted meanings through which a restless wind of life may blow.* J. Starobinski (1984, p. 150)

In the attempt to find a way for reaching the deep underlying emotions of psychic suffering, analytic research has taken a closer look at the act of playing and has gradually begun to realize its possibilities. In this chapter, I will try to bring out certain aspects of this by no means easy process, with its illuminating insights and equally strong resistances. The last stage reached was sandplay, especially when used in the analytic psychotherapy of adults, as well. Playing blows a hole in the web of accepted meanings, to use Starobinski's words, and opens the door to an aspect of "gratuitousness" that speaks of the unconscious. It is the typical comportment of the clown, an archetypal figure which, with his clownery, speaks to us of life and death.

## 1 Play and Analytic Research: A First General Survey

Play has long been remarkably underrated as a way of relating to unconscious determinants. For years, first-generation analysts felt that the children's world was unsuited to analysis and that in child therapy resorting to play was a necessity, and a not very trustworthy one, for investigating the psyche. The prevailing opinion was that children, because of their still limited linguistic skills, could have no access to "free verbal association," the instrument that had paved the way to depth psychology, nor the possibility of integrating the therapist's verbal interpretations.

Since therapy with words seemed to run up against a serious obstacle in childhood, nothing remained but play as a way (generally considered an imprecise way) of approaching that world still in the making. Therefore, what prevailed in child therapy was a distinctly pedagogical approach.

The emphasis on language, on the voiced gesture of words, long prevented the full appreciation of the significant potentialities of other bodily gestures, playing in particular. For a long while there was a dominant tendency not only to confine play to the nursery, but also to consider it not comprehensive and trustworthy enough for a thorough understanding of unconscious dynamics.

This short survey of the relationship between psychoanalysis and children confirms my conviction that the way children are, and the typical way they have of playing, gave rise at first to intense defenses among researchers. I believe that still today these defenses have not completely disappeared and arouse emotional reactions which delay the experimentation of play activities in other age groups than children. If you break with the predominating attitude and try to test this approach with adults, resistance is even stronger. The typical human need organize the confrontation with feelings into a story is still considered only on a level of verbal expression, and not in the circumstances leading up to it. Until I experimented it in my training and in my analytic work, I too was of this opinion. Now, after years of experience, I can claim that playing with objects and materials can bring about, in adults as well, an earlier level of consciousness, capable of giving representation to deep feelings that act on a physical level. Provoking that level of consciousness means releasing unsuspected possibilities of communication in the analyst-patient relationship.

The tendency to underrate the communicative possibilities of play still predominates the field of research. The doubt still prevails that it is a question of "acting-out", of a short-circuiting of energy, which does not release new possibilities of sharing, but tends only to discharge energy. Resistance to taking the communicative, as well as transformational, level of play into consideration has made it impossible to see how in those moments, play reaches a development in time and at a pace all its own, that are not to be found in the reaction of discharging emotional tensions typical of acting-out. To be sure, psychic conditions exist in which this can happen, as a natural defense against intense emotions considered to be dangerous. But we forget to stress the difference between these clearly defensive attitudes and others in which real contact is established with deep dynamics.

The difficulty of properly evaluating play was also to be found among Jungians, not only in their resistance to accepting this possibility, but also with a wholly contrary tendency: what appears in certain cases is a sort of idealization of play activities, with an undervaluation that fails to distinguish the defensive moments also clearly present in playing with objects. Both the undervaluation and the idealization of the experience signify a defense against something new that is disturbing, and prevent more thoughtful consideration.

Precisely because it is unusual, the suggestion of using play also with adults increases defenses even more. So the particular level of consciousness and of elaboration of an emotional experience, which makes it possible to awaken dormant possibilities and get around the repetitive defensive barriers, is underrated.

The first thing one notices is the temporary relinquishment of verbal language in order to listen to preverbal language, which in play assumes all its complexity and expressiveness, an apparent reevaluation of words and a return to the expressive and transformational potential of playing.

Contacting deep, often inexpressible and intensely felt emotions through touch and sight (handling materials and objects), lays emphasis on the body, which analytic research has always considered antagonistic to verbal communication. For the analyst, true to the energic model, the basic principle of analysis lies in the inducement of physical immobility and the exclusion of eye contact: suffice it to remember the use of the couch with the analyst sitting behind the patient. In view of this theoretical perspective, the body and its movements are seen primarily as vehicles for discharging wish-tensions and hence as obstacles to verbal communication.

From my point of view, a basic condition of the analytic approach is to succeed in creating an interpersonal field where the other aspect can be expanded, the one that encourages the ability to represent through play feelings not yet expressible in words, and to only later aim at shared speech. It is crucial to learn to notice how and when in the analytic field the experience of play can be a resistance, can injure communication, or on the contrary be capable of developing it. Only after an inexpressible feeling has attained representation will it be possible to restore verbal language, which is the most effective and transformational expression on the adult level of consciousness.

## 2 Significant Moments in Analytic Research

We shall now cover some of the historical stages in the confrontation of analytic thinking to childhood and playing with objects and materials. We will notice a gradual shift of viewpoint and, with time, a greater appreciation of that particular experience.

The case of "Little Hans" (Freud, 1908), historically the first example of a study centered around the play activities of a child, offers useful data for analytically understanding the dramatic fantasies at the root of his psychopathology and which he "staged" in his playing. In this case, Freud concentrated on the therapy undertaken by the boy's father, in this way reaching deep into the Oedipal core of the fantasies present in his play activities. This was a foresight. But for years these intuitions did not lead to further research.

Resorting to play was simply a necessity, given the insufficient linguistic possibilities of children, at least in the early stages of their development, and yet paradoxically in the theoretical elaboration of the analytic work to get at the roots of deep conflicts constant reference was made to childhood. Children were present in the analytic thinking, but only as imaginary representatives of the unconscious and its characteristic impulses. While there was a lot of talk about understanding adults through childhood, the possibility of applying to children the working principles which at that time were being discovered for adults was, at the same time, excluded. The main idea was that analytic treatment could be arrived at in children only when consciousness was fully formed, hence after the latence period. Determining this attitude was the undeniable fact that in this age group, the assimilative and communicative capacity was still in the making.

In operative terms, a pedagogical approach necessarily prevailed, though it contradicted the very principles that guided analytic practice with adults. In short, there was a devaluation of children's assimilative and communicative capacities which, unlike adults, are still strictly connected with physical acts and concrete objects.

So at that time, the opinion prevailed that play was substantially untrustworthy for the cognitive and transformational purposes of the nascent "depth psychology." Childhood experience appeared be too closely linked to the "primary process" to be a viable means of communication. In evaluating play, emphasis was placed on the function of discharging emotional tension. Repetitive gestures, which often distinguish it, were considered a way of lessening anguish, of reaching a possible compromise.

In the energic approach, the principle of wishing was given emphasis in the clash with reality. What lost emphasis was the representational and reflective capacity of playing, as revealed by the pace of gestures, by the choice of objects and the use of space.

After Freud's work, it was not until 1921 that in an essay by Melanie Klein we find the idea of playing with objects as an effective way for understanding and transforming the psychic world of children. For her, the actions and gestures of children began to be just as important as free verbal associations. She also deserves credit for having also brought out the relationship between verbal language and play in elaborating emotional experience. The two different levels of expression turned out to be closely connected, with a possibility of acting reciprocally in transforming the anxiety triggered by a conflictual situation. Concerning this, Klein remarked (1927):

> Representation by means of toys – indeed symbolic representation in general, it being to some extent separate from the subject's person – is less invested with anxiety than is confession by word of mouth. If then we succeed in allaying anxiety and in getting in the first instance more indirect representations, we shall be able to convince ourselves that we can elicit for analysis the fullest verbal expression of which the child is capable. And then we find repeatedly that at times when anxiety becomes more marked the indirect representations once more occupy the foreground.

Also in adults, verbal language reveals a more limited aptitude than play to express representations infused with anxiety. Going back to using objects in a play area, also in adulthood, can enable what is still far-removed from, and cannot be expressed in, words, to be approached and elaborated. As Klein remarked, playing releases potentialities of elaboration and opens the door to verbal integration. An initial possibility of elaboration, still connected to the use of objects, then gives way to the integrative capacity of words, which reveals a world of new possibilities for communicating and sharing.

So with Klein we began to catch sight of another perspective: not only does play reveal an expressive potentiality, but a corresponding possibility of transformation of the relationship to emotions. According to her, child patients, even in an early stage of development, know how to react to the therapist's suggested interpretations, both on the level of play activities and on the level of words. Children also show they are able to alter their responses to anxiety linked to an ongoing conflictual situation. Play more and more begins to assume the same importance as free verbal association in adults.

As to the prevailing pedagogical approach, greater and greater assent was being given to the significance of playing as a spontaneous interpretative capacity, which implements the complexity of a conflictual situation, an unsuspected ability to elaborate feelings up to that moment underrated. These new perspectives began to affect the prevalent stereotyped notion that till then had excluded real children from any possibility of analysis.

With the appearance of the expressive and transformational significance of playing, a new theoretical horizon began to unfold.

It was Winnicott (1971) who took a new step forward and opened up a perspective that till then had been only implicit in research. With him, the space in which the representation takes place becomes the protagonist: the play area where children encounter emotions takes on an importance it never had before.[40]

The forms appearing in the space-time of play scenes are marked by a painful differentiation between self and different-than-self. This is seen not only as a compromise between opposing forces, but more and more the result of an elaboration, a true reflection, which changes the relationship to the violence of primitive emotions and to the anxiety they provoke.

This significant changeover marks a turning point in the assessment of play and of the relationship to the emotions play brings about. Until then, research had been dominated by an approach in which prominence was given to the question of the "why" of a given form that appears on the scene: it was the mediation between a drive seeking discharge and reality. This attempt to detect a compromise between opposites and to discover what has remained hidden, led to a drastic devaluation of the forms of the representation in itself.

With Winnicott's contribution, the question was first raised as to the "where" of that "intermediate zone" in which the impact between self and other-than-self takes place. With the necessary stage of illusion, the individual gains the capacity to relate to underlying emotions and to know them through objects. In everyday language "illusion," Winnicott's term for this experience, is by no accident synonymous to a fleeting moment that has no effect on, indeed avoids, reality. But illusion (*in-ludus*), the possibility of entering the dimension of imaginal playing with materials and objects, is a physiological step in confronting emotions during childhood. As a result of Winnicott's intuitions, illusion created by play situations is not only crucial for understanding the psy-

[40] See in particular "Transitional objects and transitional phenomena" (1971, p. 1-34)

chic transformation of the individual in course of differentiation, but becomes a fundamental concept in analytic theory and practice.[41]

Since the role of the environmental, perceptual and emotional response has been reassessed in psychic development, attention has focused on the space where the encounter-clash between subject and object, between intrapsychic and interpersonal, between imagination and perception takes place. Analytic thinking, which till then aimed at discerning and trying to explain the "why" of the forms created through play and their structuring mechanisms, was in this way enhanced by a careful assessment of how the "where" and "how" of using objects were able to transform the relationship to emerging feelings. The accent shifted to the choice of materials and to the spatiotemporal organization that play scenes bring to light. Increasingly greater emphasis was laid on the preciseness of those choices and the connection of that "how" to the complexity of the ongoing emotions.

The classical approach which considered the formal aspects of play, dreams and fantasies simply a compromise between opposing forces, tried to go beyond appearances and essentially to devaluate them. In this way the sense of form was lost and emphasis laid on its tendency to distort, to make believe, which concealed the "true" that was to be referred back to mechanisms.

Consequently there began to be a breaking free of the prevailing power of an intellectual model in order to open a new chapter in analytic thinking. After Winnicott's teachings, wishing and wish-fulfillment were no longer connected primarily to the concept of tension-discharge, but to the possibility of "being there," of the individual finding his way in the encounter with the different-from-self, in the drama of individuation, which always entails coping with separation and loss. This way a vital need of imagination in the face of reality

[41] The concept of illusion is, in fact, central to Winnicott's analytic theory and practice. In this view, the illusion-disillusion changeover represents the emotional framework in which the psychic transformation is integrated, whereas disillusion marks its failure. See "Transitional Objects and Transitional Phenomena" (p. 1-34), "Playing: A Theoretical Statement" (p. 51-70), "The Use of an Objects and Relating through Identifications" (p. 115-127), "The Location of Cultural Experience" (p. 128-139), all in Winnicott (1971).

seems to materialize in the field of play. Out of concrete play emerges a sort of map that charts the relationship of the individual with his own conflicts and inclinations. The response adults experience in handling the sand, in using the pigments or objects of sandplay induces the vitality of the imagination, provokes it and facilitates the symbolization of feelings. Through the concrete sandplay scenes in the analytic field, the feelings active in the relationship discover a possibility of being interpreted. Usually, they inspire the involuntary gestures, the facial expressions and movements of the body, as well as the words of the patient, but they are less easy to define.

According to this new approach, the play scene itself appears as the form that most closely corresponds to the underlying feeling and to the possibility of perceiving consciousness. Careful research would seem to confirm how precise play scenes are in their structure, and how deeply rooted in the unconscious content.

Integrated representation *alludes* to the enigma, does not resolve it, but supplies new elements for an ever-deeper understanding of the opposites at stake. From this point of view, the play-scene form is rediscovered, revealing not only an unexpected complexity, but also that significant previously underrated precision.

In scene building, cores of experience which, congealed in the repetition of the symptom, wait to be represented and integrated by consciousness, take possession of the perception of the moment, or rather are evoked by it and organized into the wholeness of an image.

Additional to the dominion of verbal thinking, based on logic, is the dimension of thinking that seeks out the similarities and differences and which, through a crisscrossing of the emotions and perceptions of the moment, create images that correspond to, and represent, experience.

The latter is phylogenetically and ontogenetically older, but still operative and capable of surprising and unexpected syntheses, new with respect to the previous theoretical approach. As will be seen in the following pages, the aforesaid complexity and preciseness of the *mise-en-scène* are present both in the way space and time are used and each individual material and object chosen.

This short historical survey shows how a new conception of play has gradually made headway.[42]

## 3 Play According to Jung

As early as 1929, Jung wrote (1931, pars. 98, 99):

> All works of man have their origin in creative imagination. What right, then, do we have to disparage fantasy? In the normal course of things, fantasy does not easily go astray; it is too deep for that and too closely bound up with the taproot of human and animal instinct. It has a surprising way of always coming out right in the end. The creative activity of imagination frees man from his bondage to the "nothing but" and raises him to the status of one who plays. As Schiller says, man "is completely human only when he is at play." My aim is to bring about a psychic state in which my patient begins to experiment with his own nature – a state of fluidity, change and growth, where nothing is eternally fixed and hopelessly petrified

These prophetic words stress how for Jung the experience of play opened a new path for understanding the psychic world. Implicit in them is already the next stage, which some forty years later would lead to the use of sandplay also in adult therapy.

There are a number of nodal points in the attitude of anyone who places himself in this perspective. The first aspect to be underlined is the propensity to evoke, also in adults, the expressive potentialities of playing that have lain dormant since childhood. Sandplay is, in fact, a way of utilizing a level of experience, which, natural in children, can also be revived in adults.

This is a way that makes it possible to abandon closed repetitive verbal circuits, where an attitude governed by the defenses is often seen, in order to activate another level of communication. According to Jung (1940, par. 276), the

[42] On the ways of conceiving playing in analytic space up to its present-day use with adults, see the collected essays by various authors edited by Manuela Trinci (1993)

experience of playing with materials and objects brings about a particular mental attitude, and the roots of this possibility lie in an archetypal predisposition:

> The child motif represents not only something that existed in the distant past but also something that exists now; that is to say, it is not just a *vestige*, but a system functioning in the present whose purpose is to compensate and correct, in a meaningful manner, the inevitable one-sidedness and extravagances of the conscious mind.

During the formative years and in order to contend invasive feelings, children still need objects and actions, as if the capacity to face emotional events and transform them into representations demanded the typical activities and perceptive contacts of physical experience. Also in adulthood, the same need may arise in intense emotional situations to return to that way of expressing, to regress to gestures in order to elaborate disturbing feelings.

As recorded by Jaffé (Jung, 1961, pp. 197-198) Jung described his own conflictual experience and what he did to resolve it:

> The first thing that came to the surface was a childhood memory from perhaps my tenth or eleventh year. At that time I had had a spell of playing passionately with building blocks (...) For as a grown man it seemed impossible to me that I should be able to bridge the distance from the present back to my eleventh year. Yet if I wanted to re-establish contact with that period, I had no choice but to return to it and take up once more that child's life with his childish games. The moment was a turning point in my fate, but I gave in only after endless resistances and with a sense of recognition. For it was a painfully humiliating experience to realize that there was nothing to be done except play childish games. Nevertheless, I began accumulating suitable stones, gathering them partly from the lake shore and partly from the water. And I started building: cottages, a castle, a whole village.

In childhood, handling materials and using objects are a constituent part of playing and represent a level ever-present in the process of growing up we all experience. We can distinguish a first level, where children handle parts of their own bodies, followed by second level where materials and objects are the vehicles of their tendency to differentiate themselves from the world and give form to emerging emotions.

Play has an adaptive function of great importance in childhood, in that it possesses a potential for elaborating and transforming the deep emotional experiences that determine important changes in their relational and communicative capacities. Play activities express the human need to address emotions, to understand them and differentiate themselves: they reveal the oldest level of imagination's capacity to assimilate and represent. In playing with objects a process of spatiotemporal organization of emotional experience takes place, in which, through the body and through gestures, the player creates new connections, new representations or their symbolic equivalents. The vicissitudes of this process, in which the subject can differentiate the object as different-from-self, entails contacting and overcoming deep emotions like loss and separation. At this stage of life, play expresses the typically human need to "recount" these emotional events precisely in order to separate oneself from them and acknowledge them.

The next level leaves the task of elaboration and self-differentiation typical of play, to the capacity to verbalize. First play, then words, convey the vital need to create a distance between the self and the emerging emotions. The need to tell a story, which gradually becomes a sharing with others, emerges in successive closely connected levels of integration. Stories, which all games tell, just as the verbal sharing of individuals, give satisfaction to the need to establish a distance from the invasiveness of emotions and at the same time to assert oneself, one's own identity.

In the perspective of the Jungian model, offering sandplay to adult patients means helping them revive this subconscious possibility which places in the field old ways of projecting, externalizing and introjecting, viewed as the ability to distinguish, express and assimilate one's emotional experiences. Its function, therefore, is to activate and make clear, as well as truly effective (in the containment provided by the analytic space) that way of metabolizing feelings which lies on a preverbal level but which is, even so, always at work, even if unseen, in the experience of assimilating and transforming feelings.

# 4 Adults and Sandplay: A Positive Regression

In this short summary I have brought out the progressive change in the psychological perspective in play. Its expressive importance, along with its capacity to transform deep emotions, has gained ever-greater significance and importance. We have seen how, in the process of differentiating the self from the world, playing with materials and objects constitutes an evolutionary stage we have all passed through.

When sandplay for adults becomes a vehicle of analytic communication, there is a return to an old experience, a regression to a level that belongs to the past. Also in the personal experience recounted by Jung, the regression to playing with the materials and stones of his garden marked the beginning of an integrative process of the psyche, which at that moment verbal thinking was unable to put into practice in the face of the disorientation of consciousness.

When speaking of regression, one immediately thinks of pathological withdrawal, accompanied by the psyche-splitting characteristic of serious pathological disorders. But pathological regression is not to be confused with organized and controlled regression, which is basic to our adaptation to the world.

Progression and adapting to the environment, which are typical of psychic health, are closely connected physiologically to moments when we return to previous stages of development. Progression and regression are like the systoles and diastoles of our psychic development. Playing is controlled regression. After an intense emotion, children instinctively go back to playing and "stage" the emotional situation they have expressed. So they regress and confront emerging emotions through imagination, even if they can already use words intelligibly. Offering sandplay to adults activates this same level of experience. Winnicott (1958, p. 282) has well-expressed the difference between pathological and physiological regression:

> Analysts have found it necessary to postulate that more normally there are *good* pregenital situations to which the individual can return when in difficulties at a later stage. This is a healthy phenomenon. There has thus risen of two kinds of

> regression in respect to instinct development, the one being a going back to an early failure situation and other to an early success situation.

Using play in the sense of an organized regression in the analytic setting is subjectively not always an easy thing to do, in that it creates in the patient a situation that consciousness cannot control. Adults who accept the game and go over to the playing field are, I would say, people who agree to pass through a situation of need without their usual defenses. In certain cases, the experience can also seem to present the risk of ending up depending on the analyst.[43] These are moments which open up an expressive potentiality that goes beyond defenses, and the analyst, aware of the psychological situation in progress, knows how necessary the emotional containment of a knowing silence is. It is a situation which is similar to that of the patient who agrees to lie down on the couch without being able to see the analyst. Both are experiences out of the ordinary, at first even painful, which even so pave the way to emotional perception. Relinquishing the known for the unknown, furthered by controlled regression, establishes contact with emotions and feelings that are usually checked by the defenses.

The "basic rule" which opened the way to analytic research is closely connected to the activation of the expressive possibilities created by regression (*ibid*, p. 283).

> The organization that makes regression useful has this quality distinct from the other defence organizations in that it carries with it the hope of a new opportunity for an unfreezing of the frozen situation and a chance for the environment, that is to say, the present-day environment, to make adequate though belated adaptation

I think what Winnicott says can here be seen as the description of an analytic field that can activate a psychological condition open to the perception of emerging emotional contents. Sandplay, more effectively, I feel, than free ver-

[43] See also Chapter VII.

bal association, facilitates this controlled regression, and with it the perception of deep contents.

Winnicott understood, more than others, the importance of play as a path to unconscious determinants in adults as well. As he remarked (1971, p. 54):

> Whatever I say about children playing really applies to adults as well, only the matter is more difficult to describe when the patient's material appears mainly in terms of verbal communication. I suggest that we must expect to find playing just as evident in the analyses of adults as it is in the case of our work with children. It manifests itself, for instance, in the choice of words, in the inflections of the voice, and indeed in the sense of humour.

Clearly Winnicott, not having yet thought of using concrete games in analyzing adults, could not help considering words, verbal gestures, the only possible form of play. His intuition foreshadowed many of the aspects I am sustaining here; all that was lacking, in my opinion, was the last but crucial step.

After this survey of the importance of play in analysis, one can understand the gradual change in opinion that has taken place in depth psychology research. I believe that the use of concrete play, as a way of relating to unconscious determinants also in adulthood, represents an epistemological change whose potentiality for research has only recently begun to be appreciated.

# VII Looking in the Analytic Field: A Way of Listening and Understanding

*To hear with eyes belongs to love's fine wit.* W. Shakespeare, Sonnet 23

Watching something means being carefully disposed to receive its messages, to distinguish what in it seems to be similar to what is already known and what surprises us as being different, unexpected. I agree with Masud Khan (1974, p. 246) when he says:

> What I wish to discuss now is another factor, which has been totally neglected in analytic writings on technique. I have not come across any paper that discusses the contribution made to our knowledge and experience of a patient from our looking at him or her in their person as a body as against looking at merely verbal material and affective responses in the analytic situation.

In an analytic field where sandplay is used it is possible to watch not only the patient's body, his actions, as Khan suggests, but also to consider what he "stages" through playing in the sand tray. The symbolization of feelings active at that moment in the relationship finds this other way in addition to involuntary words. The analyst's watching as he follows the play activity is for me a listening, because it takes in the messate emerging from those gestures, makes them his own, following the thread of the similarities and differences with what he is experiencing in the analytic space. The visibility of the play-scene event provides new metaphors for understanding the player's intrapsychic world and the emotional atmosphere that involves us both.

In order to go deeper into the working hypothesis presented here, I would like to point out that the importance given to watching implies not only an attention paid to the exterior, to the patient's play-actions, but also to the inner theater of the analyst himself, where images are formed are in resonance with what he is hearing. By paying attention to what the patient says, the analyst not only follows the linear flow of the words which produce well-known and shared meanings, but also aims at drawing off the narrative structure of images which those same words awaken in him. He tries to stay in touch with what I would call his "dreaming state" which serves as a background to everything he hears, both in life and in analysis. As he follows the linear flow of shared verbal meanings on an only partially conscious level, he assembles what in my opinion is his representation of the experienced event. This paying attention to the imaginal reverberations that accompany the shared discourse is a perceptive condition that requires training but which is to be found in all of us, though with particular characteristics depending on the typology of the listener. That is to say that the perceptions that take hold vary from person to person, but that all have the power to evoke metaphors which can reach the visual level of mental representation. In this context, watching takes on the significance of an effort to grasp the moment and the conditions of the field in which the representation succeeds in giving shape to emotions, transforming them into shareable feelings. The attitude which I have called "antinomic"[44] aiming simultaneously at two levels of communication, the verbal and the imaginal, is in my opinion the most effective way of getting in touch with psychic phenomena. As I have already pointed out, the appearing of a representation, whether exterior or interior, bears the secret of a new relationship with feelings. What we choose to show speaks not only of the relationships between the ego and the emerging feeling-tone, of its resistances and difficulties, but also contains the inmost structure of the emotional charge that insists on becoming conscious.

[44] Regarding the antinomic principle, see above, Chapter I.

In the present chapter I would like to point out how the mental attitude of the analyst who uses sandplay always remains the same, both as he watches the messages appearing in the field, and as he establishes a relationship to the other through verbal communication. The two moments, apparently so different, show many similarities and are two different ways of integrating and symbolizing feelings. The analyst's working hypothesis is based on the conviction that the spatiotemporal construction of a play scene reveals in its narrative structure a real story, which only later will be translated into words.

Consequently the thesis sustained here may be summed up as follows: images and words, play scenes and shared speech are consecutive moments of integration of the relationship between the ego complex and the emerging feelings in the analytic field. They are two distinct levels of a single symbolic process, deeply connected and in a constant and mutual relationship.

I believe that our ability to use "effective" words to express emotions, and to transform them into shareable feelings, begins and develops in the soil of a preceding mental representation.[45] Verbal communication which effectively expresses feelings and assimilates their energy reveals a more integrated relationship with them. It is the transformation of those feelings which were already present in the initial configuration, but still shut into an exclusively subjective dimension.

Words, which are the fruit of the encounter-clash with current beliefs, perhaps precisely because of this constituent limitation, attain the greatest flexibility and capacity for placing the energy of the emotional charge at the disposal of the ego.

Sandplay makes this relationship between images and words, between representation and discursive language particularly evident. The *mise-en-scène* is the first expressive level both of the emotions that have remained isolated in the depths and of the train of defenses mobilized to contain them. An experience that pertains to the past of the individual and has been repressed, a vital need that has never found the way to verbal sharing because it is deeply split,

[45] For further investigation of this subject see Chapter VII.

can, under favorable circumstances in the relational field, overcome the defensive barriers and gain access to symbolic expression.

Jung intuited this relationship between images and words very early on if already in 1912, in the book which marked his break with Freud, he described fantasy as a "kind of thinking."[46] Fantastic thinking and verbal thinking, as ways of integrating feelings, are always active in the process of adapting to reality and in confronting the mystery around us. This is what happens in every analysis, not only when the analyst uses sandplay, but also when words are the only vehicle of communication.

## 1 Listening Field and Symbolic Activation

Listening, exactly like scene building, can be either effective and deep or superficial, can either grasp feeling-toned structures active in the field, what Jung called "active fantasies," or simply proceed down well-known paths. Our task is to see the difference between the two moments in order to understand the determining factors in the field that activate the imagination on the level of play, dreams and fantasies capable of bringing about a change and of broadening the understanding of shared events.

This is a fundamental theme that is still not sufficiently studied and developed. Personally, I believe that sandplay can make a valid contribution to research in this direction. The question is "how" we approach the complex phenomenon of communication in psychotherapy, as well as "what" we are trying to attain and "when."

In the analyst-patient encounter, the mental attitude is determined first of all by the theory, that is to say by the framework within which the therapist organizes the events. All of us, even without knowing it, apply a theory, a personal approach in the field, which however corresponds only faintly to what we have learned from books, and is conditioned above of all by the structure of our per-

[46] "The two kinds of thinking," in Jung (1912/1952).

sonality. Personal style, like the therapeutic skill of every analyst, depends essentially on his qualities and faults, on the conflicts overcome and resolved, on those that still exist.

So having one's working hypotheses clearly in mind means trying to understand, through constant self-analysis, the unconscious and never fully resolved aspect of our attitude. Going over our personal history, defining the positive and negative aspects of our conflictual issues, and enduring the pain this entails, constitute the fundamental formation for assuming an attitude that seeks an awareness of our actions. This is a first element we need for obtaining a field of listening that is clearly defined, like the tray in which patients build their scenes.

The analyst who asks himself these questions knows by experience that there is always a gap between what he says he's doing and what he happens to do, instead, when he tries to heal the other with the psychic means that are activated in the relationship. This gap demands that he constantly verify the way he responds to the stimuli coming from the field of encounter, and it is a source of endless, sometimes frustrating, but always interesting research, which must be kept alive during the whole course of his professional career. Starting from this premise, the analyst knows he is looking at the psychic world and its mystery from only one of many possible windows, and therefore places himself in a dialectical relationship with what he hears. From a sometimes passionate trust in a conscious theory it is easy to fall into a non-critical identification with it and in an automatic acceptance of it. The dialect remains alive if, instead, the therapist opens to doubt, even while recognizing the penetrating capacity of the working hypothesis which he feels to be closest to. In analytic psychotherapy the encounter with the other cannot and must not aim only at confirming one's assumptions, but at discerning the blind spots and unanswered questions which stimulate the researcher's imagination.

So our style shows the kind of relationship we have with our theory, in both its conscious and unconscious aspects. Repetition and monotony in our attitude are symptoms to bear in mind. They show that the dialectic is weakening, and with it our ability to renew ourselves and to fantasy new ways of being in the field. For a healthy attitude, it is fundamental to recognize the problematic connections the theory we profess have with our history and with our personal conflicts, those known and resolved conflicts but also those still suspended or will appear.

Awareness of a personal style is therefore connected not only to the "knowledge" learned from teachers and from clinical experience gradually assimilated over the years; it is also an awareness of the limits and merits of our personal equation. When we begin to recognize our particular style of relating to the unconscious in the psychotherapeutic relationship, we learn to define our capacity to intervene. In fact, when we admit its limits, our theoretical implement turns out to be useful in some psychopathological instances and less useful or not useful at all in others.

In this regard, Jung remarks (1929, par. 163):

> Hence the personalities of doctor and patient are often infinitely more important for the outcome of the treatment than what the doctor says and thinks (although what he says and think may be a disturbing or a healing factor not to be underestimated).

The personality Jung speaks of is the one built up in years of directly confronting one's personal conflicts and psychic pain. An acid test that can help identity a therapeutic personality is its ability to tolerate the emotional tension of the relational field. The conflictual nuclei existing between the two participants create an interplay of acceptance and distancing: the ambivalence, which is the salt of every creative relationship but is also its constant risk of breaking.

> You can exert no influence if you are not susceptible to influence. It is futile for the doctor to shield himself from the influence of the patient and to surround himself with a smoke-screen of fatherly and professional authority. By so doing he only denies himself the use of a highly important organ of information (*ibid.*)

When the analyst's personality has a vital dialectic relationship to theory a confrontation can be established in the field which, however painful, can be rich in new possible developments. The unresolved personality, or in any case the one that is out of touch with its foundation, generally tends to eliminate the painful tension of the difference and to virtually "indoctrinate" the interlocutor, forcing him to fall in line with his life solutions.

The relationship to theory thus shows the perspective from which the analyst views events and defines their course. His mode of procedure may be aware or omnipotent. The latter is the case with those apparently competent professionals, often eclectic in style, well read, but far removed from their emotional roots and from an awareness of their blind spots.

The analytical attitude is based first of all on this personal relationship with the theory that founds it. When speaking of style, I already mentioned the question of the "way" the therapist works, of the conscious and unconscious means he employ, with a constant dialectical striving to recognize what is happening. The basic approach of the therapist, who aims at being aware of his actions, is the preliminary field condition for analytical sharing.

To activate the symbolic process we know how necessary it is to have the sense, or rather the representation, of a well-defined space sustained by rules that makes it possible to distinguish the analytic field from "real" life. Ritual, which helps differentiate the inner from the outer, in this similar to the tray of sand, has a complex machinery. It consists of apparently external aspects, such as the pace of the sessions and the spatial arrangement between analyst and patient in their relationship. But the attention given to these aspects is to be seen, in a deep sense, as the expression on the part of the analyst of an ethical attitude towards the mystery of the psyche. The ability to accept the unexpected, the keen curiosity about unusual perceptions that take one by surprise, the sense of the uniqueness of shared events, are some of the elements that go to make up the emotional atmosphere which facilitates the emerging of an effective symbolization. As Dora Kalff pointed out (Montecchi, 1984, p. 20):

> To succeed in creating a free space I try to free myself of judgmental attitudes and preconceived ideas. I like being in an open-minded space receptive to the unexpected.

This attitude, when it is real, is not only the result of a conscious act of availability, but has roots that are much more complex. The atmosphere of cordiality and freedom which the analyst may be able to create is closely related to the emotional narrative structure which he has built up over the years by working on himself, a process that is never definitely concluded. So the way the analyst listens, which has such importance in the symbolic process activated in the analytic field, has an intricate and enthralling origin that is only partly known.[47]

## 2 Listening As a Scene Under Construction

The hesitating or resolute gestures of the player, like the pauses and the pace of their sequence, express a concentration and a striving to perceive, an authentic "listening," I would say, to what is happening between him and the playing field. These moments, by no accident, are often dominated by silence, just as we remain silent in order to hear a sound, a piece of music or what the other is saying. It is a complete silence, open to surprise, charged with reflections. I believe I have understood the psychic act of listening in analysis more thoroughly by watching patients play.

So the complex psychic act which the analyst experiences as he tries to understand the patient's verbal and preverbal communication bears many similarities to the experience of the person who succeeds in playing: staying silent comes automatically, being receptive to every slightest indication, like what happens with that tray of sand which as soon as it is touched sends a message, whether it be a lightly traced stroke or an object placed in the scene. As soon as

[47] In the Freudian sphere, Antonio Di Benedetto (1991, p. 405) describes a similar approach to listening: "The real obstacle is not 'understanding' but making the words of the other resound in us, as we listen to ourselves in order to give meaning, our personal, genuine experienced meaning to those messages. Wherefore what is offered is a 'maieutic' rather than an 'investigative' function, a field of semantic possibilities marked by a readiness to let a spontaneous generation of meaning occur, rather than interpret a hidden meaning."

the patient enters into resonance with the sand and the objects of all kinds, from the simplest to the most elaborate, the analyst establishes contact with his various listening levels. It is not only the contents of the story that draw his attention, but also the gestures, the facial expressions, the tone, and pace of the words.

In the act of perception different qualities of resonance can be distinguished: from the most distinct and conscious to the least differentiated. Some of them can be put into words, others strike us as an emotional atmosphere or make themselves felt as a barely perceptible physical sensation. Hence it must be possible for the perceptive capacity's range to extend from what is immediately clear, because familiar, to the color of the feelings, to the even chaotic movement of emotions, all the way to the physical responses awakened by the field.

The duty of the analyst is to train himself to distinguish and organize these levels of perception. It is a question of broadening one's field of listening in order to succeed in visualizing (in a condition I have already described as a dreaming state) whatever emotions present in the relationship which touch one's sensibility. The goal is to bring forth in oneself the first level of symbolization, to open up to involuntary images, in order to be able to "play" them in the analytic field, as the patient does when he chooses his object for the scene.

The analyst aims, therefore, at activating in his listening the two kinds of thinking, imaginal or verbal, the vague and uncertain kind of representation that takes him by surprise, and the distinct, more reliable and customary form of thinking in words. He must always question himself about this two-fold aspect of symbolic expression, and keep the two levels related. Jung pointed out this interdependence when, in his essay, *The Transcendent Function*, he sustained that the "principle of creative formulation" and the "principle of understanding" were needed for elaborating feelings emerging from the unconscious (Jung, 1957/1958, par. 175):

> Whereas aesthetic formulation tends to concentrate on the formal aspect of the motif, an intuitive understanding often tries to catch the meaning from barely adequate hints in the material, without considering those elements which would come to light in a more careful formulation

Both "principles" are an essential part of listening and of that psychic work which, in the analytic field, prepares the interpretative act in the form of representation and then translates it into words. Explaining the need for the two levels of symbolization to be simultaneously present, Jung remarks (*ibid.*pars. 176, 177):

> The danger of the aesthetic tendency is overvaluation of the formal aspect or "artistic" worth of the fantasy-productions; the libido is diverted from the real goal of the transcendent function and sidetracked into purely aesthetic problems of artistic nature expression. The danger of wanting to understand the meaning is overvaluation of the contents, which is subjected to intellectual analysis and interpretations, so that the essentially symbolic nature of the produce is lost (...) *One tendency seems to be the regulating principle of the other:* both are bound together in a compensatory relation. Experience bears out this formula. So far as it is possible at this stage to draw more general conclusions, we would say that aesthetic formulation needs understanding of the meaning, and the understanding needs aesthetic formulation. The two supplement each other to form the transcendent function.

Speaking of interpretations that make use of both these levels of the symbolic act, we shall see that, when what prevails in the analytic field is the principle of understanding, or the verbal way of organizing experience, to the detriment of a creative formulation, there is a tendency to explain things through mechanisms. This is the exclusively relational, interpersonal or "horizontal" perspective where verbal thinking is given more emphasis than the imaginal substructure. Also identifying the underlying mechanism of experienced psychic phenomena is in the end undoubtedly a move on the part of the imagination as a way of operating the field. It often happens, however, that the operator loses touch with the originally fantastic roots of his formulations, and closes himself into stereotyped repetitions. This impoverishment, this loss of the metaphorical aspect of the theory, tends to imprison what happened into vain conceptualizations in which the relationship to the vitality of an event is lost.

When instead the opposite principle prevails, the principle of creative formulation, an adequate distinction between active and passive images is no longer possible. And the analyst, setting aside the principle of understanding, assumes an attitude based on undue aesthetic emphasis, which views every image as a revelation.

The two different kinds of thinking are, I believe, also necessary for our working concepts. And with regard to this I would like to introduce a metaphor here borrowed from mythical thinking: a representation which I found was useful for amplifying and exploring the question of listening. Actually it offered me a way for keeping my bearings in the complexity of the mechanism and for describing it in imaginal terms, instead of defining it in concepts alone. I have taken a representation of Eros from Plato's *Phaedrus* whose vitality I have always been struck by:

> As I said at the beginning of this tale, I divided each soul into three - two horses and a charioteer; and one of the horses was good and the other bad: the division may remain, but I have not yet explained in what the goodness or badness of either consists, and to that I will proceed. The right-hand horse is upright and cleanly made; he has a lofty neck and an aquiline nose; his color is white, and his eyes dark; he is a lover of honor and modesty and temperance, and the follower of true glory; he needs no touch of the whip, but is guided by word and admonition only. The other is a crooked lumbering animal, put together anyhow; he has a short thick neck; he is flat-faced and of a dark color, with grey eyes and blood-red complexion; the mate of insolence and pride, shag-eared and deaf, hardly yielding to whip and spur. Now when the charioteer beholds the vision of love, and has his whole soul warmed through sense, and is full of the prickings and ticklings of desire, the obedient steed, then as always under the government of shame, refrains from leaping on the beloved; but the other, heedless of the pricks and of the blows of the whip, plunges and runs away, giving all manner of trouble to his companion and the charioteer, whom he forces to approach the beloved and to remember the joys of love.

This magnificent image catches the thrilling moment, the sudden appearance of Eros, summoned when least expected by the look of the loved one. The representation, in its dynamic complexity, brings forth the play of emotional tensions which are ignited on various levels when the possibility of a transforming encounter appears. In analytic listening, too, there are unexpected moments in which the depths of an emotion are touched that can change both.

Using metaphors to grasp the elements of a complex experience is not a rhetorical device, but a way of seeing and understanding more. I fully agree with Niels Bohr when he says:

> Our goal is not to penetrate into the essence of things, whose ultimate meaning we shall never know, but to develop concepts which allow us to deal productively with natural phenomena (...) photons and neutrons are not real (...) they are rather shadows created out of a combination of light and the position of the observer.[48]

The conceptual formulation of a phenomenon always represents a great enrichment which can nevertheless lose its value, grow old and become a virtually automatic repetition. Imaginal thinking always appears in the early stages of a symbolization process that prepares a new concept.

A preexisting poetic metaphor, like that in *Phaedrus*, is not a spontaneous representation, does not spring from my imagination, but can enrich my understanding and permit me, as well, to organize what I perceive as I listen. To state in conceptual terms that the emerging signs in the relationship between me and the other take on a charge of feeling-tone and become signals is certainly correct. In the same way, it is correct to say that I get prepared to detect the feeling-toned and instinctive messages which go beyond shared speech; but all this remains detached from the vitality of the experience which I find instead in that representation, when I apply it to the moment in which the event takes place.

In fact, the Eros metaphor enables me to distinguish and connect the different levels of listening. The two horses seem to represent drives, that emotional charge which has not yet attained symbolization in the analytic field, but which the bodies of both the analyst and the patient may experience and endure. Of the two horses, the white obedient one reminds me of the capacity to recognize the impulses emerging in the field, the ones I perceive with intensity, but also succeed in acknowledging and controlling: it is what I have learned to know

[48] Quoted in Gaburri (1997), p. 13

about my impulsiveness. The black horse can be seen as the indomitable drives which under emotional pressure can charge off independently of one's will and in the acting-out go off on their own. When I realize I am saying or doing something in the analytic field that surprises me, that does not abide by the rules I have set myself and considered definitely established, the impulsiveness of the black horse appears, which can lead the analytic position astray and lose its tracks, switch off the symbolic dimension. It is true, however, that when this does happen a possibility of understanding is also created, however painful and difficult it is to accept.

Plato stresses the fact that the horse that leaps out of control "forces them [the charioteer and the white horse] to approach the beloved and to remember the joys of love." The *daimon* that appears reduces the ego's confidence, at times its *hubris*, and exposes it to the astonishment of a look that sees beyond what is the customary and the already known. The image of the charioteer may suggest a few considerations about the role of the wish to understand experienced by the analyst when he listens. The therapist, like the charioteer, tries to open the way to understanding in the emotional turbulence of the analytic field, sustaining the impetus of the two horses. But if he favors the white horse only, refusing to recognize the presence of the black horse in himself, he risks the tedious and reassuring repetition of what others think. If instead he surrenders to the illusion and lets go of the black horse, he swerves off the road and harms the patient and himself. The chariot plays the role of the theory that has been learned and fully assimilated. It is what allows me accept my task: what to do, when and how to do it. But it is a vehicle I must always renew, put in order every day, as soon as I notice the difference between what I say I'm doing and what I actually happen to be doing.

Other aspects have enhanced the act of listening, reconsidered through the metaphor of Eros. Thinking of it at once in words and in images has made it possible to approach its vital complexity.

# 3 Listening to Mario

The encounter with Mario, a young engineer who for some time had suffered from sudden seizures of panic, offers the opportunity to grasp the vitality and the different levels of the symbolic event, in his communicating along with my listening.

Mario had only recently started his job and explained his seizures by blaming them on the new situation he was in. In particular, those seizures took place in the presence of a master builder, his subordinate, who knew the materials and the secrets of the profession better than he did. His story is logical, based also on an introspection capable of going beyond contingent facts. The choice of his present job indicates an old conflict with his father, he too an expert technician in a field not unlike his own, who would like them to work together. Mario, instead, is trying to become independent, and any failure could have serious consequences for him.

Though keeping in mind this plausible explanation, which however has not had any appreciable effect on Mario's suffering, I try to detect and single out what there is about him that strikes me. As a rule I dwell on some impression that comes into my perception like a first object chosen for an imaginary sandplay. So I wait until something appears capable of stimulating an association, a metaphor or a more distinct image.

On that occasion, I remember I was struck by the way he entered with his head down, almost as if his hooked nose were being used like a beak for pointing the way. That first stimulus was immediately offset by an atmosphere of gentility that created an almost exaggerated distance between us. These two contradictory elements, like two objects that are exact opposites, were a completely subjective choice of my listening. The first was hard, piercing, the second soft, like something that still had to find a shape. They were two metaphors drawn from the interpersonal field, a first point of reference which could be useful for organizing what I was perceiving.

The above-described attitude is like dreaming with your eyes open while, at the same time, with the watchful part of my listening, I carefully follow what he says and try to detect something in the elements of the story he tells that refers to the two-sided imaginary object I have just perceived: the "hard" and the "soft". The task I set myself is to bear the initial impressions in mind in order to organize the turbulence of perceptions on the various levels existing in the field.

What happens, and will happen in the next session, between me and the patient begins to prepare the way to understanding the distinct contents of verbal thinking as well as of those first exactly opposite images I perceived. In other words, it is a question of focusing on the possibility of perceiving the two levels of symbolization active in him and in me. By using the metaphor of Eros, I must be able to hold the reins of my listening: to balance the measured gait of the "white horse", my lucid understanding, and the hurtling thrust of the "black horse," namely my wholly subjective, sometimes apparently absurd perceptions which, among the many possible stimuli, intrudes upon my listening with a remarkable emotional resonance.

Returning now to the initial perception of "hardness," of piercingness, and setting it against the perception of "softness," I wonder where these two aspects in Mario's story can be found, in the structure of his family of origin, in the situation of the present relationships he is describing to me. I remember, for instance, that at that time I associated the violent, piercing impact of my first impression with the figure of his father. His intense description, a mixture of love and hatred, dwelled on this figure, whereas I noticed that it was more difficult to find the "soft" aspect in his words. In subsequent sessions I realized that this rarely verbalized part lay closer to the image of the mother who, though appearing only seldom in the story, had actually in real life deeply involved him.

A later step in the excavating work of listening is to try and find out what the patient is forcing me to do or say. In Mario's case, I suddenly noticed that, though having given him more time than usual, as is often the case at first meetings, I had lost touch with my sense of time, which went by in a flash and beyond the deadline I had established. Thinking back over it, another fact struck me: I had been very obliging, had met him more than halfway in accepting his dates for the next appointment, even neglecting my own engagements. I can now say that I had not realized I had become too "soft".

This metaphor, still obscure in my awareness at the time, bore instead an image that was active in the field: I was identifying with that image, without my being able to explain it. Mario, who seemed to be completely available, was introducing into the relationship something piercing which won out over my demands. It was only when I suddenly caught myself that I could take control of the chariot again. It was the "black horse" which at that moment made me lose my sense of time. When I realized that the images were active and creating an interplay of identifications and projections stronger than me, I could resume the role of the chariot in Plato's representation. The moment of surprise is always very significant, in that it gives a first general picture of the narrative structure of the emotions and feelings present in the relationship.

In my representation of the event resulting from our encounter, in the construction of my imaginary "sand scene" I now placed the "objects" I had detected between Mario and me which had before remained suspended at the level of perception, without my being able to use their symbolic value as a way of organizing the analytic field.

A confirmation of what had come about in the field was the dream Mario told me in the next session:

> Shut up in a dark pool is a large shark, it too dark, lying on its side; a soulful eye peers up through the water, I feel sorry for it.

The symbolic process that had been activated had extracted a core of pain and destructiveness, which helped me understand the emotions existing in our previous meeting. The dream representation suggested the unlivability of Mario's emotional space, to which a vital force was confined, reduced to the image of a dying shark. The representation offered a view of Mario's whole psychological narrative structure, of his story, but also gave a form to the image that was active between us. The availability which had suddenly struck me the day before, in him and in me, was certainly related to that dark core, the "shark," which, unseen, instilled in both of us fear and surprise.

A few days later Mario's encounter with the concreteness of sandplay was remarkable. Going over to the tray he said he thought it looked like a desert, and he placed a compass in the middle. Soon after, caught up in the playing, he placed marine objects on the sand, which in his eyes became the bottom of the ocean. In the end he added an upright metal figure, clearly feminine, with two protruding beasts, which seemed to have nothing to do with the representation of the sea predominant up to that moment.

In the following sessions, in reply to an observation I made about that figure, Mario said he hadn't noticed its feminine aspect: a different element suddenly emerged in the *mise-en-scéne* with regard to the chain of associations guided by consciousness. Subsequently, that feminine image seemed to us to be trapped in the iron, just as the shark in the dream was trapped: a soft emotional part imprisoned in a hard cage like the soulful look in the eye of the shark, immobilized in a pool. It was an image which in Mario's story recalled his always needing to be strong and successful in order to please a mother who had been abandoned by her husband. The figure's metallic verticalness, at the moment absurd, placed in the scene an inner persecutor who tolerated neither weakness nor derogations of law, unlike what had happened with Mario's father, who had made his mother suffer. The symbolic level reached through sandplay conveyed an experience which up to that point words could not have expressed.

## 4 The Confrontation of Words and Images

We know that words sometimes seem to go further, break the preexisting bonds of thinking and open unexpected perspectives. At other times, instead, they seem to exhaust and lose their vitality. With time and with use, they can become repetitive, monotonous, both in their contents and in their color, almost as if they were deliberately used to avoid surprises of any kind. The same happens with the images in a representation, whether it be mental as in dreams or fantasies or concrete as in a play scene. In building a scene, the first objects chosen often refer to nothing but the experiences usually connected with the materials themselves. Sand, shells, stones can open up a wholly predictable sequence of associations related to experiences on the beach or by the sea, until suddenly an irrational idea makes headway. In a structurally similar fashion repeated everyday words, the prefabricated manners of speaking with which we approach the thrill of meeting the other, all of a sudden depart from their usual course and associate a completely new element. In words, such phenomena appear as a sudden leap, alien to the logic followed so far by the thread of conversation.

Freud, who was the first to lay stress on the above event, had sensed the possibilities of this moment for research. Free association, actually quite hard to bring about in analytic practice with words alone, tries to provoke this particular aspect. As happens with images, together with words that bear out an experience, other images that shatter preexisting connections may appear.

The analogy of words and images, noticed here, brings out the defensive or transformational role which both of these means of expression can assume. Further similarities can be found, on the one hand, in the tone, in the color, in the inflection itself of speech, and on the other, in the choice of objects, in the figures that are placed in the playing field, in the pace of the gestures, which generate the feeling-toned atmosphere of an experience. In fact, the words, like the images, that constitute a representation, may be descriptive, literal, conceptual, but also metaphorical, surprising, and, at particular moments, succeed in being poetic, evocative.

The symbolic process unfolds in the same way on the above two levels: there are images and words which tend to maintain the preexisting psychic equilibrium, and others which destroy the old relations and open new perspectives. The former play a homeostatic role, the latter have a propulsive, metapoietic function.[49]

[49] For further investigation of the symbolic function in Jung, in its two-fold aspect, see Trevi (1986).

The spatiotemporal coordination of sandplay choices has always seemed to me tantamount to a highly varied and well-constructed story, even if it still moves in a wholly subjective universe. In my opinion, each individual choice of objects can be superimposed on the denominating words, whereas the placement of every element in the context of the playing field corresponds to the organization of a discourse, to a narrative that is gradually taking shape: the object placed in space is therefore similar to the naming of a feeling, and the finished representation establishes contact with the complex structure of an experience.

# VIII Building a Scene: A Story Told

*I must simply try to discover, with the patient, what acts for him - I am almost tempted to say, what is actual.* C.G. Jung (1931) par. 95

In a theoretical view of the psyche and its pathology where importance is given to the process of differentiating between the self and the world, story-telling plays a leading role. Story-telling is an act that distinguishes between self and other-than-self and, with its descriptions and delimitations, creates a distance from emotions and allows them to be dealt with. Story-telling is considered an essential human need, an activity which helps people organize and, in the end, think about and experience their emotions more fully. The analyst aims at establishing an interpersonal emotional field which facilitates and renders this attitude effective for understanding the emotional narrative structure which is active in the depths of the individual and which, unseen, determines his life.

Imprinted in the unconscious of all of us is a sort of map of our personal history. It registers both the scars produced by the encounter-clash with life and the individual heritage of potentialities, only partly expressed, which may be brought out or inhibited by the environment. Part and parcel of this deep narrative structure are the defenses built up over the years as strategies for surviving the pressure of over-invasive emotions. The gestures, the words, dreams and fantasies of the individual speak of both. Dialogue with the other becomes effective when it succeeds in bringing out the basic emotional structure underlying what is being said. In my opinion sandplay, sooner than purely verbal analysis, is able to evoke that capacity for telling stories which still eludes the dimension of words.

# 1 Towards a Borderline Experience

At times patients fill the space of the relationship with words. What is striking is the "quantity" of what they say, the unvarying tone, aside from the repetitiousness of subject matter. That "talking" is clearly not so much a communication as a way of retaining a center of assurance, a sort of reference point in the stability of the customary. But sooner or later, silence will clear a way through the jungle of words. These are moments when patients are closer to their emotions and can perceive them. In the analytic field I am describing, the patient has the possibility of returning to the sand tray which he has already experimented at least once in the preliminary stage of the analysis.

The return is not easy, laden as it is with ambivalent sensations and feelings. In the unusual play-situation, adults can experience a loss of assurance, like someone preparing to pass through a new country that lies outside of his usual control, but who is at the same time drawn to it. The analyst must know how to wait for this spontaneous return to the sandbox, because he realizes that for them agreeing to play is the same as crossing a borderline into and sharing an unfamiliar space, all of which demands concentration. Standing at the sand tray, the absence of preconceived responses may give a sense of freedom, but at the same time of something lacking. The only feasible response is the one that is set going between the patient and that delimited space, between him and a random pattern traced in the sand, which points to a first possibility of choice. The answers which consciousness expects for its assurance are, as it were, suspended, postponed. It is a fundamental ever-present psychological condition for confronting emotions that are difficult to control. We leave what is known and venture beyond habitual boundaries, towards emotional states that cannot yet be expressed verbally.

In the presence of that still empty sandbox, fear also seems interwoven with a need to let go. The illusion of a space where everything is apparently possible brings old ghosts to the scene. Early in my experience, I expected the possibility of wishing, though constricted as it was by the limited space of the scene and by the objects available, to trigger the impulse, the discharge of wishing. I realized instead that this eventuality, though often encountered over the years in situations of resistance, is quite rare. What is found more frequently, indeed almost always, are evenly-paced play actions, "without climax and not of an orgiastic kind," Winnicott would say, who described very clearly the nature of these actions in children (1971, p. 69):

> In playing, the child manipulates external phenomena in the service of the dream and invests chosen external phenomena with dream meaning and feeling.

When adults establish contact with the play area and start using it, the initial hesitation gives way to concentration and pace.

## 2 From Approaching the Play Scene to Using It

The concrete presence of the sandbox makes it possible to take a closer look at the complexity of the phenomenon, especially when the protagonist is an adult endowed with more sophisticated, introspective tools and has no trouble translating them into words.

In the stage of approaching the field it seems to me that it is the object itself (the play area, the sand, the objects on the shelves) that is given the greatest importance. It is appealing but also creates uncertainties and is sometimes frightening because of what it obscurely represents. The field can be dominated by an emotion that can be so strange and so vague that it sometimes instills a sense of persecution.

Through play, the body becomes a protagonist in the analytic field, and this fact can increase the prevailing sense of insecurity and exposure that must be carefully contained. We know that in every psychological confrontation the body is the vehicle of the deepest emotions, of phantasms only vaguely sensed in the relationship, but hard to put into words. In the play situation, movements are no longer inhibited: the patient gets up, moves about looking for a form, chooses the objects, builds the scene. After the scene is finished, the analyst, who usually maintains his usual position, also gets up to observe the scene and then photograph it. This is when old and new phantasms connected with the body are undoubtedly activated in the field, which can bring about less controllable dynamics of a seductive or persecutory nature that are always present in the transference and countertransference relationship. Depending on individual situations, moving about sometime induces levels of anxiety which the analyst must recognize and know how to contain in silence as well as by speaking. In this situation, which requires the attentive participation of the analyst, together with the aspect of wishing, and at times of need, the possible symbolization of emotions and feelings experienced on a physical level becomes present in the patient at that very moment. This is the first step towards the visual integration of feelings in the representation and towards the use of words.

So sandplay for adults means crossing the borderline of what is known and taking a step towards the unknown: patients agree to accept a free space that is wholly unpredictable where they risk being drawn to the sphere of wishes, and in some cases of finding also in themselves the frailty of old never-gratified needs. They feel they are leaving behind their usual center of balance based on words, at the risk of finding an expression that is harder to control. Fear, sometimes refusal, but also attraction, are feelings that accompany this transition. The explanations and responses used up to that moment by consciousness are perfectly useless in this situation, where the only alternative is to surrender to the present experience.

I remember that at the beginning of my work with sandplay I was struck by the intensity with which adults can take part in it, working through their fears or momentary refusals and then giving in to an unexpected capacity to let go. What was clear between them and the playing field was the aspect of wishing which was both appealing and alarming, but also the possibility of experiencing a need that up until then had been kept at a safe distance, as if it were something embarrassing because of irrational elements so distant from the positions acquired by consciousness.

What seemed to me immediately paradoxical was how an initial attitude, often marked by an uncertain and cautious adherence to sandplay, veered into being "taken" by it. As if those shapes, to all appearance foreseen, once used in the field had revealed an unexpected independence and, by reflection, triggered in the patient a need for letting go. It is the moment where "need" seems to lead the patient to seek what he finds matches him and what he senses to contrary or different. In building the scene an inner urge appears, experienced but not recognized by the patient, to choose that particular object and not another, that position and not another, that connection with the other figures in the scene and not another. This deeply-felt need leads to the invention, as it were, of spatial relationships and metaphors which are impossible for consciousness, that believes it has the experience under control.

Jung (1929/1957, par. 20) gives a good description of the attitude needed to accept contact with the emotional depths that concern and involve consciousness:

> The art of letting things happen, action through non-action, letting go of oneself as taught by Meister Eckhart, became for me the key that opens the door to the way. *We must let things happen to the psyche.* For us, this is an art of which most people know nothing. Consciousness is forever interfering, helping, correction and negating, never leaving the psychic processes to grow in peace. It would be simple enough, if only simplicity were not the most difficult of all things. To begin with, the task consists solely in observing how a fragment of fantasy develops.

## 3 The Moment of Use

When the hands, watched by the eyes, touch the sand tray and arrange objects in its space, the whole situation changes. A measured pace is established, as if the player were starting to look for the "real object." What has been chosen first (figure, concrete object, place of the scene) immediately calls up "something else," that is similar or opposite, and aims at organizing the barely suggested scene into a whole.

What happens when real contact is established with the playing field?

At present this question can be answered only partially. Personally, I believe that between the patient and that field a need for an answer is activated, a search which only seems to be conducted by consciousness. The action that animates the gestures in building a scene reminds me of something Jung said (1937, pars 242, 243):

> The richness of the human psyche and its essential character are probably determined by this reflective instinct. Reflection re-enacts the process of excitation and carries the stimulus over into a *series of images*, which, if the impetus is strong enough, are reproduced (...) Through the reflective instinct, the stimulus is more or less wholly transformed into a psychic content, that is, it becomes *an experience: a natural process is transformed into a conscious content.*

I believe that the archetypal structure of the reflective instinct, as sensed by Jung, found a possible commonly-shared account in the collective myth of Narcissus. The searching gestures induced by sandplay speak of the mystery of an identity in the making. Identity of self and other-than-self in the search for a response that meets the deepest emotional needs. The concrete response of environment to the searching psychic gesture, represented here by the "malleability" of the sand, by the variety of objects in the play-scene space, speaks of the vicissitudes of narcissism.[50] The self-reflection of Narcissus transpires in the pace of the scene-building.

The above moments, the going over to the playing field and then capacity to use it, may be seen as a possible way of distinguishing at first hand the subjective experience of the ambivalent relationship to wishing an object that is already part of personal history or of the need to look for it. Object-libido and narcissistic libido, in their complex relations, are present and alluded to in those movements.

[50] Winnicott (1965) pointed out, as few others, the role of environmental response in psychic transformation.

For the moment, suffice it to say that the stories told through the whens and hows of building a scene differentiate individual desires and needs more clearly than shared speech was up to then able to communicate.

During sandplay, emotions are channeled into both words and playing. Contact with the materials and objects opens the way to a "story" about what is still excluded from the possibilities of words: the expressive potentiality of playing conveys sensations and emotions that are still restricted to a level preceding representation.

## 4 Signs of Difficulty: The Resistances

Paying attention to the whens and hows of using sandplay, along with the tone and contents of the accompanying verbal reactions, offers a new view of the resistance to change, which is typical of every analysis and may involve both participants, the patient no less than the analyst. The similarities and differences between the two levels stress the structure and force of the ongoing resistance, and reveal the relationship with the emotions and feelings present in the analytic field. When deep emotions take shape in the scene-building there may be a tendency to react with indifference or boredom. In those moments, it could happen that I had trouble photographing the scenes or remembering aspects of them which with time would turn out to be the expression the shared emotional dynamics. Only after looking at the photograph could I see what I had previously been blind to, and recognize my countertransferential participation. The difficulty of keeping silent in the presence of an "irritating" scene, the almost compulsive urge to ask questions, are both signs of the difficulties I gradually learned to accept. It is easier instead to detect the phenomenon of resistance in patients.

Some patients fill the play scene with objects, just as they filled the space of the relationship space with words. This behavior seems to imply a merely formal acceptance of the "rule" of an environment which contemplates the possibility of using sandplay. In this case, the "borderline" is not really crossed, there is no real contact with underlying emotions: the same defense noticed on a verbal level is triggered by the gestures. What strikes the observer is the jerky rapidity of these gestures, their compulsiveness, and at the same time the lack of reflection (Narcissus) in the making of choices. A hastily-built construction unreflectively "acted-out" is a first sign of defense against an anxiety present in the situation.

A less apparent defense takes the form of a sort of aestheticism in the construction. An intolerance of discord or of hands getting soiled by the sand is like a polite conversation that avoids physical contact. In other cases, patients do not seem to be interested in discovering the particular characteristics of the materials offered, but in adapting them to experiences they have already had. I remember a painter who used the sandbox as if it were a sheet of paper and, filling it with the colors at hand, tried to create something that what was familiar to him. It was important for him to learn how to take advantage of the malleability of sand and establish a tit-for-tat relationship with the lines and figures he had traced, until he succeeded in using the prefabricated objects he had avoided before.

The difficulty of establishing contact with the world of experienced emotions is also expressed in the relationship with the malleability of sand and the use that is made of it: sometimes avoiding it, suppressing it and turning the tray into a simple support for the things placed there; at others limiting contact with the surface of the field until only a very small part of it is used, leaving all the rest empty. The dull, barely audible tone of the voice seems to be the equivalent of the cautious scene-building that not know how to take up room.

The presence of play in the analytic field offers the analyst a new viewpoint of the phenomenon of resistance, whether experienced in oneself or pointed out in the patient. Approaching the sandbox clearly means confronting the emotion active at that moment for both in the relationship. The patient's ability to move away from a familiar center of assurance, and open up to still "unsayable" emotions, corresponds to the possibility of the analyst to abandon his usual points of reference and taking part in the event. The resulting defensive reactions of either one of the participants which gradually and eventually appear are the first act of this encounter-clash with the emotional dynamics to be understood.

## 5 Signs of Willingness

By observing the building-pace of a scene other elements emerge. It reveals, first of all, the ability to wait in front of the untouched, empty space of the sand tray. It is as if the player were looking for some sort of sign, a perceptive invitation to start the representation: this may be triggered by a pattern he has traced in the sand or by some object that appeals to him more than others. The patient seems to "go along" with what is happening with reflective actions that are altogether different from the hasty, convulsive movements I have just described. Reflective pauses alternate with a series of faster activities, which to the observer look as if the player had suddenly got an idea. These alternating stops-and-goes in the building process seem to correspond to the involuntary words and meaningful pauses of a verbal narrative.

Some of the sudden connections between the figures chosen, some of them apparently very strange, are nothing less than free associations. What would seem to be happening is a dialogue, a circular movement, between the patient and his playing, which completely captures his attention. The patient, as a result of this acceptance of the play-dimension, is able to perceive the moment and abandon conscious goal-oriented representations. What reveals a true encounter with experienced feeling is the deep concentration that accompanies the playing, the pace of it in particular. The player is engrossed in organizing the scene, and every figure or constructed form appears to be the result of a carefully pondered choice between opposite tendencies. For the observer, it is clear that certain figures are chosen with no effort, whereas others, which give rise to a vague uneasiness, are placed in the field as if there were some inner compulsion to do so.

As we saw with Anna (Chapter III), some particular forms follow patients throughout the course of their scene-building, successive images carrying a meaning that is distilled, step by step, before reaching the integration of words.

Adults engrossed in playing frequently accompany their scene-building with exclamations or sudden memories. These involuntary words give the observer further information about what is happening: intense words, not only in their meaning, but also in their emotional tone. The dullness of speech, which often exists before going over to the sand tray, is replaced by a more expressive, a more colorful and straightforward, sometimes even violent language. This is the way a deeply afflicted, but alert and thoughtful patient described the different emotional field dimension he through sandplay:

> Before starting to play I was seized by a general feeling of ill-being which remained vague and also for this reason disturbing. Placing the objects was for me like focusing, even though I was the one who actually invented the whole thing. It did me good to feel more active than when I tried to communicate with words. When I succeed in expressing something it as if I were entering a dimension of my own. Now at least I know or think of the stone I put there and don't feel just a vague contradiction.

Involuntary verbal remarks during the scene-building are of great interest because, like sudden associations, they shed light on the images taking shape. What also often emerges involves matters that have never been discussed before. A dialogue can open up, become fluent, or take on expressiveness. Silence can also change the atmosphere of the relationship, and reach a never-before experienced deepness of sharing.

The task of the analyst is to pay closer attention to the words and forms appearing on the scene, wondering what effect the event has on him at that moment and what it might tend to make him do or say.

## ⑥ Sandplay: A Story Beyond Words

The actions which organize and describe these emotional experiences tell the story, in the space-time of building a scene, of consciousness making contact with emotions. Only later is the integration of verbal language grafted onto this primary basis.

I would like to remark on the fact that also verbal stories, when they succeed in expressing the alien nature of disturbing emotions, are the fruit of a particular mental attitude: its capacity to describe. A consciousness simply defending itself from an emotion looks first of all for an explanation, tries, that is, to check and even imprison the disturbing or distressing experience into a conceptual cage. Attaining a descriptive disposition implies, instead, that the usual defenses are momentarily abandoned, and offers new possibilities of expression and understanding (Tagliagamba, 1997, p. 262):

> So the advantage offered by description with respect to explanation consists in the fact that it is not anchored to claims of being unique and allows an unlimited choice between different symbolic systems and using them alternately.

What playing induces spontaneously is harder to achieve through the words of shared speech, which has trouble escaping its logical sequences and mental habits. It is not easy to abandon the known, sustained by verbal thinking, for the precariousness of a pattern, a representation through images which consciousness finds indistinct, uncertain, at times simply an arbitrary and in the end irritating invention.

Paul Ricoeur (1988) observes how two moments intersect in the act of story-telling, which I have noticed in my own experience by watching the behavior of people beginning sandplay. He introduces the notion of narrative identity, that is a sort of "mix" of historical story-telling and fiction. According to this theory, the self-understanding we all have is narrative. I cannot see myself outside of time, Ricoeur remarks, and therefore outside of the account: what I am is the equivalent of the story of my life. In this sense, the narrative aspect is essential to self-understanding. It possesses the dual characteristic of being at once historical and fictional.

An analytic field like the one I am proposing here, where words and playing with objects have the same importance in terms of communication and transformation, makes it possible to discover this dual level also in the story that is told by building a scene. Only with time and gradually-gained understanding can the specific historical connection between the patient and his choices be discovered, choices which during the scene-building seem charged with the imaginary, simple fictions also for the ones who have conceived them and at the same time paradoxically true.

In my opinion, an analytic field organized on two levels, verbal communication and the preverbal communication of playing, offers greater possibilities of escaping the defensive circuits of verbal thinking. Through play the narrative dimension is enriched by the double characteristic of "being at once historical and fictional." It is precisely this "mix," to use Ricœur's term, that, with the appearance of new metaphors, makes it possible to break free of the repetitive circuits of current speech and at the same time to lend it a greater wealth of expression and subject matter.

Heidegger remarks (1959a, pp. 120-124):

> Everything spoken stems in a variety of ways from the unspoken, whether this be something not yet spoken, or whether it be what must remain unspoken in the sense that it is beyond the reach of speaking.... What it says wells up from the formerly spoken and so far still unspoken Saying which pervades the design of language.

The attempt to recover the "original Say," to use Heidegger's magnificent metaphor, is a way of defining the goal of sandplay in adult analysis: giving form to the unexpressed, blocked by the defenses. Only afterwards can a "spoken" appear that is no longer dominated by the compulsion to repeat and capable of conveying emotions never before expressed.

The need to differentiate and at the same time to try and unite the two levels of communication in such a way that people "narrate" themselves and their experiences, is clearly expressed by the philosopher, Ernesto Grassi (1989, p. 17):

> We must differentiate between the logical, rational structure of explanatory language and purely persuasive rhetorical language. What is their mutual relationship based on? Both start off by stating principles: one the principles of *ratio*, reason, the other the principles, the images, that influence pathos, passions (...)

So does the "rational," "explanatory" language have to be placed alongside the arational, purely "indicative," semantic language, whose structure is different?

So sandplay is a way of returning to the roots, to the act of playing, which, during the growth of individuals, is the first to inspire the typically human need to tell stories, but never underrating the other side, the verbal "explanatory" side.

In this manner, emotions activated in the unconscious find a way of expressing themselves. In this context the task of the analyst is to compare the two possible levels of story-telling, the verbal and the play level, mark their differences or their converging on the same underlying meaning. I can claim by experience that generally speaking playing brings to the scene, and symbolically unifies, what is still held separate in shared speech. Analytic work therefore proposes to restore or bring to a verbal level what has remained separate or never been expressed.

## 7 The Underlying Narrative Structure of Story-telling: Indicative Signs

To claim that building a play scene recounts the basic narrative structure of a life may sound exaggerated, virtually unfounded. But the act of story-telling, as I said at the beginning of this chapter, expresses the human need to deal with emotions, experience them, feel them, and at the same time to create the distance necessary for meeting them without being overwhelmed. If play reaches this level, it brings about a deep change in the analytic field. A number of recurring clinical indications prove, in my opinion, the effectiveness of stories told through sandplay.

*Sudden recollections*. The recollections accumulated in a lifetime, which we see as our own and which always remain available in our memory, as if to confirm our sense of identity over the years, differ from the recollections that take us by surprise and suddenly emerge as vivid images. In analysis, the former are a part of the verbal account, the latter are more frequent when the patient approaches the tray, often upon first contact with the sand.[51]

The images connected with sudden recollections are both vivid and functional in the analytic field, both because of the emotional tone in which they are communicated, and the effect they have on the relationship. For example, for a young lady just the act of beginning to caress the sand triggered a deep emotion: she started to cry in silence, whereas up until then she had stuck firmly and stiffly to her verbal account. Later on, she told me that touching the sand had taken her back to the intense recollection of somebody's skin she had loved, somebody significant she had lost, who up to that moment she had described with indifference.

*Dreams as a resonance of play*. Another important element is the close connection between building a scene and the dreams and fantasies that spontaneously emerge, almost as a response. When the convergence of the different levels of relationship to the images becomes clearly visible, I believe that play succeeds in giving representation to a fundamental thematic nucleus activated in the analytic field. The emotional resonance, the reverberation of what is happening in the tray, can later be confirmed by involuntary dreams or fantasies, in which some of the feeling-tone and contents of the thematic nuclei that have appeared in the scene are picked up.

I think, for example, of one of Anna's scenes (Chapter III), the fourth of the series, with the drama of that monstrous rotting head and of the dream she had the same night, in which she had to bury a corpse coming from Africa, the place where her father had suddenly died. The two levels of representation converged in the same thematic nucleus: the dream was pervaded with history, and the play scene recast the dramatic representation of death. The appearance of this dream, as of others that emerged at that time connected with Anna's

[51] In Chapter IX, I speak of a direct clinical experience of the moment when contact with the sand tray released a sudden recollection.

other scenes, shows the "narrative" effectiveness of the process that was taking place through sandplay.

This process represents, in my opinion, a step in the elaboration or, with a metaphor I am fond of, in the metabolism of emotions. Dreams, precisely because they must necessarily be translated into words, transform into historically recognizable feelings the same emotional rises-and-falls expressed in the imaginary figures of sandplay.

During analysis with Luca, a man around fifty, intelligent and cultivated, what frequently prevailed was his brilliant conversation, like his defense in the analytic field. The sessions were pleasant, full of cultural discussions though, in the end, repetitive. I realized more and more the seductive atmosphere "in process" in the relationship, particularly when he went over to the sand tray. Swiftly and skillfully, without hesitation, he built a scene in a short time, but without ever using the sand to create a form. The sand served only as a surface to support the objects he placed there, and was never touched. The representation was often symmetrical, built out of geometric, mainly transparent objects such as plexiglas cubes and pyramids. His scenes were as aesthetic as his speech, devoid of that rhythm which indicates a pondering of choices, an active thoughtfulness, and were constructed with regular, mechanical gestures. Luca went to the play area only rarely, almost as if to please me, to fall in with my working style.

When I pointed out this behavior, what I stressed most of all was the fact that he had used the sand very little in his scenes, had virtually ignored its malleability in responding to gestures, repeating instead, with small variations, the same structural composition. He thought this over for a moment, then went over to the sand tray and pressed first his right and then his left hand into the wet sand. He stopped a moment to consider the imprints of the palms of his hands placed to the right and left of the scene, and with a rapid gesture, touched the center of the tray with his index finger, leaving a very visible dot. On his way back to the couch, he fleetingly remembered how as a child he used to play with earth in the country during summer vacation. This did not strike me as a very significant response to my observations.

The next night Luca had a dream in which an historic monument, that actually stood right outside the windows of his house, collapsed into a heap of sand like the one in the tray the day before. He himself drew my attention to that resemblance. In the dream he realized that he had caused that catastrophic event by moving a piece of his mother's antique furniture in the house. Inside and outside mysteriously connected. The dream-scene also laid emphasis on a young man secretly digging two women's portraits out of the sand like some he had seen at an exhibition. I was struck by the clear response to the "sand" of the previous day. The dream-representation he described showed, in my opinion, that feelings of central importance to Luca's structure had at that moment entered into resonance. What took shape in the imagery of the dream was a nucleus of aggressiveness and guilt feelings towards his mother and towards the feminine which with words he kept at a distance. My brief comments about his defensive behavior had had an unexpected effect. Proof of it was the immediate oneiric response, constructed within the framework of his story.

The point to be stressed first of all is the convergence between the play scene and the dream. It shows how the act of interpretation had opened a way to the perception of emotional contents far removed from consciousness and activated by contact with the playing field. In this way a different context, at the disposal of underlying feelings, was created.

Touching the sand and leaving an imprint had provoked, aside from the verbalized recollection at the moment, what in my opinion was the physical memory of a "myself" very close to the emotional tensions of childhood and by now far from consciousness. Thanks to the apparently simple act of playing, there was movement of concentration around a nodal point of that narrative structure which, called forth in the analytic field, made it possible to begin metabolizing and transforming feelings confined to complexes and never approached by words.

*Fantasies as a resonance of play.* I remember the involuntary fantasy of a young woman a few days after she had built a scene where behind a female face there was an odd fight going on between two eggs. As she played, her comments had stressed the violence of that impact, whereas I was puzzled at the time by the unusual and original character of her choice. It was hard for me to put together the drama recounted in words and the clash represented by the two eggs. It was, instead, an intense emotion related to her mortified womanhood, which had found expression in the sand scene. I realized this in a subsequent session when she suddenly said that precisely during a serious feeling of frustration she had experienced the day before, that strange clash depicted in the tray suddenly appeared most vividly in her fantasy. Our mutual surprise made it possible to associate that representation to an experience she had never talked about before, an experience connected both to an episode in her adolescence then put aside, and to the ongoing emotion between us at that moment. The play scene, with its metaphor, had made it possible to further investigate the story, but above all had brought to light a transferential dynamic which then and there I had difficulty recognizing.

Involuntary fantasies, in which different aspects that have already appeared in the tray are placed back into emotional contexts, bear witness to the emotional effectiveness of those metaphors, which recount fundamental emotions of a human event.

It is interesting to note that the forms which reappear in involuntary fantasies or dreams seem to lodge in the player's memory like signifiers of specific emotions. In other words, they act like acquired ideas, like signifiers which emerge, in equivalent emotional contexts, to give meaning to the event experienced.

*The sense of belonging of play scenes over time.* Another indirect indication of how the use of sandplay can bring about an effective story-telling can be seen in the mark which certain scenes, or particular aspects of them, leave in the player's memory and by the feeling that they will go on experiencing even years later.

I remember one patient who, coming to see me seven years after finishing his analysis and telling me the incidental reasons for his visit and filling me in on the intervening years, made special mention of the sandplay scenes he had made years earlier.[52] He said:

> You remember that female figure in my sand scenes that went on dancing even under the forbidding eye of that destructive totem? Whenever I was sick it was the only image that consoled me, gave me confidence.

I was surprised by the tone and contents of what he said. There was something extremely vivid about the way he remembered those objects, those imaginary figures. It was as if those scenes were a part of him, were an already acquired way of understanding and expressing feelings he had experienced years before, but which were still active in him. So I began to realize what takes place between the patient and his play scene, when a story told in images functions and changes the pre-existing emotional situation. The objects he remembered were spoken of fondly and with a deep sense of belonging. This clearly suggested that at the time they represented moments of integration of his anxieties and continued to have great importance for him. Reviewing over thirty "pictures," which we started to do on that occasion, made me see how complex that story by images was and how deep certain choices were. Playing offered the opportunity for telling a story which only years later could become, at least partly, also verbal and reconstructed in greater detail.

The persistence in memory and the significant vitality of certain scenes are also proved by the fact that in the "sands" by the same patient, though separated in time, it is possible to detect a thematic continuity and its development. It is as if the symbolic integration by images of an experience had left a deep trace, like an acquired idea that had been placed at the disposal of the ego complex.

[52] In Chapter XIII, I describe Enrico's first scene at length, to highlight the differences between verbal stories and stories by images. His return gave me the first opportunity for reviewing the whole sequence of play scenes after a period of time. For the meaning reviewing sandplay scenes with the protagonists has assumed with time, see Chapter XIV.

# IIX Sandplay at Preliminary Meetings

*A subject represents something to itself: this too is knowing. But this goes back to the past, in which something has not yet been represented and from which it has been taken in order to be represented.* G. Colli (1969) p. 6

As is well-known the preliminary meetings in view of an eventual analysis are of great interest, full of possibilities. The expectation both parties feel, the analyst and the would-be analysand, creates a psychic field capable of bringing out the feelings underlying the request. It is a situation in which the narrative structure of a personal story, its conflicts and operative defenses, can be more easily detected. The emotional temperature in the interpersonal field is often very high, and the prospects and fears of possible disappointment are activated in both the analyst and the patient. This ever-present anxiety, however variable in intensity, is not only an obstacle; it is also a catalyzer of attention. Communication between the two parties, still relatively free of defenses, allows emotions and feelings to be seen which later on, in analysis, tend to be hidden.

In order to create in each new meeting the atmosphere which I find most suited to this perceiving, I set a limit, similar in a way to the limits of the sand tray the patient is offered. If at the end of the first interview too many difficulties come up in the discussion of a possible analysis, I say so at once. Otherwise, I suggest a preliminary period, usually three weeks, in order to become better acquainted. The schedule I am the most comfortable with for getting the possibilities and limits of an analytic relationship into focus is two sessions a week, two days in a row. I cannot explain why this works for me, but it is like a delimitation that enables me to make out and carefully assess the feelings activated in the analytic field.

My purpose here is to describe how the use of sandplay facilitates the analyst's job. I would like to remind the reader that only in this preliminary stage do I ask patients to build a sand scene, unlike what I do during the actual analysis. I believe, in fact, that the person who has come to me must immediately see how I conduct an analysis.

For clarity's sake, I will then point out the difference between the verbal level and the play level in each encounter, in order to highlight the relationships between these two forms of expression. The emotional narrative structure is communicated on these two levels, but it is their relationship that brings out the psychic phenomenon I am looking for.

## 1 Meeting Bruno

The first impression I had of Bruno was the liveliness of his shining, feverish eyes: darting, nervous, almost afraid of holding a look. The hand he put out was, instead, firm and rigid. This first handshake transmitted a sense of emotional hardness, like a constitutional armor that tries to shield a frailty that was difficult to protect.

*The verbal level.* His words, spoken in a voice broken by emotion, were like his eyes: at first uncertain, roving, as if to accommodate me, but very soon like his hands, hard, almost violent as he explained why he was there.

Bruno had discovered that his wife was being unfaithful to him with a friend of his, and with trembling hands and trembling voice, he told me about the hellish month he had just gone through, his immediate reaction and the revenge he had taken with the wife of that unfaithful friend. The success, largely imaginary, of his having gotten even, aside from not pleasing him, had created a deep conflict within himself. What had happened to the father loved by two children, the professional businessman admired and respected? It was an unexpected collapse that aroused in him feelings of anger but also of absolute helplessness, he who had been an orderly man, good at his job and loyal in his affections.

In subsequent meetings, the galling issue of unfaithfulness took over in the analytical field, of his frustrating attempts with other women, the depression that prevented him from working. I asked one or two questions about his personal story and he replied briefly and precisely, but it went no further than that, carried away as he was by his emotions about the other story.

*The play level.* At the last of the preliminary meetings, Bruno went over to the sand tray reluctantly, only because he was asked to. He stood there a while in silence before the untouched surface of the sand, as if he wanted to do what he has been asked to do as quickly as possible. He chose four seashells and placed them neatly in front of him. I was struck by the symmetry of that arrangement and the fact that all the shells were placed face down, as if to protect them. The association between sand and seashells was natural, almost foreseeable, but the neat, precise placing of the shells was the perfect equivalent of his defensive behavior. He cleared away the sand down to the blue floor of the tray, creating something like a horizon on the sea. The picture was complete: the beach, the shells and the sea. But at this point he suddenly introduced a new association which changed the obviousness of his first moves: he put a bell-tower on the right side of the tray which seemed to upset the previous logic and which struck me as a false note.

Something unexpected had happened, so much so that he started telling me about a fond memory of his: as a child he used to walk with his father along the beach where there was a tower. A vacation spot he had gone to for many years, from childhood to adolescence. The memory had now come back of himself as a child giving his hand to his father: "It was strong, warm hand before Dad got sick," he added with deep feeling, communicating at last a fragment of his personal story, unrelated to the subject that had dominated our first meetings. Silence fell between us, if only for a matter of seconds. The association had brought something intimate to the surface, a past experience that belonged to him, in which he recognized himself. I believe that touching that emotional nucleus enabled him to take a look beyond his usual self-image. I was eventually able to understand the last act of that scene-building, so utterly different from the previous ones: without a word, Bruno picked up a handful of stones and dropped them at random next to the bell-tower; a gesture that contrasted sharply with the control he had shown before in the careful arrangement of the seashells.

Only later did we succeed in understanding the meaning of the scene and the final gesture. His father's physical and mental collapse, which he had experienced as a teenager, had been a fundamental motif in Bruno's history, along with the loss from illness of a slightly younger sister, which happened around the same time. We realized that, up until the marriage crisis, Bruno had felt obliged to be a "tower" of strength, someone who always held out against all others. So those stones dropped at random seemed charged with a complex significance, which would then become the main topic, never thoroughly explored, of his analysis.

This reconstruction on the two levels of communication in Bruno's preliminary meetings helps clarify the meaning of this combining of words and images, talk and scene-building. A situation like sandplay, strange for adults, limited in space and time but even so never "saturated," lacking, that is, the information consciousness goes by, can unquestionably lead to the emergence of deep feelings which words are as yet unable to express. As we said in the previous chapters, regression can open the way to feelings. Bruno proved this when, through the perception activated by sandplay, he suddenly felt a past memory stir. So different words appeared spontaneously, free at last of defenses, which could recount what was buried in the past, apparently remote yet still so active in the unconscious.

The overall picture that emerged enriched my understanding. In the beginning the verbal level had laid emphasis on the defense-structure. Though Bruno's words carried in their tone the underlying destructiveness, they at the same time contained and anchored the compulsive urge for obsessive one-track repetition. But slightly later, after the first moves guided by the same defense mechanism that appeared in the linear association between the sea and the lined-up seashells, sandplay succeeded in activating a deeper emotion, and with it a collapse of certainties, expressed by that random dropping of stones around the bell-tower. It was an old memory dominated by a sense of irreparable loss, but also deeply related to the present, with all the weight of a grief that only later would emerge in words.

## 2 Meeting Carla

When I saw Carla, a woman around forty, for the first time, I was especially struck by the difference between her smile and her eyes. While her lips flickered with apparent availability, her eyes were fleeting, wandered around as if to avoid meeting mine, though in them a deeply-felt need for contact showed through.

*The verbal level.* The tone and manner of her conversation showed the same difference: the descriptive brilliance and even pungent irony of some of her remarks sounded harsh at times. She would laugh at the wrong moment and there was a falsely frivolous tone in her words, similar to the tight lips of her smile. When for a moment she did not succeed in filling the whole space between us with her talk, she would fall into a silence charged with emotion, and I had the impression that her eyes were about to fill with tears. I was struck by the fact that the contents of her story, even the very painful ones, were almost never accompanied by a tone and a pace that corresponded to her words. She spoke of repeated emotional failures, of abortions, intentional but also deeply painful, with the same tone of voice she used in talking about her work as a respected professional, or about something that had just happened to her. But under the cover of harsh, sometimes almost unbearable words, beneath the garb of conventional attitudes, one sensed a great solitude and an unexpressed need for human contact.

This sensation was confirmed by a dream. At first meetings I always ask if there were some present dream, or in any case one that had been remembered. Carla told me a recent dream which had stuck in her mind, though she herself found it to be too explicit: "There was a woman sleeping at the bottom of the sea, she was alive and had to be reached and woken up to be brought back to the surface."

It may have been the conciseness of her account, or the interpretation it immediately brought forth, that for a moment made me think that the dream had been told for my benefit, or was more a metaphor than a real dream. Reconsidering it now, it was Carla's defense that had affected me at that moment, almost to the point of rendering useless and inauthentic her contact with that deeper woman-image.

The image gave expression to the silence and solitude which until then her affectivity had been confined to by her defense, an apparently successful defense needed for adapting to the demands of the world. It was difficult to bring the woman in the dream back to the surface because she was too exposed and vulnerable, something Carlo had often experienced in the past. By no accident, after the first interview and having agreed to go into analysis, Carla disappeared for several months. Feelings had apparently been activated in the field that still needed to be kept in silence at the bottom of the sea.

*The play level.* A few months later Carla returned and the analysis began. I wondered if her need to go away was perhaps connected to the prospects of using sandplay, appealing but also new and hard to control. I was, in fact, struck by the way she threw herself immediately into the experience of playing, as if to overcome some difficulty by rushing at it.

There was almost no pausing before the empty tray of sand, as if she had already partly decided what scene she was going to build. The first thing she did was to choose a starfish and place it far away from her on the left side of the tray. As often happens, the first choice was associated with something familiar, something she already knew: the bottom of the sea. But suddenly, as we saw in Bruno's case, an "irrational" choice: she sprinkled a large amount of red powder on the starfish. I too was so impressed by that unexpected intrusion that I don't remember the content or tone of what she said at the moment. Subsequently, the use of blue on the left side of the tray and then of yellow to outline a sea-urchin shell on the right showed that some emotions had been mobilized.

I now felt that my lack of attention to what she said was no accident: the field was pervaded with a very intense feeling-tone which I myself had perhaps shunned. This is proved by another move Carla made: immediately, without letting herself be seen, she took a little jar, the smallest one available, and buried it next to the starfish, as if trying to hide it from me. Only with time did we realize that she had entrusted her fragility, her feeling at certain moments small and helpless as a little girl, to that little jar, which needed to be so carefully protected. Another important element was the dream she told me the next day:

> A woman was photographed with a gangster; for which reason she risked being killed.

The dream revealed how intense the experience of the first sand scene had been, of the movement it entailed and of my photographing it. Reference was clearly made to a world of violence, the violence perhaps which Carla had experienced in life, but which she also turned against herself. The red powder on the starfish revealed an intense emotion, normally contained by the defenses which dominated her verbal communication. Feelings which would gradually emerge during the actual analysis, were condensed into that first scene: I am thinking of her denied need for contact, her anger, the protest, at times the violence, which the dream about the gangster's woman began to represent and make available to consciousness.

In this sequence, where the expressiveness of the color and of that buried jar suddenly intruded upon the logical association of her first moves, Carla had really let herself go. The emotions expressed on a personalized level, with the woman in the first dream at the bottom of the sea, now appeared in the play scene on a more primitive, exquisitely physical level. The color red drawn from the scene and that little jar, hidden out of a need for protection, had brought to the surface a deep emotion, probably connected to the intentional and at the same time painful experience of abortion, which in life she had always held at bay and removed from consciousness through splitting.

When during the following session Carla told me her dream, which I said nothing about, I had the feeling she had gone too far. It was as if in that first contact with sandplay she had reached a level still beyond her capacity for symbolization and verbal communication. I said nothing about the dream, not only as a deliberate choice, but also because I still knew her too little, and it seemed important to give her the chance to find the way on her own, while at the same time offering her my full participation. It was the right decision, because feeling an experience too intensely would have exposed her to a danger: the woman in the dream could be killed. Indicative was her immediate return to the tray, where she built a scene which was the exact opposite of the one she had built the day before. The need of the defense seemed to have led her back to the tray in order to assert a vital right.

In her second scene, Carla reestablished the silence of feelings and an atmosphere of solitude, in a representation that reminded me of certain De Chirico paintings of the metaphysical period. Far to the left, a church, to the right a mosque with a minaret and between them a barely outlined road with a bench and an abandoned cart.

I was struck by the two places of worship which created an even more rarefied atmosphere, far different from the previous scene teeming with emotions. What I felt most was the sensation of a desert: there were no human figures, and the chosen objects spoke of shared experiences but were void, like hallucinations.

Words, play scenes and dreams opened a new perspective on the narrative structure of her life. The crisscrossing from one level to the other threw a more specific light on a complex emotional situation, which words or play by themselves could not at that moment express as effectively. So that later on, I thought that the church might represent the image of femininity introjected into a family context, where the prevailing importance of maternity implied the sacrifice of other vital aspects. Carla's abortions may have been the violent and self-inflicting response to this superegoic psychic presence. The mosque spoke of the same thing, belonging as it does to a distant world where, as Carla remarked, woman's role is subordinate to men. Actually, this scene restated the main characteristics of a defense whose strong points were surrender and solitude.

The novelty of sandplay had made it possible to arouse the capacity to represent emotions that were far from consciousness. Her dreams offered concrete proof of the activation brought about by the symbolic process that had been set into motion and which would then proceed in analysis. In two consecutive meetings, Carla had expressed her psychic world, both verbally and in sandplay, a world dominated by a defense mechanism based on splitting. The conventional language, the facial expressions and fleeting looks suggested emotions almost impossible to contact. The first play scene, after the surprising associations of the colors and the hiding of the little jar, had created an unexpected contact with archaic, destructive and split emotions relegated to the unconscious. As was proved by the subsequent dream and her need to reestablish a distance in the representation of the second scene. Once again, the physical aspect of the experience had made possible what could not yet be expressed on a verbal level.

Contact with the sand, even if limited to only a few gestures, had given expression to the sense of emptiness and depersonalization she had suffered from in adolescence, in an alienating passiveness which had left an indelible scar on her.

## 3 Meeting Dario

In our first meetings, Dario flooded the field with words which seemed to be saying, most of all, how socially powerful he had become in his work: "high-sounding" words, as it were, which suggested a vertical dimension, a distinction between above and below, between himself and others. I immediately wondered what that loftiness was steering clear of, what there was down below, but I could not see it. I could not even understand why he had asked for an analysis and in that sea of words, I felt confused. As a psychiatrist, I felt that the right term for his behavior was "hypomaniac" but that was no help. Aside from what he actually said, what I felt most of all was the pressure of his talk, which was invasive and penetrating. Along with the psychopathological term, I had another useful concept at hand for assessing the way that verbalization affected me: the concept of resistance. But the "below" I was looking for remained obscure, and it continued to escape me however much I tried to represent it.

*The verbal level.* It was above all on a physical level that I began to feel a vague sense of oppression, without succeeding, however, in visualizing an image that would help me to keep a distance and make something out of it. The force of that talking left me little space for thinking or perceiving. But by concentrating on the physical sensations I was feeling I was able to become aware, little by little, of some difficulty in breathing. And as I was questioning myself about that weight on my chest, a first association suddenly came to mind. Dario was describing, in a tone of voice that smacked of showing off but also of pain, his relations with women, his going from one to the other, driven by a compulsive need to possess them rather than establish an emotional bond. It was as if what he said had at last given a recognizable form to my sense of oppression.

The emotional tension of his words which tended to fill up the space, to make the air unbreathable, to take possession, was very much like the tension which, to my ear, the women he was talking about must have had to put up with. In my physical and psychic discomfort, while I felt drained of all thoughts, and in a situation which I supposed was like what his women had experienced, I had at last found an "active image," a significant metaphor which opened my eyes.

Up until then, there were only the two of us in the analytic field: he active and invasive, me passive and drained. After this association, which introduced a first recognizable form into the field, there were three of us: that vague and oppressive force, that presence which acted on him as it did on me, found a first representation. At that point, the questions could change: who was speaking in him and who created that effect on me? What dynamics were dominating the field that made us its actors?

*The play level.* The next day during our second meeting, Dario went over to the sand tray at my request. He dealt with it briskly as he went on talking. To build the scene, he used no objects but only the sand, working with his index finger as it he was drawing. He quickly drew a rectangle almost as large as the tray itself, then taking a longer time he added something else: he said it was a door, and the detail on the right-hand side was the handle and the keyhole.

I said nothing, though the "door" and the "keyhole" he had drawn in the sand seemed to coincide with the image I had noted in silence the day before. His rapidly moving index finger that lingered on the keyhole, as if it were a key for opening it, further confirmed the feeling of penetration his words had aroused in me.

I eventually understood the meaning of his doing nothing but draw. I think it was a way of containing an over-intrusive emotion by keeping it on a two-dimensional level. Using objects necessarily involves three dimensions, and so an emotion, as the other-than-self present in the representation, takes on the characteristics of real space, is there in front of the patient as a concrete presence, no longer confined to the two dimensions of a drawing which held it at a greater distance and made it easier to control. On many other occasions, I have noticed that when a sequence of play scenes is exclusively two dimensional, there is a deeper need for defense, which is only later overcome by going back to using objects.

At first, with Dario, I wondered what was on the other side of that door, which seemed to point to something hidden that still escaped my perception. But a new metaphor enriched our relationship: in the previous session I felt as if I had been forced, like that door. Any reference to the feminine compelled Dario to start looking for something he himself did not know. On the other side of that door there was implicitly a hidden space which had to be opened, explored. Only with time did I understand that he, in the few signs he gave, had provided the interpretation that corresponded most closely to his deep inner situation and to the reason why he had come to consult me about an analysis.

At the moment my understanding, still very limited, had seen that door as nothing but a symptom, the one he acted out with women. That there was something else on the other side of that door I intuited a little later, when he told me about a dream he had had that same night: he was perched precariously with his older brother on the cornice of a very tall building, like the ones that stood near his house when he was a child.

He told me how scared he was of high places, but said little about his brother, except that he had done well in life. The height of the building reminded me of the feeling his words aroused in me; and the brother made me think of an ambition which might for him be dangerous. Only some time later, when Dario had greater trust in me, did the real reason for the dream-choice come out. For years during adolescence, that brother had forced him to have sexual relations. So the emptiness on the other side of the door could conceal precisely this passiveness, which he endured but in some way also shared. Consequently his need to be always and at all costs active, accomplished and strong, took on an altogether different meaning.

Also for Dario, the play scene had triggered a deep emotion that had been hidden for years. He had locked that allusive door also against himself, because he still could not touch that absolute sense of impotence which, unseen, always forced him to outdo himself, indiscriminately, with every woman he met.

These examples of preliminary meetings illustrate the expressive possibilities of sandplay and their reflections on verbal communication.

As we have seen, Bruno tended to restrict what he said to only one theme, while entrusting the deepest narrative structure of his grief to his gestures and facial expressions. After his first conventional gestures, corresponding to his verbal defense, sandplay succeeded in drawing out an old memory that exposed the roots of his agonizing feeling of loss. The perception of the sand-beach and the tower opened up a chain of associations which led to the verbal communication of an old nucleus of pain, which up until then had been compensated by defense.

In all three of the above cases, it is clear that building a play-scene had outflanked the defenses, touching complex-nuclei that had been held off. In the last chapter, I remarked that the narrative effectiveness of a play scene is confirmed by distinct clinical indications. As we have also seen in these brief sequences, dreams follow sandplay sessions much more frequently than during the analytic work itself. To be sure, when an active emotional nucleus is approached in analysis, an often very significant converging of play-scenes and dream activity is often to be found. In my experience, active involuntary fantasies with elements of play are rarer, but they too are relatively more frequent in the first stages. The activation brought about in the analytic field on a physical level of symbolization emerges more distinctly in preliminary meetings than at other moments of an analysis.

Communication, on the two levels of words and play, emphasizes the narrative structure of emotions that are particularly active in that moment so full of expectations, hopes and fears, but also makes it possible for the usual defenses to be seen clearly. The activation of images, sparked by the novelty of being faced with the untouched surface of sand and the objects at hand, facilitates associations more closely connected to the emotions and feelings peculiar to that specific person in that interpersonal field. The usualness of the situation, which places the player's consciousness in an "unsaturated" state, is certainly crucial, precisely because it is new and unfamiliar, therefore lacking prefabricated responses. What seems clear in all the above meetings is that through sandplay verbal communication, primarily defensive in the first stage, assumes colors and tones, but also contents never before expressed.

# IX Scene-building As the Activation of Symbolic Expression

*With the birth of the symbol the regression of libido into the unconscious ceases. Regression is converted into progression, the blockage starts to flow again, and the lure of the maternal abyss is broken.* C.G. Jung (1921) par. 445

One of the most prolific aspects of the theoretical model resulting from Jung's research is the concept of symbols. Sandplay, which has only recently become a part of Jungian analytical practice, finds a valid support in precisely this theoretical model, especially as concerns its distinctive outlook on symbolic function. In fact, sandplay may be said to be, first of all, a way of activating the visual representation of dim, but still operative emotions in individual lives. The goal is for deep emotional contents, repressed or rooted still in bodily experience and therefore far distant from words, to find symbolic expression. In my experience, sandplay is particularly suited to creating a psychic field where this transition can take place. By using it with adults, new research possibilities have opened up for studying the way symbols are formed and the determining psychic factors that help activate the process.

## 1 Jung's View of the Unconscious

To understand what Jung meant by symbolic function at least some reference must be made to the broader view of the unconscious he developed. His concept of the unconscious was influenced not only by his personal story, but also by the instructive contact he had with the serious pathological disorders of patients in the Burghölzli psychiatric hospital. It is surely no coincidence that the troublesome and difficult book, *Wandlungen und Symbole der Libido*, which in 1912 marked his break with Freud, was written as an account of the fantasies of a prepsychotic patient (Jung, 1912/1952). Psychotic manifestations, with the sense of drama they arouse in researchers, necessarily open the way to a different perspective: the typical distance and incommunicability of psychoses left an indelible mark on Jung's approach to the psychic world.

In short, with Jung the emphasis moves away from the opposition between wish and reality (launched by Freud as the key for interpreting psychic life and which allots an important role to the mechanism of repression in the irreconcilable conflict between drive and consciousness) and towards that process of differentiating the individual self which Jung called "individuation." Of central importance to this new perspective is the course, which every human being has to follow, from an initial undifferentiated stage, completely dependent on environment, to an ever-greater definition of self and autonomy. With this change of perspective, which Jung was the first to bring about, a new approach was introduced into psychological research, subsequently picked up and explored by many other writers, however different their individual slants.[53] For example, Loewald (1979) remarks, regarding this, that the problems of differentiating between self and objects, with the intrinsic polarization between individuation and fusion, are probably more universal and deeper than the psychosexual conflicts of the Oedipal core of neurosis.

In the early years of his research, Jung shared with Freud both the energic model and the respective theory of repression. But with time, dealing with the world of psychoses in particular, he laid more and more emphasis on the fact that, along with mental phenomena related to the repression of drives and wishes in the clash with reality, there existed an unconscious, protomental dimension constantly in the making. So for Jung the unconscious was no longer

[53] Among Jungian analysts I am thinking in particular of Neumann and Fordham and among writers of the Freudian school Winnicott, Kohut and Mahler.

the "crucible of seething excitations," which, in Freud's concept, is countered by the ego (seen as a structure for controlling drives) in order to adapt to reality. The unconscious becomes, rather, a psychic dimension with an autonomous reality and activity of its own, sustained by the structures and dynamics peculiar to a collective unconscious that is the very foundation of psychic life.

As of that moment, the unconscious and the repressed could no longer be considered coincident. The reappraisal of repression as a basic mechanism of the unconscious dimension offered a larger framework in which to set psychic suffering and its treatment. The resulting analytical approach, though aimed at reconstructing individual stories and overcoming defenses, also tends to carry what has remained imprisoned and unexpressed in a protomental dimension to the level of representation and then of thinking. Thus "reconstruction" and "construction" as equally important moments for achieving psychic equilibrium: reconstruction for freeing energy blocked by repression, construction as an opening to the "thinkableness" of the never-expressed.

So with sandplay, the analyst aims at constructing a "text" through images which gives form and visibility not only to emotions rejected by individual consciousness, to hidden wishes, but which also expresses vital needs not yet experienced.

In Jung's research, the unconscious therefore appears on two levels: the unconscious dimension, connected with individual stories and repressed aspects, is called personal whereas the collective unconscious is the transpersonal structure of the psyche. It is a basic unconscious organization, pertaining to every human being, endowed with an inexhaustible creative activity, a continuous mythopoeia which, like organic metabolism, regulates our functioning and maintains its stability. In other words, a sort of psychic metabolism in which those recurring models of behavior, in particular those typical ways of structuring experience, that Jung called "archetypes,"[54] appear in different people,

[54] "The *a priori*, inborn forms of 'intuition,' namely the *archetypes* of perception and apprehension, which are the necessary *a priori* determinants of all psychic processes." This is where Jung (1910, par. 78) uses the term "archetype" for the first time.

from different, even geographically remote cultures. The basic ever-present archetypal structure emerges quite clearly in cases of serious psychic pathology. On a collective level it finds expression not only in themes that keep returning in human history, but also in the spatiotemporal organization of the fantastic creations that have always characterized myths, religions, fairy-tales and art in its various forms.

## 2 Notes on the Symbolic Function

In this perspective, the symbolic function (in the sense of an endless process of organizing the experience of self and the world, aimed at creating the new responses needed for adaptation) takes on a role of prime importance. According to Jung, there is in the unconscious an ongoing instinct to create new images when previous associative connections are no longer capable of answering vital needs. So that the transition from dissociation to integration, from destructiveness to creativity, is renewed in every new acquisition of consciousness.

Representational life – the go-between for understanding the psyche – is no longer determined exclusively by childhood events in the encounter-clash with reality, but bears the traces of the creative autonomy of the unconscious. Instead of Freud's dramatic view of a struggle between Ego and Super-ego, between instinctual drives and the limits of reality, what we get in Jung is a way of conceiving psychic suffering as a confusion between self and other-than-self, as a painful loss of meaning, which separates and dissociates the individual from self and from reality, to an extreme degree in psychotic pathologies.

Mental representation takes on the significance and pregnancy of "meaning" when, in a particularly tense emotional field, it succeeds, by means of a new representation, in relating the conscious and the unconscious, the known and rational dimension, and the unknown and irrational one which even so seeks to make itself known. Expressed in it is the attempt to find an attitude that more closely corresponds to inner and outer needs, a goal never fully attained, since the representational and operative meaning of the previous symbolic image ages, and becomes insufficient, as the subject and its reality change.

In this perspective, symbols are, on the one hand, the expression of the mythopoetic activity of the unconscious, but, on the other, are germinal ideas which correspond to the deepest intuitions of consciousness. Their appearance in the life of the individual is a primary experience where joy over the inner correspondence is accompanied by the sense of one's limits, because what has occurred remains elusive, transcends the possibilities of consciousness. It is an essential moment that can be reached only by expressing, not avoiding, one's conflicts. The ensuing sense of loss, the bewildering insecurity, at times fear, are some of the emotions that must be put up with in order for a new level to open up. The first act that can bring about a new symbolic form, charged with energy and capable of influencing consciousness, is the fruit of this moment. The symbolic image thus obtained bears in it the energic potential and the key of a new conscious attitude.

Jung gave the name "living symbol" to this particular form of imagination, which grips consciousness and by its action transforms it; he remarks (1921, par. 816):

> As long as a symbol is a living thing, it is an expression for something that cannot be characterized in any other or better way. The symbol is alive only so long as it is pregnant with meaning.

His concept makes a difference between "sign" and "symbol": the former refers to something known in that it has already been experienced, even if it is, at the moment, repressed by consciousness, whereas the latter conceives (both in the sense of a new birth and in that of a new concept or idea in the making) something barely foreshadowed. Mario Trevi remarks (1986b, p. 43):

> A symbol does not reveal a repressed drive (for this the symptom or symbol-symptom suffices) but the 'not-yet' implicit in existence and closely connected to the particular structure of the human animal. While in Freud a symbol reveals

> the not-experienced in that it is repressed, in Jung, a symbol reveals the not-yet-experienced in that it is implicit in the already-experienced.

An "implicit" that appears for the first time and reorganizes thinking by giving new meaning to experience as a whole. By bringing together opposites, symbolic forms contain a program that takes refining. It suggests possibilities not yet put into practice which the individual feels driven to seek. Trevi goes on to say in this respect (*ibid*, p. 50):

> What is held together in a symbol are the opposites which rational and nullifying thinking rightly keeps separate and, in their mutual exclusion, disjoins and distances. The character of this kind of symbol, a particular favorite with the romantics, makes the symbol itself inaccessible to reason and portrays it as the product of an intuition that cuts through and tears the logical and rational fabric of thinking. In this sense, a symbol expresses creative tension and antinomy, but also unity and relationships

From this viewpoint, symbolic activity is the spatiotemporal organization of experience which, once activated, aims at restoring the unity of parts which till then were separate. The purpose of analysis is to delineate a psychic field capable of activating the symbolic function that has been paralyzed by the defenses. Sandplay is a method that helps this goal to be reached.

## 3 The Spatiotemporal Unfolding of a Scene

The gradual spatiotemporal organization of a scene makes it possible to follow the different stages of an ongoing symbolic process. I would now like to present the sand-scene sequence of a 23-year old student, with the choices he made, the subsequent placings of objects and his involuntary remarks. With respect to the interpersonal situation that facilitated the emergence of symbolic forms, it should be remembered that it was his first "sand." So the emotional field between us was particularly charged with expressive possibilities which the physical experience of sandplay succeeded in communicating, whereas the dialogue was still dominated by the defenses.

After the first impact with the empty tray of sand, and the disorientation caused by the new situation, the young man succeeded in concentrating and taking part in the new experience.

The first thing he did was to divide the tray into two parts by digging a furrow down the middle (Fig. 10, Images). It is a move that nicely reflects his need to distinguish and mark off differences in an initial state that was still magmatic and confused. On a personal level, dividing space may also be seen as a fundamental experience: a double aspect of the self still only dimly perceived. The furrow was the first protagonist of an experience and opened the scene. As we shall see, as the last move in his composition, the young man will, significantly enough, return to this same point.

After establishing contact with the sand, the young man went on to scatter some yellow powder on the right half of the tray, a color he himself called "sunny." He followed this by placing the riders and, in the upper right-hand corner, the pointed stone. I was struck by the way the riders looked as if they were galloping off to conquer the peak, though the patient felt the need to block the way by sticking red sticks in the sand. So far his moves had been smoothly executed, as if had a precise idea in mind. This was followed by a pause to think.

Then he quickly dug a line in the sand between the riders and the peak, almost as if to further bar the way, obstructed as it already was by the red sticks. "It's a bleeding wound," he said suddenly, as he scattered some red powder around it (Fig. 10a, Images).

This remark revealed a basic emotional core. An extreme uncertainty suddenly pervaded that sunny-yellow field of conquest. Imagination gave birth to a representation that emphasized a vital loss: the wound. It is as if by describing the act of conquering the peak had allowed the patient to look beyond the boundary of the image which at that moment dominated his consciousness (the ideal he wanted to reach) and created the condition for a different-from-self object to appear. The clash with emotion was emphasized by the tone of his exclamation and by the sudden irruption of the wound-image, as if that battle-ground had all at once become his wounded body.

It was precisely the activation of the two-fold level of communication, verbal and preverbal, that proved that what was actually being told was a story. The young man was bringing to the scene an emotional narrative structure which words could still not communicate at first. Only later was I able to see more clearly the reason for that "wound" when he succeeded in showing me his agonizing doubts about the size of his penis. He told me how he would find himself looking at the crotch of the men he met, almost obliged by his insecurity to make constant comparisons. Until then he had spoken only of his shyness with women and his difficulty in going into public places. It was some time before what had emerged in that first contact with sandplay could find expression in words.

He was a student who was respected by all, reliable and open in his behavior, though isolated by his agonizing secret. In the riders galloping to conquer the peak, his search for a vital space, his attempt to win out in comparison with others, materialized, but his anxiety emerged clearly and distinctly in the representation of the wound. That red wound, which suddenly seemed to impose itself on its own, changed the whole picture without the patient being able to see what he had happened to be expressing and without my being able to recognize it when it appeared.

His use of space was even more eloquent. The peak of the ideal was set against the deepness of that bleeding cut. What was dark and mysterious, the nameless suffering, was represented at the bottom whereas at the top, on the peak, was the seat of gods. In this case, as elsewhere, elements appeared to the right that involved his relationship with others, while those to the left, as we shall soon see, involved his relationship to himself. To be found here are the archetypal structures of spatial imagery, which, in details like these, offer the possibility of approaching the deep experience of the patient.

Like the use of space and time in building the scene also the choice of objects bears traces of modes of expression that recur among different people.

The peak, made by using the heaviest stone at hand, placed the accent on the hardness of the experience, and possibly on its weight, as well, as a sign of the psychic effort it involved. So what an object is made out of expresses other emotional aspects. In these peculiarities and differences lies the secret of the expressive potential of sandplay.

The moment the young man described his need to be strong like those riders in a concrete and, at the same time, imaginary representation, he could also give shape to his wound. Agreeing to play, to pretend, for him meant accepting the possibility of describing, but without identifying himself with, a vital need. In this transition, the path was opened to the transforming possibilities of the symbolic function.

It was precisely that first move, seen as a self-representation but also implying the relinquishment of a defensive identification with the hero, that led to the possibility of perceiving, in some still obscure way, what laid beyond. The formulation of an experience he had suffered only in the agitated confusion of introspection whenever he met other men was foretold in the symbolic form of the wound.

On the left side, as well, another attempted conquest was shown. The woman at the top established contact with the allure of a summons, but the past was as cumbersome and dangerous as the dinosaur in the foreground was out to possess her. The young man confronted it with another animal just as strong and primitive (Fig. 10, Images). Choosing these archaic figures referred to a most remote past that had apparently disappeared, but was still present in his instinctive drives.

At this point the recollection of a childhood fantasy emerged which had all the flavor of a fairy-tale. He remembered his passion for pictures of those big and powerful animals and at the same time the fantasy he frequently had as a little boy when he went to bed at night: to comfort himself he would imagine a friendly dinosaur coming to protect him in his sleep. Involuntary remarks reappeared at the very moment deep contact was established with his emotions. The fight he put on between dinosaurs, one good and friendly, the other a devourer of the feminine, recalled his emotional ambivalence towards women, between aggressiveness and obedient passivity.

The older impulses appeared on the left, suggesting perhaps an Oedipal setting, where the disproportion between his littleness and a primitive and destructive force that could devour him was emphasized. Here too the use of space alludes to an obscure or, perhaps, as they say, to "sinister" (left) past.

His last move was the most deeply symbolic. He took the only goldfish then available in my consulting room and placed it in the furrow, the canal, he had dug out at the beginning.

In my experience, the color red always turned out to be the essential element for expressing something pressing in from the depths. So I was struck by his need to paint the little boat the same color, to place it too in the furrow, but I was able to understand why only later.

The free association, fish-boat, that emerged suggested that the color red, experienced as a libidinal hemorrhage, could be condensed into a double image. What came from the unconscious – the goldfish – presented itself as something that could be reached by means that consciousness had devised – the boat. It is the implicit blueprint of an individual wholeness, of the self, as Jung would say, that appears in the middle region which at first separated the two opposed worlds. The space carried, therefore, the colors of the feelings, revealed their complexity and their tendency to integrate, much more than the words between us could have at the time. The boat and the fish, both red, set into the imaginal flow of the canal separating the opposites foretold, or rather conceived, an as yet unthinkable relationship with the anxiety. They brought the invasive "red" into contact with the integrating potentiality of consciousness, as was possible in that situation. In the following sequence of scenes turned the color red into a leitmotif of the elaborations activated by sandplay.

With time I have realized more and more clearly how the spatial distribution of objects in a scene, and the mutual relationships with subsequent choices, indicate a highly significant structure. The spatiotemporal organization of the whole not only opens a perspective of the patient's intrapsychic world, but offers, as well, suitable metaphors for understanding the interpersonal dynamics that are activated in the relationship. There were two particularly intense moments in the student's scene-building: the wound and the recollection. In both, there was first a pause, virtually a halt, in his series of moves and then the words which exploded spontaneously as a commentary.

Thinking back over what happened between us in three years of analysis, my constant point of reference was this, his first "sand." It helped me at first to get my bearings without speaking and subsequently, by reminding the young man of certain details, to indicate the emotions we were experiencing between us. I mean, in particular, the fighting dinosaurs and the riders whose forward rush was hampered by the wound. Indeed, first "sands", like first dreams in analysis, carry the basic elements of a story: the ensuing process may be seen as an ever-deeper elaboration of the same subject matter.

Then and there I had not realized that the dynamics of transference and countertransference that would emerge during the analysis were also clearly depicted in that scene. Sometimes I felt almost irritated by some of his behavior, at others the tension was so high that it triggered in me a symmetrical response that I found hard to control. Only later was I able to rediscover in this first scene the metaphors for what I had experienced with him. The fighting dinosaurs in the foreground and the placement of the more emotional and sensitive aspects, like the woman, in the background, were representations that struck me as being charged with meaning and anticipating what was to take place between us. His transference was, I believe, determined by his perceiving me as that weighty, unattainable peak, and by his feeling, in comparison, small and helpless. The wound placed as an obstacle was a living metaphor, an active image we both perceived. For the young man it was the reoccurrence of a castration anxiety, and for me the frustration I felt in the difficult moments of the therapy.

It might be said that at the moment of the composition our conscious participation, of both patient and analyst, was still partial, linked to single moments and not to the scene as a whole. Only gradually did we discover how much he had succeeded in saying about himself in his scene-building. The story the scene told greatly anticipated, in fact, our possibility of understanding and speaking. On the "play" level there was in him "a dim foreknowledge"

(Jung, 1947/1954, par. 402) whose meaning was to be revealed only after a long analytical process. An important step in this direction was when, polite and responsible as usual, the young man began to display a timid critical attitude towards me, so that an aggressive dynamic was subsequently to emerge between us.

In the representative choices so far considered the different levels of the young patient's self-experience were brought together in the unity of a scene. Some were recognizable indications, like the riders or the friendly dinosaur, others living metaphors of experience which the young man had still not said anything about, such as the bleeding wound or the violent animal that wanted to possess the woman. I tried to show how this organizational impulse rose from the depths. The way elements were placed in the tray expressed different psychic parts and set between them boundaries that also suggested possible relations. Shared speech gave voice to this or that emotional content, but still did not tell the whole story; only with time would it acquire the symbolic penetrativeness which had appeared in the playing field right from the start.

The symbolic function is evident in the above scene precisely in the presence of the contrast between the urge to conquer and the impossibility of doing so, between the self-ideal and the anxiety of loss, while at that moment the player's reflective consciousness tended to separate the two aspects. The symptom is, as Jung remarks, "a suppressed antithesis" and implements what is rejected, repressed or suppressed by consciousness. The symbolic function proposes this antithesis again and depicts it as a whole, as in the above scene, opening a way to the synthesis of opposites and to reflective thinking. Through psychic acts of symbol-formation, the energic field is modified and the relationship changed between consciousness and underlying emotion.

Jung's view of symbolic activity invites further investigation but, in my opinion, sandplay helps distinguishing in its complexity. The act that portrays as a whole what the defense of consciousness keeps separate has, as I have said, an energizing and stabilizing effect on psychic life. By joining together the urge to conquer and the bleeding wound, or the clash between dinosaurs, a relationship between emotions which consciousness had split became visible and took on unity in the representation. The symbolic function was even more evident in the enigmatic red objects, the fish and the boat, that were placed as a final move.

According the hypothesis I have sustained in these pages, the student's ability to respond to the emergent emotions had, with the representation in the sand tray, attained a first level of integration. A new energic event had occurred: this was first reflected in his verbal outbursts and the emerging recollection. Only later was the vitality of the figures that appeared in this first scene clearly born out in the analytical field. Of the greatest importance was the moment when we discovered the relationship between the narrative structure of the scene and the emotions we experienced between us. Being able to talk about it helped us get a clearer picture of what we had shared.

# X The Vitality of an Event Between Images and Words

*In the immediacy of sensorial interpretations, the vital process represents an indissoluble unity which subject and object may not be detached from.* E. Grassi (1989) p. 153

Building a sand-scene, as we have seen, offers a significant perspective of psychic phenomena as they unfold. In the present chapter, I want to focus on the moment when, through contact with the sand, an involuntary memory came to a patient's mind. This event, which deeply changed the emotional tone of the relationship, is given particular emphasis by the sequence of words and gestures, where the feelings aroused can be seen in an antinomic perspective. Recalling the composite narrative formed by the words and the building of scenes in space and time is the best way for giving the reader a glimpse of the vitality of the phenomenon just as I perceive it in the clinical situation.

Ada had barely begun her first sandplay when she remembered a trip she had taken many years before in the Kras region: "I was a little girl and was deeply impressed by a river that suddenly plunged underground into a cave". The fact that this 34-year old woman, upon touching the sand in the tray for the first time, should recall a childhood experience, did not particularly impress me then and there, but, shortly after, that memory would become more and more intense, forcing itself upon our attention.

> I can see the blackened ceiling of the cave the river disappeared into. It was left by an explosion that had taken place years before. The retreating Germans had blown up an ammunition depot there.

I report this clinical fragment as an example of how the representation of a "reexperienced moment" (Aite, 1976, p. 101) can surface during the analytical investigation. In current usage, memories and reexperienced moments would seem to be synonymous, both indicating the moment when the dimension of time is perceived. There are so many different ways this can happen that a sharper distinction must be made, both of the phenomenon and of the terms used to refer to it. I will limit myself to describing two different ways memories can appear in the analytical field.

In our previous sessions, Ada had given me a detailed account of her past history. Intelligent and meticulous as ever, she did this in an orderly series of memories, together with the apprehensions, the intentions and the hypothetical explanations she herself gave to explain her discomfort. At that moment, the vivid representation of that river, unexpected and surprising for the patient herself, went against the memories she had collected over the years and had arranged carefully in her verbal account of them. What she had told me about so far was part of a world Anna usually identified with, rather like the things she surrounded herself with at home; the last event was different in that it appeared suddenly, and also because of the tone she used to communicate it: the river-image immediately showed a particular vividness and operative capacity in the field of our relationship.

The activity I wish to stress as an important feature of this phenomenon is expressed on different levels. In the first place, the representation itself imposed itself on our attention because of its inherent dynamics: the calmly flowing water, its plunge into darkness, the blackness caused by the German explosion. It was a wide-ranging scenario, filled with events, which evoked war and peace, the security of belonging and the sudden possibility of loss. The image that appeared in her memory depicts the disappearance of a vital element, like that water flowing in the sunlight, and links shadow to light, the unpredictability of something that can happen at any moment to the stability of the known.

The scenario is "strong" because of the very nature of the representation, which arouses emotions also connected with the sensorial level. The ceiling of the cave, blackened by the explosion, and that river plunging into the void, opened up a more intense and more dynamic range of perception that made itself felt. To consider the image first of all a significant fragment of the story, and in that way delimit it, comes almost automatically. But if greater attention is paid to the expressiveness of the scene and at the same time to the way it appeared, Ada's recollection can be read as the description of an experience that was active at that very moment in the analyst-patient couple. Intrapsychic world and interpersonal world, too frequently viewed as separate entities, are to be seen as a single unit. In other words, the suddenly appearing configuration is the representation of a single psychic event that is to be considered on both levels.

So the image that appeared in Ada's recollection is also "strong" for me, the listener, precisely because it was not only an expression of the other's world but was also the fruit of a shared moment. That story opened up a perspective and gave shape to a representation, a "form" in which, according to me, a perception of the emotions, the thoughts and sensations existent between us, was expressed. What is active, but still indistinct in the relationship, was thus brought to the level of "visibility." Consequently, the image that surfaced in the sphere of memory may be seen as the way Ada organized, by drawing upon her mnemonic and perceptive heritage, her confrontation with the emotions present in the field.

Does not the nature of "reexperienced moments," where images take shape and reach visibility, offer a special clue? The sudden assertion of the dimension of time could be the expression of a particular and privileged condition in which the deepest structures, always active in the individual, reach the level of imaginal visibility and story-telling. In other words, a new possibility for apperceiving and confronting one's emotional life: from a vague state of fusion to facing something for the first time and looking.

In this perspective, the event contained in Ada's recollection, precisely because it was perceived subjectively as image of her personal history and characterized by a specific element of time, could be considered the "dramatization" of a central structure of personality, of a particular way of being and reacting.

So it is not important to ask if what appears has really happened, but rather to investigate the historical connotation of that imaginal event that forced itself upon consciousness. When active images appear in the dimension of time the individual story is, in my opinion, set into a broader framework. The sense of continuity and of belonging, together with a feeling for what no longer exists, which the perception of "reexperienced moments" always entails, reveals the vast psychic territory condensed in the image that has appeared. This approach makes it possible to give greater depth to the understanding of the recollection that has surfaced in a relationship, distinguishing between a possibility of its being an "active image" operating in the field or a "passive image," like the representations that usually and automatically form a part of the way we recognize ourselves.

## 1 Signs of the Activity of Images in the Analytical Field

We have seen how Ada's representation leapt forth suddenly, almost instantaneously triggered by contact with the sand, replete with details, taking us by surprise and completely capturing our attention. Other indications detectible in the analytical field confirmed this first impression of an active image. Ada went on talking as she dug down to the blue floor of the tray. She carefully traced the course of the river she was describing in words. Her tone of voice was different, softer, more intense than usual, so as to inspire in me, as well, in my inner theater, the capacity to vividly represent what she was saying. I too clearly saw a river of my own, with the cave, the plunge, the darkness: I was completely taken by what she was communicating, with no distractions.

In her next move, tense, almost rigid, she placed four white stones in successive order in the middle of the tray. Though the presence of stones seemed logical in the description of a river, what struck me was their order and the way she placed them. They gave me the impression of a foothold, looked for and found, since what she was talking about was the river's plunge into darkness. It was as if, in the presence of the emotional event of the plunging stream of water, that gesture expressed the need for a contact that would restore a sense of security: that void was there between us, and demanded a reassurance of some sort.

I realize that my "listening" and my sharing through the images produced by the patient might prove puzzling or be seen as a descriptive expedient. The most congenial way I find for working in the analytical field involves the use of visual metaphors that come up in the context of a session as a means for understanding and taking part in what is going on. By listening through images and remembering what I had been putting together in previous sessions, it became spontaneous for me to associate the images that appeared with a previously experienced sensation.

Ada's verbal approach, in fact, gave the impression of invading the space of the person she was talking to. Her words filled all possible silence to the brim, as if to prevent a reaction of any kind. Between her fast, non-stop talking and that stream of water, I perceived a significant connection. My sense of having no space in which to think, to exist and to react against this flood of words, found a pertinent association in the stream she was describing. On a verbal level, her endless flow of words countered my being reduced to silence.

As I said before, the images afforded by memories, just as in sandplay scenes, suggest a way to describe and understand the present psychic situation. So though Ada's attitude in the relationship was compatible with the stream of water, the stones more appropriately expressed my role. Emotionally, I felt I myself was that "stone," or rather the sense of oppression and immobility previously experienced in the midst of Ada's flood of words, corresponded exactly to those stones.

At that moment, as Ada was remembering her "river" and representing it in the sand tray, that sensation began to fade. Her words were no longer invasive and I found room again to feel and think in. I wondered what the easing-off Ada's new words and gestures inspired in me could mean. It was as if the "plunging-river-and-stones" image, till then separated into its opposed component parts, had taken on a unity of expression in the sand scene and in what Ada was saying, organizing itself into a new form through words and play. The easing-off I felt was probably due to precisely that unity of expression which the two elements had reached in the representation.

The separation previously experienced in the analytical field, but not yet visible as a representation, found expression only in the dynamics of the roles Ada and I unknowingly and uneasily played: the flowing stream and the stones holding it in were the parts experienced and acted out by both of us, in the face of the agonizing "blackness" which had not yet reached the level of visibility. The hypothesis taking shape is that, through the remembered event and the "re-experienced moment," unity had been restored. But what I particularly want to stress is that the construction of a "form" corresponded to a distinct shift of energy in the field. By reacquiring the unity of its parts in the representation, the image, until then separated out of a need for defense, also changed the transferential dynamics.

If this way of thinking makes any sense, and I am more and more convinced it does, what is meant by "image" is a *dynamic presence in the relationship*, which leaves its mark on everything that happens in the field, from what is said to the apparently most insignificant behavior, up to the playing and the individual gestures of scene-building. When, through analysis, this "operative" dynamic is carried to the level of "visibility", the field of the relationship changes: in the image thus formed, where a synthesis has taken place, the organization of the parts at stake in the transference and countertransference can be seen. Precisely by attaining visibility what is in progress in the relationship can be recognized and treated. A new operative possibility is created, similar to what happens on an energic and structural level, thanks to a successful interpretation. When it works, the act of interpreting opens up new perspectives and further elaborations. Therefore, “finding the images which were concealed in the emotions,” as Jung remarked (Chapter VI, p. 98), is already an act of interpretation, even if *per figuram*. So Ada’s image was the possible interpretation of the moment, a first integration of thinking, to be carried gradually to the level of shared speech.

The moment the “river” image appeared between us, the pace and tone of Ada’s story gave me the impression of conveying and communicating what she had before held at a distance. This first indication of an “energic variation” in the field, was, for me, also confirmed by what she did. After placing the white stones as a foothold in the middle of the tray, Ada added two black stones to the scene to indicate the exact spot where the water disappeared. This move was not only descriptive, but seemed to endow that plunge into the dark with an emotional consistency. The consistency I am speaking of is not simply the concreteness of the black stones, but applied also to the secretive way she buried a little animal beside them, it too black. It was precisely in that act of hiding, which I noticed only at the end of our session, that the gesture turned out to correspond to a not yet “sayable” emotion. Shadowed forth there was something the recollection activated in the field had foretold, but not yet expressed.

Ada then remarked at the end of the session.

> It’s a proteus. My child took great interest in this animal which, in order to get used to living in the dark, has lost its sight.

Listening to her, I thought that in the depths evoked between us by her recollection, there was some living thing which, by adapting to the darkness, had lost its ability to see. Analytic fantasy immediately finds here a suitable concept: a *repressed conflict* had been engaged, on both the level of play, with the stones and the dark animal, and of words, by that “blackness-plunging-explosion” in Ada’s recollection related to her childhood, hence also to the relationship with her parents. The peaceful sunniness of the stroll with her parents and that flow of life disturbed by the plunge into an at once horrible and alluring void, almost automatically brought the “Oedipus complex” to my mind. The blindness of the primitive salamander buried in the sand also fitted nicely into the archetypal Oedipus scenario.

Ada's mention of her child and of his interest in those remote, rudimental animals, opened up further perspectives on the implicit meaning of her secretly hiding a black "something" which could not yet be brought to light. A scenario opened up where one could sense the dimensions of guilt and punishment condensed in the desiring animal-son.

Interpretative fantasies by analysts can also be perfectly legitimate, as long as the desire to contain the totality of the phenomenon, to understand it in order to dominate it, is kept under control.

Thinking back now on her gesture and the words that accompanied it, I wonder whether a deep experience of death and destructiveness, which Ada refused to get closer to, was not condensed in that obscure animal. Only later did it emerge, in fact, that for her childbirth had been a victory over the depressive certainty, after two painful involuntary abortions, of not being able to have children. Against the background of these experiences, disturbing glimpses of other "black" aspects of her childhood opened up, like the feelings of jealousy, anger and aggressiveness towards her younger sister.

Since lying beneath our symptoms there is a network of unconscious determinants, it is, to say the least, naive to become attached to our explanatory hypotheses, the principle still remaining valid for me that the successful representation of images, corresponding to our experience, prepares the way to research and transformation. As we have seen, contact with the playing field, perhaps because of its very unusualness, also released in Ada the possibility of remembering and of interchanging words and play. The individual parts of this simple scene, from the river to the white and black stones, to the hidden primitive animal, are the points of a woven fabric in which the multiplicity of Ada's determinants are condensed. The important thing is that from a state of indistinct fusion with these component parts, Ada succeeded in portraying before her what she had lived in total unawareness in a concrete, visible representation. This prepared the way for confronting her suffering.

But let us return for a moment to the Oedipus hypothesis as the underlying archetypal structure of the representation. I remember that this way of assessing it (actually almost a foregone conclusion, given the central importance of oedipal dynamics in its development) imposed itself almost automatically, coming quickly to my mind and emotions. Why this need to set the emotions present into a convincing, certainly pertinent theoretical cage? My countertransferential reaction, as well, was probably a sign of that vitality of imagery which I wish to stress here as the salient feature of that clinical event so charged with "reexperienced moments."

The way I grabbed hold of the theoretical "rock" struck me as the perfect reflection of her placing of the white stones I described as a foothold. This latter aspect also shows that the image of that dark void which the water was flowing towards was an active presence in the relationship. Both of us reacted unconsciously with the defenses we had at our disposal. Mine took a theoretical turn, was a tried and tested conceptual framework and, all things considered, a familiar and reassuring image, which allowed me to keep my distance from that void charged with emotion. That at that moment I ended up realizing this probably depended simply on the fact that Ada's emotions, still running free in the field, had found a corresponding form in her recollection and playing.

The "plunge into the dark" that appeared between Ada and me in the sphere of memory had opened a path to the process of elaboration. To be sure, the image could be seen as a "screen-memory" (Freud, 1901) that needs to be seen against the light, in which that particular conflictual story is at once revealed and concealed. The anxieties and wishes set into motion in Ada's earliest contacts with the world, and, at that moment, also present in the relationship, are inscribed and condensed into the scene that emerged.

From another point of view, it may be observed that the representation retraced a recurring structure in mythic thinking, namely the archetypal motif of the innocent maid carried off to the underworld. Ada was experiencing a typical moment in the evolution of every woman, also told by the myth of Kore. The underground journey of the river suggests the vital need to establish contact with experiences confined to darkness, to touch the very roots of the conflictuality and to try and transform it. Later on, being aware of the analytic progress and the dominating motifs of her story, I am better able to understand the significant preciseness as well as the latent outline of development of these apparently casual acts of playing and remembering.

Analytical elaboration can take many different paths, all of them potentially effective. In a certain context, every theoretical framework reveals an operative validity of its own, so long as it does not pretend to exhaust phenomena in their totality, or correspond to the direct and painful personal experience of the analyst. What I feel is essential to emphasize is the moment which opens the doors to elaboration. We must increase our capacity to differentiate, in what we perceive in the field, between "active" and "passive" images. In my experience, it is a question of taking a decidedly semiological approach: stopping to consider every detail, describing the signs and their interconnections, such as was the case with Ada's recollection. In short, it is a critical exercise with a view to recognizing those operative forms known as "active images."

# XI Self-identity: Play Scenes As the Representation of the Confrontation With Ideational Feeling-toned Complexes

*Fantasy it was and ever is which fashions the bridge between the irreconcilable claims of subject and object, introversion and extraversion.* C.G. Jung (1921, par. 78)

What I want to bring out in this chapter is the fact that the work of extracting a form in play scenes, viewed as the fruits of the confrontation with emotions active at that moment, evolves in a way that aims at rendering the ongoing emotional experience more and more personal and recognizable. The transformation of the way successive parts of a scene are formed and experienced by the patient tends to take a course which, from an initially impersonal nature, ends up differentiating itself more and more as other-than-self. It is a process to be found in the sequence of each individual scene as well as in the overall succession of play scenes. The unfolding of the representation shows a gradual transformation of the feelings experienced in the relationship, but at the same time modifies the experience of self-identity which the player is ever more clearly aware of. The tendency towards the gradual identification of the narrative structure of feelings present in the analytical field, perceived as "other" in a more and more differentiated way, is closely connected to the variations of self-experience.[55]

[55]In self-experience, Paul Ricoeur distinguishes between "self-sameness" and "ipseity" or selfhood. With the former he indicates the kind of identity we all preserve during our life, despite changes. With "ipseity" he means the moment of opening up to diversity as a surpassing of self-

Sandplay offers extremely important indications of this unfolding which, dominant in the development period, reappears in the course of life in all moments of impact with new emotions and feelings. Jung applied the term "individuation" to both this spontaneous occurrence of representation in intrapsychic life and the corresponding differentiation of a given individual from others (1946, par. 448):

> Individuation has two principal aspects: in the first place it is an internal and subjective process of integration, and in the second it is an equally indispensable process of objective relationship.

When a patient actually starts building a sand scene, he undergoes a moment of more or less deep instability, which can alter, sometimes radically, the habitual sense of self. Self-identity becomes experience with the gradual change in the relationship to emotions: from the initial identification with them, it passes to the recognition of them precisely through the act of representation. In the process of the spatiotemporal organization of the play scene a new point of view opens out onto the process of differentiation between self and other-than-self and on the storm of emotions and feelings this entails.

## 1 Emotions and Feelings as Successive Integrations

In my presentation I have often realized that "emotion" and "feeling," which analytical research often treats as synonyms, should be considered quite distinct terms. "Emotion" bears the meaning of a generalized movement of the psyche, dominated by automatic physical reactions, triggered by an outer or inner cause. Feeling differs from emotion in that it presents a recognizable organization of the prime emotional impulse: it is, in fact, linked to a form, to a

sameness. This is the transition that inaugurates the narrative act. It is also what happens in my experience also at the moment of playing. See Ricoeur (1990), Martini (1998).

mental representation, seen both as the organization of previsual perceptions, and as a visible form of things or words, that stand out against the background.

Analytical research has emphasized more and more the crucial role emotional/feeling-toned dimension plays in the process that shapes the individual out of the initial undifferentiated matrix. Using the two terms as synonyms, however, makes it hard to distinguish the different levels of integration and their corresponding functions. In my opinion, emotions and feelings are, in fact, successive stages in a single metabolic process, in which the individual's responses to the environment substantially change: from the automatism of his initial emotional reactions, to the selection of more adequate emotional responses and in the end to sentiment, seen as a cognitive function that gives value and allows the individual to respond to experience consciously and act reflectively.

From this point of view, sandplay can be an operative tool of great interest for research. With this method, the significant moments in the psychic process taking place in the analytical field can be brought out and studied. In fact, when emotions are activated in the relationship, they set off a contagion that involves both, but when these emotions are linked to a form, their influence changes. Attaining visual perception creates a greater distance, what I would call cognitive. Studying the mysterious link that joins emerging emotions and perception in the organization of a representation can be further investigated through sandplay. Experience teaches that sandplay representations can take place in the analytical field which substantially alter the shared emotional tone.

I believe we must return to and further explore the Jungian concept of ideational feeling-toned complex in order to understand the dynamics of the event that lead from emotions to feelings. It is a theoretical perspective that helps detect the relationship between representations and feelings. The transition from the modality of representation through "things" to the capacity to give a distinct and personalized form to feelings, opens the possibility for the representation of words, which already includes the relationship with the other, recognized as other-than-self. In my opinion, sandplay provides reliable evidence of the interrelation between levels of representation and feelings. What occurs in the construction of a scene makes it possible to study the relationships between the ego complex and the feeling-toned charges confined to secondary complexes. As we shall see shortly, it is precisely this relationship that constitutes the phenomenon of "consciousness": the subject, from the condition of being dominated by emotions, reaches the possibility of giving form to feelings, ultimately succeeding in being able to reflect upon them, and communicate them to the other (Marozza, 2000).

## 2 Complexes in the Play Scene

According to the point of view sustained here, the play situation, precisely because it is new and unsaturated, devoid, that is, of preordained responses, brings about a change in the tone of consciousness in the player and fosters the emergence of subconscious and unconscious feelings.

The basic characteristic of sandplay, namely its capacity to activate a physical level of relations with emotions and feelings, is situated at a nodal point of analytical research: the close relationship between psyche and physical experience. Jung remarked (1957/1958, par. 180):

> Often the hands know how to solve a riddle with which the intellect has wrestled in vain.

So yielding to the tactile and proprioceptive sensations of the hands playing with the materials and to the visual perceptions that accompany it in shaping the sand scene, means returning to the primary theater of the relationships with emotions: sandplay reactivates this physical level which in the more advanced stages the mind tends not to recognize and to dominate, as if to break free of it. Eugenio Gaddini (1989, p. 560) catches precisely this aspect when he says:

> In fact, the fascinating discovery of psychoanalysis was the enormous importance the body as a whole, its various parts, its functions, occupy in the mind in the course of development and later in adult life. One might say, paraphrasing Freud, that the mind can never forget being based in the body. But the im-

plications of this discovery are even more fascinating: that is to say the tendency, inherent in the mind, to dominate the body's dominion, to go beyond the biological, which even so makes it exist.

From the earliest stages of development, the individual may be seen as an intricate physical and psychic entity, that organizes the different levels of his sensations and capacities to respond into a unified perceptive whole.

In Jung's view, the "ideational feeling-toned complex" is the basic physiological structure of the psyche; it is here where the emotional experience provoked by the individual's relationship, in his physical and psychic globality, to the environment, is organized. Each complex-unit bears the signs of an attempted and laborious confrontation with emotions which, by overcoming the ego's possibilities of adaptation, were not at the moment assimilable. It must be remembered that these feeling-nuclei of the psychic structure preserve traces not only of emotional and adaptive failures, but also of those individual potentialities which have never had the chance to emerge. The representations that take shape in dreams, in active fantasies or in concrete play, indicate the complexual narrative structure active at that moment. Present in the organization of the configuration are forms which "stage" these nuclei of experience linked to a particular story of adaptation, but also the personal style, that way of perceiving, recognizing and metabolizing the feelings which bears the special character of every person.

In the concept of ideational feeling-toned complex, we find the traces of a natural tendency to establish unity. Every emotion experienced is inscribed in the mind, first of all with a physical code, consisting of still vague primary sensations and subsequently of more and more differentiated perceptions. So we might say that the perception of the materials and objects offered by sandplay reactivates above all the physical memory of the relationship with the world introjected by the individual. What I want to point out is precisely the tendency of the individual to organize the various levels of response into units. Inscribed in all of us is our personal physical and psychic "story," as a potential predisposition to a certain development, as well as the consequence of our experiences in life. Each complex-unit contains and organizes the oldest strata, linked to the biological, and at the same time the feeling-toned and ideational responses to the encounter-clash with life.

But besides the ordinary, familiar affects there are subtler, more complex emotional states that can no longer be described as affects pure and simple but are fragmentary psychic systems. The more complicated they are, the more they have the character of personalities (Jung, 1929/1957, par. 49).

The dynamic and structural view of ideational feeling-toned complexes, conceived by Jung, opened a new path in the approach to the psychic world. Alongside the prevailing drive-model of the time, a perspective that placed at the center, as we have already indicated, the process of differentiating the individual from the other-than-self and its vicissitudes, appeared on the horizon. Researchers began to direct their attention not only to the dynamics between drives and reality, the result of the energic model of the mind introduced by Freud, but also to the relationship where the individual's self-experience gradually develops out of the initial indistinctness.

The hypothesis of the complexes foreshadowed a line of research which would later be picked up by other writers. I am thinking, in particular, of the contributions of Melanie Klein and Winnicott who, while preserving the model inherited from Freud, have given an increasing importance to "object-relations." As is often the case in the history of thought, ideas full of potential reemerge spontaneously even if under different names.[56]

The experience of confronting emotions incompatible with the acquired stability of the individual is the field of onsetting secondary complexes. Repres-

[56] The concept of complex, neglected, in my opinion, even in Jungian circles, may be seen as the introjection of an "object-relation," to use a term that emerged from the research of post-Jungian writers. I am thinking in particular of Melanie Klein (see Segal, 1988), of Winnicott in *Play and Reality* (1971), frequently quoted in the present text, and of Erikson (1987). The vicissitudes of feelings are, in fact, no longer viewed as derivatives of drives, but rather basic motivational and adaptive elements linked to unconscious fantasies. In my opinion, the concept of complex includes the unfolding of an "unconscious" or "active fantasy," as Jung said, but also the relational field of its onset.

sion or splitting hold these feeling-toned nuclei at bay, which even so remain active in the unconscious. Both mechanisms play a defensive role with regard to the charge of anxiety triggered by responses that are not adequate to primary needs or bound to unfulfilled wishes.

The structural and dynamic model described here lies at the basis of the formation of the ego, it too viewed as a complex (Jung, 1920/1948, par. 582; Jung, 1921, par. 706).

> According to this theory the ego-complex forms the centre characteristic of our psyche. But it is only one among several complexes. The others are more often than not associated with the ego-complex and in this way become conscious, but they can also exist for some time without being associated with it.

> By ego I understand a complex of ideas which constitutes the centre of my field of consciousness and appears to possess a high degree of continuity and identity. Hence I also speak of an *ego-complex*.

The ego, as a feeling-toned and ideational complex, assumes a central role with respect to the secondary complexes, the bearers of repressed or split experiences. The somatic basis of the ego complex lies in the totality of the physical framework, and is distinguished by the stability of its structure and by a particular capacity for assimilating which, on the highest levels of integration, we call "consciousness." The other complexes, similar in structure but less integrated, remain autonomous, are activated in special situations in the emotional field and distinguished by automatic behavior: as long as they remain split and do not come into contact with the ego complex, they continue to repeat their response to stimuli.

The ego complex therefore appears as the central structure, bound to the experience of the totality of the physical framework, which has the possibility of establishing that relationship with the other complexes we call "consciousness."

The network of relationships between the various parts of a play scene is the representation, in my opinion, of the dynamics that are active between the ego and the secondary complexes. The choosing and placing of the individual objects "stage" the level of emotional relationship reached with every single aspect.

Patients who, as they play, believe they are at the center of their consciousness and in control of events, are actually living the experience on a subconscious or unconscious level, as well.[57] Variations in the attitude of consciousness, its partiality, the automatism of its responses or its achieved reflective capacity, point to a change in the emotional experience of relating to the complexes, the unfolding of which sandplay makes it possible to follow.

When adaptation is in a state of apparent stability, the ego complex appears compact, its feeling-tone seems to be governed by emotional circuits, repetitive and reassuring precisely because they are familiar. The fundamental task is to create in the analytical field a relationship with the patient which, overcoming defenses, activates the expressive potentialities of the disposition to represent. Making a deep emotional experience personal means not only introducing it into the continuity of one's story, but also to be able to use it reflectively in adapting to reality.

The unusual situation of sandplay, in which the feeling-tone of the ego is altered and the player becomes open to perception, facilitates types of response which bear traces of the emotional nuclei active in the unconscious. In the rapid give-and-take of gestures and materials, between sensation and perception, the individual's habitual self-experience slackens. And perceptions corresponding to the ideational feeling-toned representations of the complexes slip through the loosened web of consciousness: in the choosing and placing of the single elements of the scene, it is the autonomy of the unconscious complex that takes over and supervises the scene-building.

[57] Many areas of ambiguity in the theory of complexes outlined here remain to be cleared up for researchers. It seems to me that there is still no definite theory of the structure of the ego complex and its dynamic relationships with the secondary complexes, which conceal the mystery of consciousness and its various degrees of integration. Sandplay seems to me to be a highly useful means for further investigating these themes. For a theoretical elaboration of these problematic issues, see Tarantini (1992), Castellana (1991), Castellana and Malinconico (2002).

The shapes made out of sand or the chosen objects are often insufficient or correspond only in part to the emotional pressure in the individual. In my opinion, it is precisely this shortcoming, sensed as diversity, that fosters research and sets going a resymbolization process of the underlying emotional contents. The particular context of sandplay and this gap, which patients sometimes have trouble accepting and with a feeling of personal inadequacy, force their way into the ego complex and prepare it for a new and never completed symbolization of the complexual emotional charges present.

What then, scientifically speaking, is a "feeling-toned complex?" It is the *image* of a certain psychic situation which is strongly accentuated emotionally and is, moreover, incompatible with the habitual attitude of consciousness. This image has a powerful inner coherence, it has its own wholeness and, in addition, a relatively high degree of autonomy, that it is subject to the control of the conscious mind to only a limited extent, and therefore behaves like an animated foreign body in the sphere of consciousness (Jung, 1934, par. 201).

## 3 Mental Representation and Metabolism of Feelings

So from this viewpoint, mental representations assume a central role in the psychic economy, precisely because they allow a transformative relationship to be established between the ego and the activated complex. The purpose of using sandplay is to create a field in which this encounter becomes visible. The analyst pays attention to the building of the scene and the verbal communication, in order to detect the presence of these structures endowed with autonomy: it is the moment when representation takes shape both in the play scene and in the tone, the pace and contents of involuntary words. Whereas before, under the pressure of emotions, the automatism of somatic and psychic reactions prevailed, the possibility now opens up for finding an imaginal form which by its very nature implies a deferment of the response to the stimulus. We know that the energic charges of the complex may be so powerful as to prevent this essential passage, and that in certain psychic fields their strength may end up submerging the ego, of breaking it apart, as is the case in psychotic states.

Jung remarks (1935b, pars 171-175):

> I am looking for what *the unconscious is doing* with the complexes… I want to know what the *dreams* have to say about complexes.

The mental process shown by the imagination in dreams, fantasies and playing with objects, reveals the successive integrative levels of the relationship between the ego and the secondary complexes. A development, this, which starts with the organization of the most primitive, still indistinct sensations (between self and other-than-self, between inside and outside the individual), reaches pre-visual perceptions and ends up with the full-blown visual representation of objects in space. Only later does personification appear, such as occurs in the fantasies that accompany children when they play with objects. We must remember that in both ontogeny and phylogeny, mythic thinking through images, where personification plays a dominant role, accompanies the first appearance of words on the level of emotional exclamations.[58] Verbal thinking, which moves according to the principle of non-contradiction and has the capacity to form and use concepts, which are the basic instruments of consciousness, appears only later (Jung, 1929/1957, par. 385).

> Many of the earlier gods developed from "persons" into personified ideas, and finally into abstract ideas. Activated unconscious contents always appear at first as projections upon the outside world, but in the course of mental development they are gradually assimilated by consciousness and reshaped into conscious ideas that then forfeit their originally autonomous and personal character.

Jung always connected this view of complexes as feeling-toned units on different levels of integration to the phenomenon of consciousness. Personification is to be understood as integration, on a higher visual level, of an initially

[58] In Chapter XV, I will show how verbal symbolization is a necessary passage in the expression of feelings.

confused emotion, but at the same time reveals the attainment of the reflective capacity of an evolved consciousness. This development starts off from the oldest levels, where emotions are still associated with primary, purely sensorial physical experiences, before becoming perceptions, recognizable forms, and lastly ideas communicable also in shared speech.

Dream psychology shows, with all desirable clarity, that complexes surface in a personified form if they are not suppressed by an inhibiting consciousness, like the gnomes in fairytales who turn the house topsy-turvy at night. The same phenomenon can be noticed in certain psychoses in which complexes "re-sound" and "voices" appear of an absolutely personal nature (Jung, 1934).

Just as sandplay makes it possible to bring out the different expressive levels, from using the sand only to the most specific personalizations, so in the analytical field there is a transition from experiencing indefinite emotions to the identification of feelings in the other's facial expression. I mean: the tendency to personalize representations is manifest in the projective identification onto the interlocutor of the complexual feeling-toned charge. The metabolism of emotions, set forth in Jung's concept of complexes, finds similar aspects in other writers, as well. Remembering Freud's famous remark (1932, p. 80), "Where id was, there ego shall be," Eagle, for instance, has suggested something different from the classical model of the id as an instinct-drive, as a "crucible of seething excitements" (*ibid.*) which is offset by the ego, as the control-structure of drives (Eagle, 1984, pp. 203-204).

> In the context of a conception of id as impersonal "it" and of ego as personal "I," the idea of the ego appropriating to itself portions of the id can be understood to mean that what was impersonal and disowned comes to be owned and experienced as part of oneself [citation omitted].... According to this latter version of the id-ego concept, the ego's appropriation refers, not to greater control over the inherently chaotic and "ego-alien," but to the transformation of an impersonal "it" (e.g., an unbidden obsessive thought; an hysterical or phobic symptom) into the personal realm of "I desire," "I want," etc.

In other words, individuals pass from a state of identity with experienced feeling to the domain of "I wish," "I fear," etc., which implies recognizing the independence of the experience from themselves: it is the premise of a confrontation which reduces the Ego, but opens the way to new capabilities of response. Central to this point of view is the unfolding of the representation as the expression and at the same time the motive of the change in one's self-image and in one's relations with others. As Eagle observes, psychic pathology may be considered the failure of the ability to represent: what ends up lacking in this expressive void is the emotional distance needed for the reflecting of consciousness, which can change sometimes disruptive and invasive emotions into feelings.

## 4 Representations of "Things," "Persons," and "Words" as the Expression of the Relationship Between the Ego and the Secondary Complexes

The aim of stimulating the disposition to represent emerging emotions in the analytical field is to try and put the ego in touch with the emotional charges confined to an independent and autonomous complex. Which brings us to a discussion of fundamental importance of how the function of mental representation in the psychic economy should be conceived.

Sandplay can make an important contribution to research on this central issue. Direct observation of sandplay activities makes it possible to detect the underlying narrative structure that unites the representations of things, persons and words as they unfold. This method opens the possibility of studying the shared feelings in the analytical field more thoroughly. Relating the unfolding of representations of scenes in space and time to the experience of the patient and the analyst makes it possible to see how, where and when the various levels of representation appear on the scene, influencing the feelings and leading to significant variations in the analytical field. Choosing objects, using and placing them, building the scene, are indicative gestures of the representative event underway: patients intent on individuating what corresponds to them is, for me, the expression of a confrontation with still indeterminate emotional pressures. What happens establishes contact, therefore, with a representative phenomenon in the moment that precedes giving a structure to of a visible form.

Using an energic model, I may say that drives invest the available material to the extent that they choose an object which seems to correspond to the dominant feeling-tone.[59] The predisposition to represent, which introduces the emergence of what Jung calls an "active image," is about to reach the level of imaginal visibility. In other words, emotions are transformed and, with the appearance of the representation, alter their intensity and become feelings.

Sandplay is an effective instrument of research primarily because various levels of "representation of things" can be distinguished. Natural objects, abstract forms or forms charged with the mythic imagery human history has produced with time, up to the personifications that most closely correspond to reality, "stage" different, successive integrations of the process of representation. The change of feeling tone in the interpersonal field, experienced from moment to moment during scene building, confirms that what can take place in this transition is a change in the metabolism of feelings or, according to the present theoretical model, a modification of the relationship between the ego complex and the secondary complexes.

Studying the forms placed in the sand tray and their emotional impact in the analytical field gives an idea of the complicated unfolding of feelings, about which very little is still known. With the help of sandplay we can discern the successive levels of a process aimed at bringing about a modification of our capacities to respond to inner and outer stimuli. When emotions turn into feel-

[59] I believe Freud senses this moment instinctively when he coins the phrase "instinctual representative." The complexity of the event emerges when he uses the term "ideational representation" as if it were a synonym. In my opinion, the first term applies to the phenomenon that precedes visualization, the second indicates its presence. Making them synonymous reveals an approach in which the transformational importance of the coming-to-being of forms that stand out distinctly against the background becomes impossible to detect.

ings, the attitude of the individual changes, passes from an initial automatism to an evermore precise discernment of his experience and ability to function. Conscious participation in the feelings also changes; from being indefinite and scattered it can finally become reflective. Communicative expression can pass from the symbolic visual register alone to the verbal one, in an endless succession of the expressive levels of words.

This is the path typically taken by the metabolism of feelings, as I have asserted time and again in these pages: from an initial condition of identity with an emotion, the individual succeeds first in conceiving a representation of "things," then passes, in a transformative continuum, to the representation of "words." So the range of expressive possibilities offered by sandplay makes it possible to detect the successive forms that emerging emotions take on in the play scene: from using materials only (sand, pigments) to the natural or miniature "things," to personifications. The verbal resonance with the representative event in the tray, from involuntary exclamations to the possibility of a dialogue, also shows the relationships that are taking shape with the representation by words. We have already seen that words seem to rise spontaneously in patients the very moment a figure is distinguished in the representation.

The characteristic sequence of the representative process may be summed up as follows: initial relationship with the materials only, use of objects, personification. In correspondence with this evolution, verbalization in the analytical field changes in form, in tone and contents. The objects, the human or animal figures, used to describe feelings already known to consciousness do not instead induce changes worthy of note on the emotional or dialogic level.

## 5 Levels of Conscious Participation in the Event

The symbolic process, activated by contact with the materials of sandplay, is an experience in which patients enjoy the possibility of being surprised at themselves. By taking part in sandplay the psychic experience of self, of that "oneself" which, despite constant physical and psychic changes, each of us perceives as being the same throughout our lifetime, comes across a more or less deep moment of instability. Perceptions occur, in fact, which, experienced in a state of partial awareness, influence the patient's choices, even if unseen. In building a scene, patients barely sense the presence of a more or less intense pressure guiding their actions, even if what prevails is the sensation of being in command of their choices. So when, after a period of months or even years, they chance to review the slides of their representations, certain aspects come as a deep surprise.[60] It is not so much the incompleteness of what they remember that is surprising as the significance certain parts of the representation have taken on in the meantime, which at the moment were executed without any particular intention, almost automatically. The revisited scene assumes a different character in the patient's eyes, one that clashes with what is remembered and is suddenly charged with meaning. But what seems perfectly obvious during the revision was already present, on a partly conscious level, at the moment the scene was being built.

As I pointed out in the previous chapter, emotions begin to be confronted the moment the player barely intuits the presence of an "other" dimension. The capacity to let go and start playing, overcoming the initial defenses, always leads to the encounter-clash with this experience. Intuition makes headway into the players' choices, in placing in the tray both what they sense to be similar to themselves and what is, on the contrary, different and foreign in character. In other words, the emotion, at first indistinct to consciousness and experienced through gestures, changes with time into an event that is perceived as other-than-self, as an emerging feeling, in the innermost core of oneself.

The model of the psyche proposed by Jung provides a conceptual tool for assessing the above phenomenon. I refer to the psychic dimension we call "consciousness," and which is to be seen as a process of integration that aims at bringing unity out of incompleteness and fragmentation (Jung 1947/1954, pars 385, 387).

[60] I will go more deeply into this experience in Chapter XIV, devoted to the "reviewing" of sand scenes years later.

> Between "I do this" and "I am conscious of doing this" there is a world of difference, amounting sometimes to outright contradictions. Consequently there is a consciousness in which unconsciousness predominates, as well as a consciousness in which self-consciousness predominates
>
> As we know from direct experience, the light of consciousness has many degrees of brightness, and the ego-complex many gradations of emphasis. On the animal and primitive level there is a mere "luminosity," differing hardly at all from the glancing fragments of a dissociated ego. Here, as on the infantile level, consciousness is not a unity, being as yet uncentred by a firmly-knit ego-complex, and just flickering into life here and there wherever out or inner events, instincts, and affects happen to call it awake. At this stage it is still a chain of islands or an archipelago. Nor is it a fully integrated whole even at the higher or highest stages; rather, it is capable of indefinite expansion. Gleaming islands, indeed whole continents, can still add themselves to our modern consciousness – a phenomenon that has become the daily experience of the psychotherapist. Therefore we would do well to think of ego-consciousness as being surrounded by a multitude of little luminosities.

The dynamic image of consciousness suggested by Jung, with the metaphor of a chain of islands which can gradually integrate into a whole continent, always seemed to me closely related to the gradual organization of play scenes and their striving for completion. It is like watching an integration of parts which, precisely in their relationships, let transpire a new way of being and of recognizing oneself. Each individual choice and each arrangement recalls what Jung calls "little luminosities." Jung, 1947/1954, par. 402:

> A dark impulse is the ultimate arbiter of the pattern, an unconscious *a priori* precipitates itself into plastic form, and one has no inkling that another person's consciousness is being guided by these same principles at the very point where one feels utterly exposed to the boundless subjective vagaries of chance.

In the scenes described so far, the player's choices seemed like "gleaming islands" of partial lucidity. They occurred on a level of consciousness in which the unconscious prevailed. Reviewing the same play scenes at a later time gave me the possibility of detecting a new level of the patient's reflective participation in his representation.

In those cases where reviewing has taken place, I was able to detect a close connection between the narrative structure of the scene, the player's conflictual history, and the shared emotional experience in the analytical field. I was surprised to see that single parts, as well as the scene as a whole, appeared as metaphors particularly suited to representing the experience of both. By joining together those "gleaming islands" in time, consciousness had succeeded in integrating what had been active and present in the analytical work into an overall view.

The old alchemists bear witness to this same process of integration. Jung (1947/1954, par. 389) quotes what Gerhard Dorn said in his *Theatrum chemicum*:

> Thus little by little he will come to see with his mental eyes a number of sparks shining day by day and more and more and growing into such a great light that thereafter all things needful to him will be made known.

So Dorn seems to have also sensed the psychological significance of his experience. By using a poetic metaphor, he brings out the same process of integration, which from incompleteness and initial confusion, leads to the moment when reflective consciousness emerges: "now I see."

As we have seen, thanks to the psychic model based on the theory of complexes proposed by Jung from his earliest research,[61] we can better understand

[61] This model, which is one of the most important legacies of Jung's thinking, is being explored in recent Jungian studies. Amedeo Ruberto (1995) offers a perspective of the levels of integration of consciousness which confirms what I have been observing in my research on sandplay. He says, among other things: "There is something in consciousness which, though in touch with the ego, is still recognized as extraneous, non-belonging, other-than-self. That's not the end of it: insofar as this something is perceived by the ego as 'self-referring,' it is conscious, but insofar as it is 'felt extraneous,' it is unconscious. But for us this means, very simply, that there is something in consciousness that is *relatively unconscious* to the ego. So we can ask: what is it there in consciousness of the mode of extraneousness and of a relative unconsciousness, with respect to the ego? Well, nothing but a *symbol*, in the Jungian acceptance." (p. 157). The same writer

the integrative process of consciousness which, from this point of view, corresponds to the very relationship between the ego complex and the activated ideational feeling-toned complexes. Its gradual development from an initial fragmentariness, to the capacity for reflection, and from there to the highest levels where Jung speaks of awareness, is expressed in its integrative unfolding towards unity.

## 6 A Complex Activated in the Analytical Field

While watching a play scene under construction, it often happened that I sensed an emotional heaviness, sometimes a downright refusal, which led me to disparage what I was seeing and sharing with the patient. With time, however, I realized that those moments of difficulty in my emotional participation, in my countertransference, were the manifestation of an active, though still indefinite, complexual charge in the field. On those occasions, there would appear on the scene a particular form, which I perceived only on an indistinct emotional level: for the patient an object became the barely-sensed foreseeing of a person. Usually it was a matter of forms that were felt as parts of a body, as partial aspects of a still incomplete and obscure personal unity.

The vitality of an event I shared with Lorenzo, a forty-year-old man, gives me the chance to approach something I want to now try and explain. It involves a significant moment in our analytical relationship, that had been going on for two years now, which brings out the phenomenon I would like to stress. Lorenzo began the session by mentioning that in a cafe he had accidentally run into an old man known as "the satyr," an ambiguous figure who was said to have committed crimes during the war. Lorenzo went on to discuss other matters, his talk became descriptive, vague, and his tone of voice also struck me as being flat.

(1999, p, 81) observes: "The products of the activity of complexes appear to the ego as symbols to be deciphered, and the product of the ego's activity, the result of its deciphering, are signs: objects no longer bound to the biological necessity of the complexes, which the ego can dispose of in order to increase its awareness." See Marozza (2000) pp. 65-81.

In previous sessions, through dreams, we had approached aspects of his relationship to his father that had never come up before. That way of speaking seemed distant to me, ponderous, almost a letdown, compared to the interest we previously shared. I remember I tried to listen to what I was perceiving, and after a prolonged silence, I told him about this difference in tone and participation.

Lorenzo did not answer, but shortly after he went over to the sand tray. He touched the surface of the sand, dug a hole on the right-hand side, and quickly placed a dark, twisted piece of wood, a toy ring-around-a-rosy and two dead leaves at the bottom, as well as an overturned box. In the end, he poured some water on the right-hand side as if to create a sea. His hasty execution gave the impression that he was acting superficially, just to be doing something. My uneasiness, almost annoyance, did not diminish even when Lorenzo told me that the overturned box was a crib, and that beneath the dead leaves he had put two good-luck charms. He finished with a reference to the piece of wood: according to him a face could be seen in it. "It resembles the satyr," he said, referring to the man he had met shortly before at the cafe. I remember photographing the scene automatically, without participation.

It is amazing how blind we can be in certain moments! As I realized the next day when Lorenzo started off by telling me that, on his way to the session, he was thinking about the name of a place he had visited as a child. The memory of the place suddenly reminded him of an episode. Lorenzo did not know whether it really happened or was a pure fantasy made up on the spot, but in some obscure way, he had associated the recollection to the uncanny, nebulous image of sexual violence at the hands of his father. He was puzzled and incredulous.

Two other recollections immediately followed. The first was related to his stammering and to the fits of rage that appeared precisely during the period he visited that place. The second was what a cousin of his told him years later about a similar experience she herself had had with Lorenzo's father. These associations astonished him, and at the same time bore out his fantasy, but most of all reminded him of places and episodes of a period of his life he had not thought about for years. At that moment, a possible meaning of the first fits of rage and the stammering, which had been treated by psychiatrists with drugs, surfaced between us. His story took on a different logic. And the face of the satyr he had seen in the piece of wood he had placed in the tray the day before now acquired an unexpected connotation.

The above episode made me realize once more that the representation of a "thing" used as a part-person, as a part of a body, has a deep emotional impact in the analytical field. I believe that on an intrapyschic level, it expresses a dread of self-fragmentation, or the feeling of an unattained or lost unity, which the analyst vaguely senses and experiences in the countertransference. Sandplay, placed in relation to the emotional storms that can invade the analytical field, makes it possible for this significant moment to be seen.

I have noticed on many occasions that my emotional reaction regularly accompanies these images of part-persons, though I do not realize it at the time. The shapeless piece of wood had brought the structure of an emotional complex to the visibility of the scene. The oppressor, the empty overturned crib, the hidden good-luck charms, now took on considerable meaning. Lorenzo's communication of his recollections and the involuntary fantasy of the next day confirmed that the same dramatic narrative structure that had appeared in the scene had been activated in him and in the analytical field, also influencing my countertransference. The two antinomical aspects of his communication, one through the images of sandplay and the other verbal with specific references to his personal history, revealed the same organization of the feelings.

A dream some days later seemed to reflect the same event. Lorenzo dreamt that in the distance he saw the psychiatric hospital blow up where as a boy his father had frequently taken him for his stammering and his fits of rage following the episode he had recalled. The dream seemed to suggest that his rage, for years confined to symptoms, had found a first representation proportionate to its intensity.

The appearance on the scene of an object representing a part of a human figure, a "part-figure," precisely when intense emotions are activated for both in the analytical field, is an experience that has imposed itself more and more on my attention. The study of the levels of the representation of "things," associated with the variations in the emotions and feelings invading the analytical field, offers a new perspective on transferential and countertransferential dynamics.

In Chapter XIII, going back over the narrative structure of Enrico's first scene, a part-figure will also appear whose presence both of us felt: by me with at times an almost unbearable sense of countertransferential heaviness, and by Enrico with deep levels of suffering which also transpired in significant dreams. Through these examples, the continuity of the symbolic process becomes clear, from the material level to the level of words. The change of expressive register indicates, in my opinion, deep emotional variations that are felt in the analytical relationship.

The analyst who uses sandplay has, as we have seen, a two-fold perspective of the psychic phenomenon in progress in the field. His attitude aims at detecting the relations between the experienced emotions and the objects appearing in the play scene, between the level of the representation and words. From his point of view, the metaphors that appear in the play scenes are the expression of the shared feelings in the relationship and of the player's intrapyschic world, as well. The task of the analyst, which I will return to later when speaking of interpretation, is to discern and at the same time contain crucial transitions in the symbolic process, in order to facilitate transformations from the level of the representation of "things" to the level of the representation of "words."

# XIII The Narrative Structure of a Sand Scene: A Story Shared in Analysis

*The player knows very well what play is, and that what he is doing is "only a game;" but he does not know what exactly he "knows" in knowing that.* H.G. Gadamer (1960) p.92

By carefully observing the spatiotemporal unfolding of a play scene, one can get a close-up view of the complexity of the emotional event that animates the play-gesture. All things considered, what transpires from the building sequence and from the involuntary words accompanying it is a detailed account. Underlying the spatiotemporal sequence of the construction is a living fabric, in which we find not only the structure of an individual, distinctly personal story, but also clear indications of what has been shared in years of analysis. When this significant fabric sheds light on the patient's intrapsychic dimension, it offers the analyst many metaphors for understanding the feelings that have emerged in the interpersonal field. With the clarity stemming from knowledge accrued over the years, we can see how overdetermined and at the same time exact the play gestures were at a certain moment. Present in the player's choices are feeling which, active at a certain moment, in the transference and countertransference, both of us would become aware of only later.

I now want to reconstruct a scene a young woman built, in order to focus on the emerging signs of her story, but also to show her capacity to put herself at stake in the relationship. I remember that Eva went over to the sand tray with enthusiasm. She was very intrigued because she had already heard about my using sandplay in the analysis of adults. I can remember the freshness, the immediacy of her first gestures, as if she took pleasure in touching, in taking possession of something she had desired and eagerly looked forward to.

Eva sunk her hands into the sand (which was made more compact by adding water) as if seeking a form. She did not seem to show the ambivalence of someone approaching a material identified with children for the first time, and which could therefore give rise to a momentary sense of regression. She stepped over to the playfield at once, without hesitation.

At first kneading the sand down till the bottom of the tray was uncovered, she shaped two rounded areas on the right-hand side. Then she began sprinkling light-green pigment on the nearest one. The two pieces of land were separated from each other and from a still untouched area to the left. Adding trees on the one furthest away immediately confirmed the meaning of the light-green which now, along with some moss, gave the impression of a meadow with a haystack. The light-blue floor of the tray gave the idea of a river dividing the scene in two from top to bottom. To the right, the gully between the two mounds of sand she had piled up in the beginning now looked like the tributary of the main river (Fig. 11, Images).

Eva's expressive impetus was apparent not only in her determined gestures but also in what she said while she was at work. She had described a place which, because of its beauty, people would often make trips to. In the distance there was a spring among the trees and next to it a group of figures, men and women, arranged to look like excursionists to those appealing haunts.

So far she had worked only on the right side of the tray, leaving the rest untouched. At that point, her playing, smooth and flowing as her words, was interrupted by a long pause. After which Eva turned her attention to the left side, sprinkling a copious amount of dark-blue pigment which she then covered in the foreground with some yellow pigment. "It's the moon in a night sky," she remarked spontaneously.

It was the first significant change. A new associative reference had suddenly intervened, altering the choice of objects. Her play movements, which until then were in keeping with the first prevailing representation (woods, spring, excursionists), now testified to a sudden change with the appearance of a new representation: the night sky with the moon. What had suddenly emerged was no longer related to the perceptive concreteness of the materials at hand (sand as land and blue as water), but superimposed, virtually imposed itself upon it. That part, until then untouched, assumed the aspect of a night sky. So the play scene was divided between the sunny woods on the right and the moonlit sky on the left.

As Eva worked on this latter area, what was intentionally meant to look nocturnal turned brighter and warmer. Thanks to the superimposition of light-blue, the dark-blue was fading into a daytime sky, and so the chilly yellow called "moon," was embellished with sprays of red, sharply contrasting the former prevailing colors. As if attracted by those ever lighter and brighter colors, Eva started touching the surface with her hands, soiling them in the process. After another long pause, a slower pace of construction and an increasingly noticeable silence drew attention. In contrast to the excited words she had used only a moment before, that silence seemed to have left room for more careful reflection. Eva, more and more concentrated on what she was doing, added the figure of a seated man to the left, and sprinkled it with some more light-blue pigment. The whole scene took on an unreal flavor, which was stressed even more when, turning back to the right-hand side, she removed the excursionists and started sprinkling black pigment on the meadow in the foreground and the woods at the back.

During her silence a change had taken place that had turned the so-far almost idyllic scene into something different, something dramatic. While in the beginning, an emphasis given to the beautiful with a sort of elation, had dominated her playing as well as her words, in the last part, after the night sky suddenly imposed itself on the scene, a configuration opposite in meaning appeared in rapid succession. Now all the brightness was concentrated on the left-hand side, where the figure of the "statue" man (as Eva herself called it) had appeared, immersed in its unreal blueness, while the scene to the right, with the sudden invasion of black, had fallen from brightness into darkness (Fig. 11a, Images).

## 1 The *Mise-en-scéne* Reviewed

While reconstructing, with the help of the notes I had taken, the whens and hows of the scene that was taking shape, recollections emerged, emotional resonances, thoughts connected with our four years of analytical work.

I am struck by Eva's first gesture: sinking her hands into the wet sand to divide it in half, to separate the right from the left side. A gesture she immediately repeated to further define, in the field to her right, the two rounded forms that first evoked associations in her words and in her playing. It is a significant way of handling the available space, especially if seen against the background of the elation of the moment, as expressed in her facial expression and verbally.

Her first contact with the playing field, dominated by the dividing gesture, seemed to be in sharp contrast with her prevailing attitude of acceptance. The play sequence makes it possible to see that only after dividing the field did the profusion of green pigment and the scene of the woods appear. It is as if that first involuntary gesture were eclipsed by the elated and literal description that followed. I remember how in difficult moments Eva tended to keep her emotions at a distance. It was a way of negating the ambivalence of an experience, in a sort of camouflage in which, under the appearance of a full participation, a fundamental detachment prevailed.

I have learned with time to realize that my interpretations of what was taking place between us, apparently accepted with the attitude of someone who had been impressed emotionally, would then vanish without leaving a trace. The gesture of dividing, of separating, manifest in the play situation, seemed to me to reflect the defensive way Eva repeatedly separated herself from every possible opposition. Avoiding contact constantly reemerged every time we approached a sensitive area of her conflict. In her story, cutting emotions off from herself was a way of surviving. The damage she had endured from her congenital displacement of the hip, with the long treatments it involved, and the still visible after-effects in her movements, seemed to find no place in her communication. The great difficulty she had of fitting into school, the agonizing dependency on her mother and the present-day reverberation in her as a woman, of that injury to her motility, emerged only later.

The associations triggered by successive contact with the play materials stood on a different level.

The sand preserves its character as earth, and is followed by the color green, the trees and lastly the excursionists. The light-blue bottom of the tray also leads to an obvious association with water, without fantasy stepping in to combine the perceptive stimuli in its own way. In these gestures there is a need to remain consistent with the perception of the moment, with the most literal questions offered by the field, with equally foreseeable answers. Fantasy is, as it were, restrained by the "duty" of the moment, and consequently every request must be handled the way others expect it to be.

I remember that at home Eva had to muffle and quash all the conflicts that might emerge. Her immediate way of adhering to others forced her to act against her own will. As a girl, she played the role of "decisive factor," with her compulsive need to immediately restore peace in the family. Even at the age of 25, when she was building this particular scene, she still went on saying yes to others' expectations, negating her own wishes in order to reestablish the lost equilibrium as soon as possible. As happened with the companion she lived with, but also with the analyst, whose words were often taken as if they were always and only explanatory and comforting, like the spring water in the woods of the scene. The superimposed landscape tended to reestablish a unity between the two separate mounds of sand. Likewise, a basic impulse to escape contact and to separate herself was often covered up by an only apparently sufficient acceptance. That sunny, idealized woods nicely reflected the atmosphere of certain moments in analysis when contact was lacking, even though the contents and tone of the verbal communication seemed to indicate the contrary.

The words that accompanied her playing, like the last objects placed, tended to simulate a unity there where distance was indispensable. Actually, no misunderstanding of the scene was possible. Between the excursionists, at that time in the foreground, and the spring in the woods which seemed to be their goal, the full depth of the stream separating the two initial mounds was clearly portrayed. Nodal points of the attitude that dominated Eva's life, seemed to be already concentrated in these first gestures: the scene sequence showed the defensive modalities she set into motion in both her life and our relationship. In other words, the emotions aroused by her first contact with the playing field had reactivated and then "staged" these modalities, thus making it possible to see the two-fold defense level required at that moment. Remembering the stages of the scene-building, I now believe I understand better the pause that followed in her words and actions. Reflective contact with the field was finally possible; in particular, with the still untouched left side of the scene.

The defense present also in these initial gestures created a distance from anxiety and in this way offered a possibility for underlying contents to be represented. The silence of that moment of reflection, all the more perceptible considering the atmosphere of excitement of her previous communication, struck me, and still strikes me even now, as the central moment of the representative event that materialized on the play scene. Here we can see at first hand that antinomic process of the psyche always to be found in the reflection on feelings. A sudden and different circular movement replaced the linearity of associations so far pursued in the construction.

As of that moment, a change in the configuration and a quick succession of actions began. Let us follow them in the free associations of my recollections. Dark-blue invades the left-hand scene. It is the first move in which the patient's fantasy breaks free. That illogical blue, illogical precisely because it is set at a level with the meadow and the woods, subverts the space that has so far been respected. A "down-to-earth" sky, an unfathomable depth brings the familiar, the habitual, close at hand. Out of this background, where an element is introduced into the scene in which the usual parameters no longer hold, the intense yellow emerges and plays a leading role. "The moon," is Eva's immediate association.

My first memory concerns Eva's wanting to be "blonde" at a certain point in her life. In high school, she suddenly changed the color of her hair, from brown to platinum blonde, turning herself from a "normal" brunette, who probably passed almost unnoticed, to a free-spirited young woman with lots of boy friends. For me, in the "moon-yellow" was condensed the experience of a femininity that had exploded boldly, but also in a chaotic, almost self-destructive way. I remember that Eva had turned back from that impulsive expression of vitality just in time before being overwhelmed by it.

Years after that period, in the first scene something emerges in the intensity of the yellow flaring up out of the blue, which, suddenly taking over, subverts the previous order of the scene. There is a striking analogy between the way the moon appeared, radically changing the entire scene, and that deliberate change in the color of her hair, which marked a period of Eva's life.

The night-sky element bursts onto the scene, and the patient is caught up in it. As of that moment, her attention is completely absorbed by what is taking place on the left side of the tray. The yellow is immediately followed by the light-blue, which, sprinkled over the dark-blue, turns it into what looks like a day-sky. It is an increasing brightness that culminates in the appearance of the seated man in the background. I remember the deep silence of that moment, the magic, I might say, that the prevailing light-blue gave the image. Only when the scene was finished did I realize that the male figure was the only one, among those available, to have broken legs.

Color was the protagonist of a sequence in which a painful experience in her relationship with masculinity seemed to be condensed. What prevails in the present-day association is the sense of a hemorrhage that dissipates vital energy, rather than the sign of a possible fertility. The intensity of the red was set against the man at the back, by no accident chosen from among the other possible figures only because it was clumsily made, indefinite, with broken legs. I now believe that the red immediately followed the appearance of the man as its counterpart: with the appearance of that enigmatic male figure, the dominant moon-yellow became tinged with red. The disempowered man at the back now also seems clearly connected with the suffering of that red which invaded the moon like a wound. My mind is filled with recollections of that particular story as well as with the symbolic amplifications connecting the moon, the bleeding wound, to the part of her that was physically and psychically disabled.

From my notes one significant element emerges. The night after the session when she built the scene, Eva dreamed that the analyst had a tumor in his legs. The pain, the fear, the uncontrollable aggressiveness of that disease, as well as the prospect of a coming separation, invaded the analytical field. In the sand scene, Eva had evidently given form to an invasive, primitive psychic experience, still impossible to express in words, unthinkable. But she had represented it, placed it there before her eyes. For the first time in the relationship, she had touched it, similar to the way she put her hands in the pigment scattered in the playing field. Still visible in the photograph is the imprint of her open hands in that sought-for and feared contact. By no accident, the dream of the next night involved the figure of the analyst. The "tumor in the legs" appeared in the relationship as an utter helplessness, an impossibility of moving forward: an experience which Eva felt to hers, was indeed herself.

At certain moments, forgetful of both the play and the dream, I myself could not help experiencing, and sharing with her, the impossibility of any psychic movement which that "color red-disempowered man" part had also caused in me. Later, with sufficient distance and clear-headedness, it becomes easy to see one's complete blindness in the moments of most intense emotional involvement, but it is always astonishing to ascertain the force of psychic phenomena.

It is amazing to realize how explicit the "staging" of the sand scene was. All the depth of suffering that Eva hid, first of all from herself, was condensed, with great representative effectiveness, in the quick succession of gestures that we went over again together. Evidence of those moments was to be found not only in the dream that followed her playing, but also in the photograph of the scene. In the foreground, to the left, the yellow she had touched is no longer intact, and lets the displaced sand show through. Clearly visible further up, where the statue-man is encamped, are the signs of fingers impressed in the red, which Eva ended by covering over with more light-blue pigment (Fig. 11a, Images).

So began the last part of the drama. It is as if a contact too close to that conflictual issue forced the experience, the attempt to fade it into the background, to be cancelled out. By covering it up, the light-blue pigment tended to wipe out the differences and contrasts between the man and the red; so what had before been vivid and violent diminished into a sort of dampening and soporific sabstraction. This psychic movement also appeared in the relationship. The analyst sometimes felt reduced, he too, to a "statue", petrified into a total detachment. An unmotivated, invasive drowsiness was the clearest sign of this psychic condition induced by the patient. So from the intensity of certain shared moments, there was a fall into the coldness and distance of a rarefied atmosphere that tended to make the male presence fade into the background.

This defensive modality was closely linked to a recurring dream: Eva discovered under her bed a young man who seemed to be asleep, like an ancient mummy for he was covered with dust; but when touched that presence outside of time woke up and started to move again. Her initial fright, the sense of horror at the foreignness of that sudden discovery, gave way to the warmth of a love relationship.

In the play scene I have described it is as if the over-intense encounter with deep emotions had provoked the return of that male figure situated outside of time and in a different space. The structure and dynamics of an identical psychic event found similar expression on different levels, in the play scene and in the dream. The convergence of dreams and "sands," which has frequently occurred in my analytical practice, makes it possible to approach and get a clearer idea of the type of experience that is activated by playing. On the one hand, we may state that in the sand scene a psychic state, comparable to a dream, was brought about. But the dream is a daydream: the psychic work that produces it can be seen. On the other hand, the converging of themes and dynamics, on the level of dreams and play, proves that a "nodal point" of that psychic experience has been touched, an experience condensed and portrayed in an individual form that is to be gradually probed and understood through the analytical work.

The last move in the scene-building is symmetrical to the first. Differences were cancelled out on the right side, too: where there had once been a woods and a meadow, black pigment seemed to wipe everything out. It was as if by unifying the color and concealing previous distinctions, Eva had tried to do away with a disturbing representation. The gesture was repeated symmetrically. Whereas to the left the light-blue served to blend the "statue" into the background, to the right, the black covered up the distinction and restored the absence of color. Where a sentiment, or a sensation, had appeared, it was replaced by a void. As for the man at the back, it is again a negation, a wanting to turn back, to avoid the representation that had been formed.

That thick black on the original forms reminded me of a symptom that was dominant at the time. Eva found lumps in her breast and despite regular check-ups had recurring hypochondriac doubts about their possibly turning malignant. The intense anxiety in those early stages of analysis diminished to the point of disappearing when her emotional life substantially improved. Covering the play scene with black pigment seemed to be an act of negation, a drawing back from, a suppression of the mental representation. Consciousness seemed to deny a contact that had been established and testified to by representation. Analytical thinking teaches that what does not go the way of consciousness can sink down so deeply as to leave a mark on the soma, finding only in the body the possibility of expression. From this point of view, Eva negated the possibility of representation to a primitive conflictual situation, anchored in the experience of her body, wounded both by the congenital injury and by her story.

Eva's first gestures in contacting the field had "staged" her drama and an attempt at compensation, precisely in the splitting and the successive idealization of the woods represented. The destructiveness negated was therefore able to reappear in the somatic symptom and in the hypochondriac resonance.

In research aimed at finding out the relations between psychopathology and sandplay, the connections between psychosomatic symptoms and the constructive peculiarities of the scenes could be further investigated. "Psychosomatic signs" generally tend to appear with the simple impression of a gesture in the sand, without using objects. This sometimes happens in an action that tends to eliminate the relief between the figures and the background, to the detriment of a distinction already acquired, like the black in Eva's sand scene.

# 2 Final Notes

Following the narrative structure of Eva's sand scene, certain salient features of her story have gradually returned to memory. With them, the intensity of that analytical relationship made itself felt, with the moments of sharing, the resistances of a long dialogue, the transferential dynamics with the corresponding emotional responses. By studying the successive changes in the scene that led to the final configuration, I was able to bring out and discern elements I had experienced in the relationship. That male figure, for example, that remained a "statue" in order to ward off the overwhelming power of the red, played an active role in the relationship, a very precise metaphor of situations shared in an alternation of identifications and recognitions.

The sequence of the *mise-en-scène*, like the forms the protagonist chose from time to time, set a well-constructed story before me. At the center, as the main feature, was the unexpected change in the configuration. In a matter of moments, the story took a dramatic turn. The characters, the atmosphere, the color, the brightness of the background suddenly changed, in a swift reversal of tendency. To the right, where the human figures and the sunny woods were located, the desert, the color black, had taken over; to the left a diffuse glow stressed the presence of the "statue" where before there had been a peaceful moonlit night. Considering the spatiotemporal sequence of the scene-building, it is the sudden dynamics of this change that attracts attention, almost as if the situation had gotten out of the patient's control. This was what happened to me, too, in certain moments of the relationship. I might say that the lure of resembling that spring in the woods struck me as being dominant, since everything I said seemed only interesting and gratifying, I then suddenly felt that my capacity for reflective thinking had been obscurely blocked, exactly like the statue with the damaged legs.

I realize that I have barely entered the territory of this image which determined the configuration of the sand scene. I have only given an overview, a pan shot, which could be further investigated. Indeed, in light of what came before and after, every single scene seemed overdetermined.

The spatiality of the scene also opens a path to understanding. I will limit myself here to considering the sequence of colors on the left (*sinistra*), the place where what is dark, "sinister," like the unconscious, is located. Aside from its location, each individual color of the sequence, ranging from dark-blue to light-blue, from yellow to red, could open a way to the underlying emotional significance, through the amplification offered by symbolisms, partly already known. For the moment, suffice it to point out that careful research can only confirm the preciseness of the *mise-en-scène*. Story-telling by images is much more complex and articulated than it seems to be at first sight. I would say that the scene the protagonist created is itself the interpretation that most clearly reflects the complexity of her experience. The purpose of subsequent analyses, in years of confrontation, was to try and carry what had already been condensed in the precise configuration of the sand scenes to the level of words.

# XIII Objects and Characters in Enrico's Scene: A Well-constructed Story Discovered Over Time

*What has become identifiable by means of a name is raised out of its unfamiliarity by means of metaphor and is made accessible, in terms of its significance,* by telling stories. H. Blumenberg (1979/1988) p. 6

Seven years after our last analytical session and nine after the scene I am about to describe, I saw Enrico again briefly. The images he had obtained years before with sandplay cropped up again in his memory as comments to the conversation we were having: for him they seemed to be something vivid, still obscurely significant, however. As is usually the case, during analysis we had discussed only single aspects of his play scenes regarding particular emotional moments in his life and in our relationship. So seven years later, in the meeting arranged for incidental reasons by Enrico, we both felt the desire to take another look at what had happened during the process and which we only partly remembered. It was a chance to reexamine the whole sequence of sandplay scenes: not only a way of recalling situations we had experienced together, but of also making new discoveries, for him and for me. Enrico's collaboration in the "review" gave me the opportunity to realize, with surprise, how overdetermined the symbolic process was in his play choices.

I am now going to discuss his first scene only, dwelling on the individual objects he used to create it, which, during the review, turned out to be charged with meaning. In fact, the chosen forms, seen years later in the total framework of the scene, struck us as the metaphors most suited to representing not only the experiences that pertained to Enrico's story which we became acquainted with in the course of the analysis, but also the feelings we shared and underwent together. The objects and the characters, either clearly defined or only hinted at, as well as their placement in the space of the scene, revealed significant similarities to the emotional dynamics that had been active between us, sometimes so intense and so intrusive as to threaten us both. As we have just seen in the previous chapter, complexes can, under certain field conditions, act like "independent characters," severed from consciousness, which suddenly emerge in their autonomy.

So we discovered that, through sandplay, and on a level of consciousness still vague and incomplete for both of us, Enrico had me share overwhelming emotional experiences that had distorted his perception of reality, sometimes elating him, at others frightening him to the point of isolating him from everybody. Reviewing the whole sequence of images was the moment when the by now almost forgotten forms that had appeared in the play field showed all the independence of emotional presences which had been endured and often unseen in the countertransference.

## 1 The Objects and Their Relationships

I now want to describe all the forms that appeared in the first scene, as a way of showing how every one, compared to Enrico's experiences and mine, turned out upon reviewing to be a part of a complex emotional narrative which then and there neither of us had suspected.

Taking the scene as a whole, what is immediately striking is the primarily "vegetal" character of the representation (Fig. 12, Images). On the left side there is a broken tree-trunk and a lichen, in the center two pieces of bark. On the right side, a seashell fossil in front and at the back the only human figures in the scene, two clowns and nine ballerinas. I would like to point out that the plant objects are fragments of a whole. The paradoxical presence of human characters gives the representation an inconsistent character, like an unexpected shifting of expressive level. The fragments from the plant world, placed significantly like an unsettling presence on the left side of the scene seem to indicate a lost unity, whereas the clowns and ballerinas are, for me, the expression of a deliberate search for figures suited to "staging" deep emotions physically and through the gestural and verbal incoherence and quips of clowns. Compared to the other scenes we have examined so far, the narrative structure that appears here bears the mark of the borderline structure but also the great compensatory resources of the protagonist.[62]

For my present purposes it seems important to report, aside from the description of the single elements of the scene, what Enrico said, based on the notes I had taken at the time, as well as on what he himself wrote during the review, in order to see how he perceived himself in the two situations. As we shall see, his words testify to a level of integration of consciousness reached in the course of time. I might say they represent the verbal interpretation of what we had experienced and shared only through images in that first sand scene.

*The lichen.* On the lower left side of the scene there is what looks like a dead, half-dried-up leaf: a lichen. I remember that during the session Enrico mentioned how vigorous this plant was, despite its appearance. There was something in the physical aspect of this young man, who was 24 at the time, that this element brought to mind. Enrico was lean, but beneath his fragility there was an exceptional capacity for resistance.

When he made this first scene, Enrico had already left home. It was a very painful step, but for him absolutely necessary, which forced him to face the "coldness" of solitude and all the hardships connected with having to approach new environments for trying to live and work in. He wanted his independence with all the determination of someone who says: "The essentials, nothing more." He had deliberately chosen to abandon the wealthy middle-class background he came from, even quitting university to look for the meanest jobs: he

[62] I believe that every psychopathological structure reveals significant choices and placements. The narrative structure of the *mise-en-scène* and its unexpected approaches are indicative of the suffering in progress. I will refer to this subject only in Chapter XVIII. It is research that is still waiting to be carried out, which for the moment I am unable to go into and which lies outside the range of this book.

had been a waiter, a window-cleaner, in order to touch something concrete and make himself independent. This determination to lead a hard, simple life was backed up by a great resistance, but then his difference from fellow workers would often suddenly make him run away. So another round of searching would begin, a new work environment be found, always with the same characteristics, but the sensation of being out of place and the painful contact with others still prevailed. He could not tell others how he felt or reveal his feelings of guilt that he drew upon a private income his family had let him have to get by on. This need for the money his father sent was, despite all his efforts, an irremediable contradiction, a distressing secret he had to keep to himself. Enrico disguised himself among others, becoming so silent, so obliging, and passive that he was often called things like "sissy," "pansy" or "baby." We will come back to this later. If analysis could be the place where these problems could be shared and communicated, it was even so not easy to accept the contradiction of paying, of the "luxury" he indulged in, mostly thanks to the money from home.

What we are for the moment reconstructing, with the lichen analogy in mind, is this impulse to stay grounded, with the meanest jobs, to live on little, also in "cold climates," with a great capacity for resistance; an impulse that Enrico had to give in to at all costs, as if he needed to salvage a self-image that was for him indispensable.

In the harder moments, this impulse had totally taken over and even influenced his eating habits: to live on the absolutely necessary became a difficulty and then an incapacity to eat for up to fifteen or twenty days. Starting to eat again was felt to be an insult to himself, to his own integrity. My notes of what he said at the time illustrate this very well:

> I didn't want to eat any more.... but I didn't succeed... the feeling stayed with me that that was the only way I could be cured. It was like a defeat. Like an alcoholic who, after having tried, starts drinking again. When I don't eat I feel freer... with the girls too. Eating is a way of finding myself unloved again. If I eat I'm seized by something like a yearning that separates me from others. I feel

> I'm becoming like that boy in *Death in Venice*, the effeminate boy attached to his aristocratic mother... for me it takes the proletariat.

In these words there is the sense of vital necessity connected with the refusal of food. To me this symptom, which cropped up in the moments of greatest entanglement and conflict, signifies his way of reestablishing his threatened integrity, which, in my opinion, finds expression both in his words and in the representation of the "lichen" placed next to him in the sand tray.[63] In life this unconscious way of being and of reestablishing his balance was projected and realized by choosing lowly jobs. So deciding not to eat was the "lichen" countermeasure to the threat at that time identified with food. We shall come back to this threat later, because it too had found representation in the scene.

Other plant-forms, real or copied, were available in my consulting room. So why lichens precisely and not a tree? With time, I realized more and more that these apparently accidental choices are very specifically determined unconsciously. According to me, the attitude Enrico showed at the time, both in his choice of jobs and when he felt that, to save himself, he absolutely had to go without food, as if restricting himself to a minimum in order to survive, had found an explicit representation in the primitive aspect of the lichen. This conviction is also confirmed by another characteristic of lichens: in Italian woods lichens live not only on the ground, but also on trees as parasites. Enrico, reviewing this scene years later, told me:

> For me it's a primitive plant capable of living and resisting at very low temperatures, in unfavorable climates. But it's also a plant without a trunk and roots, which needs a trunk, even a dried-out trunk, to lean on.

The present context lays the accent on the consequences this impulse to be in the "lichen" state had for him: his determination was so intense as to isolate

[63] In my experience, objects representing the self-image in the relationship to the world are always placed in the scene next to the player, unconscious ways of interacting which are projected and identified with the external.

himself completely from his environment, from human relationships, creating little by little a situation he had to run away from. Even when he found a job, this dynamic prevented any kind of adaptation. He wavered between the need to be independent, which was expressed in his isolation, in his forbearance and refusal of food, and his need of support. The only known support, kept at the same time secret, because of the sense of guilt it gave him, was his being a rich bourgeois pretending to be a proletariat and actually living off his father's money: a parasite.

But lichens, due to their vital character as plants that implies development and growth, also well represent the evolutionary impulse to break free of former bonds. A striking aspect, which we observed in reviewing all the scenes, is precisely the progressive evolution of plants; from lichens all the way to a leafy tree with a trunk and roots. While plants contain this sense of a vital impulse, "lichens" express all their primitiveness, the still elementary level of the time.

Enrico obeyed this impulse without being able to distinguish and differentiate it. As we have seen, his relationship to food confirms this. Then as he gradually succeeded in giving imaginal and verbal form to his lichen, it was no longer necessary, even in difficult moments, to refrain from eating in order to be, to exist. At that time, Enrico acted out this impulse with force and determination, sometimes to an absolutely non-reproachable degree, but everything remained indistinct. It was something that imposed itself from within, according to the typical all-or-nothing law of unconscious dynamics. Placing the lichen to the left of the scene confirms its inner dynamic nature that imposed itself unconsciously.[64]

All this was not apparent from the outside. Enrico was a silent youngster, shy, gentle, obliging to the point of passiveness, who never expressed a wish or a feeling of his own. But suddenly, and quite unexpectedly, something was triggered that made him stiff and unyielding in other people's eyes, capable of extreme behavior. We shall return to this point presently. Suffice it to remem-

[64] This ascribing of meaning is also confirmed in research on "experienced space" by writers who have studied the "Village Test."

ber now that in that period, he also kept these moments to himself, in his silence and solitude: he preferred disappearing until his usual passivity returned. By no accident people of all sorts at that time felt obliged, as I have already remarked, to call him things like "sissy" or "pansy." Which brings me to the fossil seashell he placed in the lower right-hand corner of the scene.

*The fossil seashell.* Enrico carefully chose a fossil seashell, petrified with time, the only one I owned. The stereotype passivity he showed in his relations to others gave the idea of armor, of petrifaction. I find in my notes something he said a few months after the scene:

> Renouncing myself, my expression, was the stone I built myself on.

This building process is his story, and some "layers" of this story are connected with the petrifaction of sensations and emotions. Enrico frequently told me about the "curls" he wore until he was six. His mother attached great importance to seeing him with long ringlets of hair and dating from that period was an episode that made a deep impression. A woman exclaimed upon meeting him: "What a pretty little girl!" Enrico remarked at the time:

> I believe that from when I first realized I existed, maybe before I was three, I never knew whether I was a man or a woman. It's a doubt that cut me in two; I couldn't recognize myself. The very moment I felt the doubt, as a reaction I had to do something that made me feel terribly strong.

And so when he was of school age, his long hair gone, Enrico stood out for his progress in the classroom. He had to be one of the first, and when he succeeded he regained his self-confidence. He also remembered a cross-country race with some schoolmates, his heart nearly bursting from the effort: not coming in first was a tragedy for him. Even so, in those years, and up to puberty, he found a way of fitting into the social group. But doubts about his identity were only momentarily sheathed in a compensatory armor, like the layers of that seashell.

Something he said a little after this scene refers to the contents represented by and contained in the seashell:

> Other people can flow over themselves, over their phallus, both when active, in erection, and at rest. For me, letting go means falling into a soft, watery sensibility, that is distressing because it is at the mercy of others... The phallus has become an endless race forward.

These words remind me of the way Enrico introduced the figures of his parents into his analysis. To my listening, "a soft, watery sensitivity... at the mercy of others" suited his mother, but also the coldness and abysmal remoteness of that seashell. His father fits the idea of "an endless race forward," of someone who never stops and tends to force on others the principles he himself had abided by to build his fortune.

We have outlined two aspects of the seashell. The first, the petrified casing, corresponds to Enrico's not allowing himself to feel in order to find solidity, his needing to be "dead" in order to live. The second is the cavity, the hollowness which petrifaction circumscribes and tries to contain. Something else Enrico said at that time helps me sense this cavity, which is soft, watery, passive:

> If I draw out what I have inside I feel like a woman. I lose my bearings, I panic.

The twofold aspect of the seashell placed in the scene is a good analogy of his relationship to the world: non-feeling, as a way of surviving, and the stone, constructed in the course of time, to check an always-lurking possibility of upheaval and panic. During the review, Enrico added something new:

> The shell reminds me of the ability to collect sensations, emotions. Under "normal" conditions they are suggestions that become part of a vital circuit: they nourish it, make it grow, or wear it down, but all the same enter into circulation.

Here the seashell is a fossil, no longer alive; it's as if it held nothing but stagnant water that no longer circulates, that was once alive and no longer is. By now, it becomes the capacity to receive only from the outside, to listen without the possibility of assimilating, of owning, of changing into something mine, that passes through me. As such, it is something stagnant, constantly overwhelmed from the outside, like relationships which no longer exist either on a social or on a personal emotional level, and which send nothing but unusable, uncontrollable, overpowering suggestions [like when they called him "sissy" and he wept helplessly]. This is overwhelming on the inside, with an anxiety which seems to exist independently of everything, with cycles that seem disconnected from any external cause.

With these words, he succeeds in substantiating his "feeling like a woman," to what I might call a sense of death, concealed by petrifaction. So the seashell aspect strikes me as the exact opposite of the lichen: the former a primitive, indistinct vitality, a being in the world according to the law of all or nothing, the latter a feeling of being passive, unable to assimilate and integrate what happens, a "having to be dead" in order to live.

This new element of the scene, considered in relation to the lichen, makes it possible to better understand the mortal threat projected onto food, opposed by the "lichen" mode in a spasm of vitality. In moments of serious conflict, food was the container of death, the poison, the deadly stagnation. The axis I see as connecting the lichen to the seashell in a dynamic relationship, seems to represent the way in which Enrico at the time felt active (the lichen) and perceived himself as existing (the seashell). This condition is expressed at the bottom of the scene, where the "good" and the "bad" are experienced, acted out and identified projectively outside and not yet recognized as parts of self.

Petrifaction seems to nicely represent the way Enrico learned how to escape the anxiety of an uncertain, confusing and depersonalizing identity. It appears in the seashell, the "hard" container for collecting the impressions, the shocks, the frustrations resulting from the contact with reality. But as his words of the time make clear, there was in him also a deep reaction to all this:

As a reaction, I had to do something that made me feel terribly strong.

As we have seen, he had already put this compensatory behavior into effect in his early school years.

The moment has now come to speak of the vertical dried-out tree trunk standing in the upper left side of the scene.

*The fragmented tree-trunk.* The compensatory reaction of being "good," "bright," "terribly strong" had functioned successfully during Enrico's early school years, but already at puberty the edifice cracked.

> At fourteen I still felt like a baby; when I took a shower I always looked at other guys' penises. Mine seemed small to me...

His friends had long been going to dances and playing around with girls, but Enrico held back. He acted the bully, the faultfinder, but again feeling himself different was agonizing. At home, he kept up his role, but outside emotions tended to overwhelm him. So his isolation began. A crisis was building up that would explode at the age of seventeen, when, during spiritual exercises, he felt the "calling."

> It was like a thunderbolt, God called me.

The overpowering emotion of that moment found expression in words only in the last years of analysis:

> It was something outside I had not discovered inside... something magnificent that demanded my annihilation in order to be.

At twenty he entered the novitiate. Attacks of anxiety alternated with doubts about having answered the call of God properly. A priest, the head of the monastery, realized the situation only much later and sent him home. He was twenty-two and came out with the sensation that nothing had meaning any more and the fear of going mad. He no longer felt anything; not even women, earlier the source of fears and hopes, aroused any reaction in him. In analysis, he remembered certain experiences of that period: one day he rushed to the kitchen and started asking the woman doing the cooking if what he saw were really zucchini, green beans... he spoke in a loud voice, non-stop in order to hear himself, to prove he existed. Episodes like this, which psychiatrists call depersonalization, followed one upon the other.

> I remember the first time I felt queer: it happened while I was reading in the paper about a transvestite arrested by the police; I was aroused and scared of myself. I couldn't look at my body. After that I didn't want any mirrors in the house... I remember that at that moment I saw myself either as a woman, an old man or a baby...

Condensed in these few lines, necessary for the information they give, is the account of years of torment. Only at the age of twenty-four did Enrico find the courage to enter into analysis.

The form of the "dried-out" tree-trunk set in the scene expresses the idea of verticality. And everything he described in the story of his "calling" strikes me as an irruption of "verticality" into his life, verticality as the "equivalent of spiritual activity and self-detachment" (Arthus, 1947, p. 291).

The verticality of the tree-trunk is the exact opposite of the cavity of the seashell. The tree-trunk is dried-out, and this attribute also turns out to be the opposite of the seashell, which, according to what Enrico says now, contains stagnant water that is never refreshed. Something vertical, something elevated, which in its dried-outness refers to a prevailing, inhuman sunniness, devoid of contact with the humors of the earth, opposes the moist, soft and stagnant depths of the seashell. Enrico said when reviewing the scene:

> This tree-trunk is the most painful sensation of the whole picture. The hardest thing to describe, to say. Strongly built and with sturdy roots, this dried-out tree-trunk I feel is still connected in some way with the father figure. It's austere, stiff, lifeless...

It is one aspect of the scene which even after nine years painfully forces itself onto his perception and fails to find a suitable form in words: "the hardest thing... to say."

The tree-trunk, with its attributes, represents, but also qualifies, an overwhelming, almost unbearable experience: the experience of the holy invading the human, an image of light that appeared in Enrico's life with the crushing force of an archetype.

> It was something outside I had not discovered inside... something magnificent that demanded my annihilation in order to be.

I repeat this remark in order to focus on the word "outside." In my experience, these images are the ones that subjects recognize as alien to themselves, endowed with a power of their own. They force themselves upon the imagination with an altogether different kind of otherness than that expressed by the "lichen" or the "seashell," and are distinguished by the influence they exert on the feelings shared in the analytical field. In the previous chapter I described these images as a different level of the relationship between the ego and the activated complex, where feelings tend towards personification. At the time of Enrico's analysis, involuntary fantasies were still unleashed that revealed this compensatory impulse towards verticality: he felt like a saint called by God to redeem mankind. Or he said:

> It comes to mind that I have to be the head of a new revolution... I feel like crying, but then I remember thinking: I really am mad.

In this remark what is formulated in words was expressed in the scene by the relationship between the "tree-trunk," omnipotent and vertical, and the "lichen" which defensively leads back to earth, to the horizontal plane. Now that the reader begins to know this story, he or she can see the deep meaning contained in what I called the "lichen" mode, which Enrico projected into the simplest and most undemanding manual labor. What is expressed in images of the "tree-trunk"-"lichen" relationship is the wavering between the omnipotent delirium-fantasy of the savior, represented by the tree-trunk, and the adherence to reality of the remark: "I don't let myself be carried to the heights, I think I really am mad." Enrico's involuntary fantasies at that time revealed his identification with verticality, with power, to escape anxiety, and they leapt up like a sudden rupturing.

Enrico found self-recovery in isolation, in remaining silent and also in abstaining from food. But this was sometimes not enough, and to survive and reconstruct himself he needed his "lichen" mode to fasten onto a less vertical, more concrete "tree-trunk." In those moments, the analyst could become the "tree-trunk" he needed, with all the ambivalence, the love and hate that involved. The partial personalization was identified projectively with the analyst, as is revealed by this highly significant dream:

> I phoned my father, but Aite answered instead. I apologized. The analyst replied: "Did you let the magistracy know about the phone call?"

The dream preceded a momentary interruption of our relationship, and it seems to me revealing because the need for a father figure and the menacing shadow of the lawmaker are condensed in the image of the analyst. The power of the image expressed in the space of the tray also broke out between us frequently during the session. There were moments when Enrico, unable to bear the silence, would shortly get up and leave:

> I've got nothing to say so I'm leaving.

Today I would say that the "tree-trunk," in its negative aspect, had come between us. For a while, Enrico was punctual and attentive and would then exclaim: "I'm always coming here to give a report...;" this marked the beginning of hostilities and explanations. Sometimes I became aware, often after the fact, that I was deeply touched by the free-playing emotions in the analytical field. Without realizing it, the tree-trunk had also taken possession of me: this was when I feared for his life because of his going without food and the isolation he used as a defense. Only later did I see my patronizing attitude and my attempt to give advice about his behavior. He said one day:

> I sometimes have to have a drink of wine before coming to you.

I now know that the wine served to diminish the power of that tree-trunk projected onto, and identified with, me. Reviewing the scene years later with Enrico I realized how that deformed, vertical wooden object brought to the visibility of the play scene, and therefore into the analytical field, an "active image" that prompted intense feelings between us, in the transference and countertransference: it was a suitable metaphor for understanding the psychic atmosphere of the emotional paralysis we had long shared.

But already present in that object was the level of representation I have previously called "part-character." Over the following months, an African wooden figure, it too distinguished by verticality, appeared in another scene Enrico built. Only later did I realize that this formal definition of the character went hand in hand with an improvement in the emotional atmosphere between us. Today I can say that the personalization of the initial tree-trunk indicated a different relationship to the feelings experienced in the analytical field. With its appearance, the emotional storms between us dwindled away, in fact, and our dialogue more and more favored the emergence of feelings that had never before been expressed.

Thinking about the "tree-trunk," it spontaneously occurs to me to include its relationship to the "lichen," as well: proceeding in my reading of the image, in this case the scene in its entirety, an interweaving of their relationship inevitably appears. So I make mine something Patricia Berry said (1974, p. 63):

> So to be faithful to a text is to feel and follow its weave... image in itself has a texture.

I described the tree-trunk as the vertical opposite of the soft, stagnant and petrified cavity of the seashell. An opposite which offsets that death, and is experienced with the intensity of a great psychic charge that invades and takes possession of the ego. As an illustration of this relationship, I remember something Enrico said:

> I've always felt the fascination of being a victim...

A need for self-annihilation that brings to mind the period of his "calling" and at the same time the attraction of that dark cavity. Opposite, a fantasy of puberty recounted in analysis:

> If I imagined having intercourse with a woman, I saw myself being extremely violent, to the point of sheer malice.

Here again we see the "tree-trunk" in its violent, destructive aspect.

This contradiction, so radical and deep, is activated in his relationship to women. The petrifaction of his feeling or his delirious isolation in the omnipotence of imagination seemed to be the only way of containing the power of the violent charge in progress, at the time, between the two poles. Gilbert Durand (1963, p. 179) says something that helps describe this situation:

> Definitive male verticality contradicts and dominates black, temporal femininity, the elevation is the antithesis of the fall...

It seems to me no accident that Enrico first felt love for a girl who had been anorectic from the age of twelve. He met her a year after leaving the novitiate.

I succeeded in understanding her language of somebody who didn't seem to be of this world; we understood each other, I succeeded in knowing what she needed.

This relationship was a meeting of two people who had much in common, especially their will to live. And it was also an exchange, because Enrico, for the first time, approached a girl outside the juggling of impotence-omnipotence that invaded his life. He frequented the young woman a long time, shared with her the conflicts springing from her family environment, from her repeated hospitalizations, with love and irritation. The girl then entered analysis and this is probably what led Enrico to do the same. Subsequently, he had other affairs, infatuations, but what is striking is that most of his girls were foreigners, just as his emotions themselves were foreign to him. Another characteristic of the girls he dated: they were children of the earth, came from farming or working families, and in one way or the other had something to do with dancing. At the time of the scene we are examining here, this broadening of the sentimental front had not yet taken place, but it is highly significant that clowns and ballerinas appear in the upper right-hand corner.

*The clowns and the ballerinas* (Fig.12a, Images). During the review, Enrico said:

> I remember that when I put in this part of the scene I imagined it to be much more remote than all the other elements, way up there at the back. It was also, in a certain sense, the most pleasant and for me completely new. For me it was human society, the others I finally saw, though at a great distance, in my own way. I would say I saw them being capable of joy, of expression, of harmony.

These words came later and actually, at the moment the scene was being built, clowns and ballerinas struck me by their sharp contract with the rest of the scene. I remember that at the time I noticed that Enrico chose figures capable of expressing feelings and emotions, which in life he still seemed overwhelmed by. With time I understood that the personifications represented a special aptitude of his for introspection, for self-recognition, for an unusual way with words, confirmed by what he said then and years later during the review. Today, clowns and ballerinas seem to represent the healthy part of his personality, whereas the primitive, fragmentary aspect of the other parts expresses his deep difficulties of that period.

The clowns give voice to emotions and arouse them in the person listening to or watching him: they establish contact with the other side of ourselves. In the scene, they are placed between the group of ballerinas and the vertical tree-trunk, as if they were intermediaries between that verticality, which brings to mind the logos, the introjected law, and dancing, the rhythm that engages the body, the harmony that is embodied in their movements and makes them the vehicle of deep emotions. I would say that, through clowns, logos and eros find here a rapport and a possible intermediation. The clowns, by virtue of their red juggler's baton, seem to be male but they are figures of which myth and folklore reveal many different aspects. They combine normality and madness, ambiguity and wisdom, demonic and truthful aspects, pungent irony and apparent stupidity.[65]

Clown- and ballerina-figures express themselves, moreover, in a social context: they say the things to everybody which each and everybody say. If we think of the scale of the isolation which Enrico was doing his best to survive in, this was a really positive prospect, a favorable prognosis for our work.

Around a year after creating the scene, Enrico spontaneously felt the need to use paint and clay. He started painting on his own, then took a course at the Academy of Fine Arts. Until then he had never taken a brush in hand or tried to sculpt: it was something he never thought he had a gift for. Then he said:

> Every so often, some content, some impression appears; it's a way of feeling things. I feel I have to express it somehow. It feels new and I'm in a hurry, otherwise I lose it. If I don't do something about it right away, I can't believe it's real.

In these moments, painting was a necessity. It was his thing, which he liked talking about it, but never showed me: in his eyes I was still too "trunk-like." Painting, he noted, lessened and balanced out the feelings of severance and demoralization that eating gave him. "Painting," he said, "balances out eating," in other words, being poisoned. In that period, he started making the rounds of art galleries, loving Chagall and Gauguin, in particular: Chagall's colors, Gauguin's children of the earth.

[65] See Moretti (1979).

> When I paint I'm somebody else... If I lose Chagall I feel awful.

To my listening, it was as if he were saying: if I lose the expression I'm beginning to find, I'll fall into the dark cavity of the seashell. Not only: relating himself to Chagall was like saying: I can let my contents emerge, even if they are ambiguous like clowns or feminine like ballerinas, because they lead to a new expression, something which consciousness, or the principles so far predominant, have not allowed.

At certain moments, he was so elated by this discovery that he really did believe he could become a great painter. The contents which by analogy had been expressed in this part of the scene invaded him completely. At certain moments, I too was enthusiastic and fascinated by this new path which had so unexpectedly opened up which balanced his isolation and added a new flavor to a life that until then was devoted exclusively to trying to survive. If I happened to say what I felt, losing for a moment my analytical position, I realized that my involvement led to a coldness and detachment on his part. I "acted out" his image and he reestablished the familiar balance represented by the petrified seashell. A few months before finishing his analysis, he said:

> The artistic period's probably over, I want to go back to university. If I hadn't gone through this experience, I wouldn't have saved what I succeeded in saving. The last illusion of grandeur has fallen.

In the scene, "ballerinas and clowns" on one side, and "tree-trunk" on the other, represent images which had a powerful effect on his life. They were also a source of fascination, as is shown by his "calling" to verticality and the spontaneous fantasy of being a saint or a leader of men (the tree-trunk), as well as by his attraction to the expressiveness of colors and shapes which he sometimes felt in his possession (the fantasy of being a great painter) and which, instead, he was possessed by. They are certainly opposed images. I associated the tree-trunk with strictness, the sterile law against sensitivity, a "spirituality" he forced upon himself at the cost of living. The clowns and the ballerinas are, instead, the expression of deep motives, a communication on the horizontal plane in the space of sociality, of the group. This aspect of the scene seemed remote and so it was. It took years to fully understand, to approach it. At the time it was only a prospect, something new to offset the law of renunciation (the tree-trunk), the petrifaction of emotional resonance (the seashell), the constant struggle to grow (the lichen). This something "new," still remote and only anticipated in the representation, was a supporting and positive element in our relationship. In the analytical space, as well, the clowns opposed the "verticality" and acted as intermediaries, opening the way to a world of "dance" (the ballerinas). I mean: even in difficult moments, Enrico ended up finding the path of communication, through the concreteness of sandplay and verbal expression. I am convinced that "tree-trunk" and "clowns" are suitable metaphors for representing the feelings, the even violent feelings we shared. Today I find in them all the ambivalence of the contents experienced in the transference.

*The pieces of bark at the center.* Moving randomly from one element to another, and letting myself be guided by the thread of involuntary association, I have reached the center. But I believe it will be easier to approach now. There are two elements, two pieces of bark half-buried in the sand. Enrico called the straighter one on the left the "male;" the other one, a curved piece of bark with a hole, the "female." Enrico's remark at that moment was:

> A man and a woman lie embraced but don't make love yet.

Let us listen to what he had to say during the review:

> The vital concern of this scene is the need to "speak" the central part. The two pieces of bark at the center are a male and a female element, and represent, if not of a love scene, a distinction between the two elements, and their closeness, and I would say a very primitive vital circuit. I remember that for months in analysis there was an attempt to single out these elements, to separate them, to characterize them. In effect, at that time my affair with X [the anorectic girl] was over, I always dreamt of two women sleeping together; any "male" residue

> in me seemed to have completely disappeared, been swept away. Feelings of sexual impotence and homosexuality were very strong. The fact that these two elements were shown close together and "distinct" is something very important, which in this case words would not have been capable of portraying, representing, circumscribing. In particular, the representation of a feminine element, the bark with a hole, as something self-standing, seemed very exciting. The two elements are close to each other and yet, as I said, they are not joined in a complete, more advanced bond of love like whole people; they represent, however, a more primitive state of an authentic relationship, of a first vital circuit, of exchange, of "repose." In other words, something lives and life circulates, even if in a very primitive state.

Enrico's gestures and involuntary remarks, as well as his written words, during the review, allow me to sense the meaning of the central embrace which "staged" a fundamental need. It may have been the blueprint, as it were, of an experience where union was no longer a vague fusion, and the differentiation no longer a total separation. There was an allusion to a possibility of being and of meeting the other, the diverse. In the "bark" object used to represent his self-image deeply painful experiences were condensed; I am thinking of how uncomfortable he was with his body, of seeing himself as a sissy: his feeling split, without a recognizable identity.

What is apparent in his remarks about the lichen, the seashell and the tree-trunk, also considered in terms of their relationships, is how each of these elements represented a way of being which at that moment excluded its opposite: to be identified sometimes with the tree-trunk, at others with the seashell or the lichen, whereas the opposite came through in the symptom. They are experiences interiorized in his personal story and constantly active. It was a still unconscious blueprint, I would say, of being "centered" so that every aspect had the right to exist in a new totality.

For a long time, Enrico still wavered between one aspect and the other, in a fragmentation that excluded all the rest. His blueprint of the time is still being carried out in his life. That central element, the embrace, seems to unite dynamically, and at the same time to differentiate and recognize, a male and a female, up until then indistinct, which has been the main theme of this story. We can now see that the terms "sissy" and "pansy," applied to himself, were, in his vocabulary then, the expression of this non-differentiation, with the terror that entailed his no longer being and losing himself. And it was a vocabulary built up through his experience as a divided and bewildered little boy-girl.

The embrace at the center, so far explained in the terms of a personal story, suggests many amplifications, it is a typically human, imaginative analogical expression of that "center" which gives meaning, which in analytical psychology is called Self. I am thinking of the fifth image of the alchemical process Jung commented on (1946, figure 5a, par. 460) where the union of King and Queen takes place beneath the water and is a representation of the work of transformation being carried out in the depths. The central elements of the scene under consideration have the same primitive character of something taking shape on a deep, vegetal level, like a pregnancy.

I would now like to describe in a less general way the relationships of this center to the rest of the scene. Each of these relationships can be seen as an imaginary "axis" joining opposite aspects. I find two of these imaginary axes particularly interesting: the one connecting the seashell to the tree-trunk and the one that relates the lichen to the clowns and ballerinas, both of which pass through the center, in fact. My hypothesis is that that center represents a perspective which at the moment of the reviewing had not yet been brought into focus. Enrico himself seems to sense this when he remarks:

> Only several years later would I realize that my person is made up of all the elements present in the scene and that therefore the dried-out tree-trunk and the seashell must also be made to enter the circuit.

In my hypothesis, the central image of the embrace is the point where those two deeply opposed aspects find a balance. In other words, a point that maintains the contrast, where both dimensions can be present at one and the same time. I wonder whether this axis, which I would call the "death" axis, where the tree-trunk negates the seashell, expresses the fluctuations of Enrico's pathology, with its alternating impotence and omnipotence. The other axis, linking the "lichen" defense to the "clowns and ballerinas" aspect, strikes me as being, instead, the vital one that enabled him first to defend himself and then to start expressing, at least to a certain extent, what was unspeakable and blocking his life.

The purpose here of my free reading of the objects, characters and words of Enrico's first scene has been to describe the narrative structure of a story and at the same time communicate the feelings we shared in the analytical space. The perspective drawn from my notes of the time and the review subsequently undertaken with Enrico years later, touch on the complexity of the representative act. The researcher's eyes can find a way to approach, study and understand the metabolism of feelings subtending the possibility of obtaining new integrations of consciousness.

# XIV Reviewing Play Scenes Over Time and the Resonance of Feelings

*Between us and events, between the doer and the deed, there is a reflective moment – and soul-making means differentiating this middle ground.* J. Hillman (1978) p. xvi

As we know, the visual register dominates our experience of the psychic world. We are used to "seeing" our dreams and fantasies. What brings about in us this psychic act of inner perceiving, similar to seeing? What role is played in the psychic economy by the integration of experienced feelings into visibility, of representations that stand out clearly against the background?

I believe sandplay can contribute to this research, precisely because it transposes and materializes the moment of seeing, making it possible to perceive the resonance of that moment on the feelings present in the analytical field. What led me to emphasize the relationship between play scenes and verbalization, and their transforming effect, was reviewing with a number of patients (by means of slides) play scenes that had been created years earlier.

In the previous chapter, I tried to describe how, when reviewing Enrico's first scene with him, I realized with surprise that it offered a possibility for reading not only his story but also the narrative structure of feelings and emotions experienced in the analytical relationship. All I expected at first was a simple recalling of moments we had shared years earlier, and it seemed to me that it would not take much time. Instead we found ourselves involved in a much more intense and complex experience than expected. What was supposed to be a simple comparison of recollections, which the slides would or would not confirm, aroused an unexpected resonance of feelings between us.

There was a further surprise: what seemed to emerge was a sort of anticipation, quite unnoticed before, of the choice of materials, of patterns traced, of recurring personifications in the sequence of the process that had followed the first scene. The building time, the way the forms of every scene were placed in space and their mutual relationships, as well as the sequence of scenes over time, struck us as being extremely meaningful. Was this an illusion, or did those discoveries put us really in touch with an unexpected preciseness, with a surprising overdetermination?

Along with elements that were vividly remembered, objects, forms, colors appeared that had been forgotten with time. And it was precisely these objects that gradually assumed the role of metaphors particularly adapted to expressing feelings we had experienced. The images we were looking at together also brought back in those forms our blindness at that time, when neither he nor I had noticed what was now perfectly explicit. The scenes as seen in the slides not only offered the opportunity for a more careful rereading of what had happened between us, but seemed to become emotionally pertinent today. It was as if those forms had dropped the role of recollections from the distant past to touch us as living things.

A new view opened up not only on the past, but for the present, as well. Signs of the nodal points of Enrico's personality, of the crucial and characteristic conflicts of his personal story, appeared as perceptible feelings between us in the present, while the review was taking place.[66] I realized little by little that even years later viewing the whole sequence of his sand scenes caused unexpected modifications of feelings between us. What I began to sense was a new perspective in which past and present were woven into a single thread. I was becoming more and more convinced that that scene-by-scene examination described an act of assimilation by the complexual nuclei which had been active between us and which also showed up again by reviewing the slides.

[66] The description of reviewing in all its aspects will be the subject of a future work. I need only indicate here the complexity of the experience.

The close connection between words and images, remarked on time and again in this book, is perfectly clear in the reviewing experience. I am also referring to the appearance of mental associations which are seemingly irrelevant, secondary so to speak, to the ongoing thread of discourse, but which threw light on what is being said about single details or a sequence of scenes. I am thinking of the different tone and pace of involuntary words, of the use of uncustomary expressions or witticisms.

The psychic activation induced by reviewing is also revealed by clinical signs that were less common, but by now described in many case histories: dreams immediately following contact with a scene that has given rise to associations and recollections, or is surprisingly meaningful. Less common is the surfacing of involuntary fantasies which, under particularly intense emotional conditions, pick up aspects that have already appeared in the sand scene. The individual forms recalled in fantasies, or that return in dreams, appear as active signifiers in the subject's psychic life. In my opinion, these signs prove that together with already known metaphors that have become the property of verbal thinking, the scene also contains "active images" still charged with emotions that are only hinted at in the relationships between the parts of the scene and which have not yet reached a level of differentiation. The appearance of a sudden recollection, a dream or a spontaneous fantasy, expresses these free emotional charges not yet fixed as objects or personifications in the structure of the scene.

These phenomena impress and surprise the observer because they are completely unexpected. The mingling of sensations, images, feelings and thoughts set in motion by reviewing shows that the relationship between the patient and certain nuclei of his emotional experience is changing. Seeing the slides seems to carry the relationship between the event and consciousness to a different level. It is as if the sequence of scenes brought out a gradual transition from thinking that symbolizes through images to thinking in words. Feelings that are only partly integrated when building the scene may, with reviewing, enter the sphere of shared speech, capable of modifying the interpersonal field. As I have tried to show in the previous chapters, going back over the scenes reveals the complexity and the significant preciseness of the organization of the representation but also casts light on the relationship between the act of reviewing itself and the appearance of further, even very intense energic variations: precisely because they have the scene as a reference point, the feelings aroused by those forms are distanced differently, which makes a new story possible, one that up to that moment had been hard to express.

## 1 Notes on the Hermeneutical Aspect of Reviewing

In its structure, the scene itself can be seen as the possible interpretation of a given moment in a relationship between consciousness and the unconscious, or rather between the ego complex, in its conscious and unconscious aspects, and the secondary complexes which conceal feeling-toned charges not yet metabolized and therefore sustained by automatism and unsettling. The autonomy of this particular organization of experience (the finished representation of a sand scene) long escapes the consciousness of the patient and of the person observing him. It always conceals an "other" meaning which only careful and never-ending study will reveal with time. Access to the question is created in the field, and what I consider a true "hermeneutical circle"[67] emerges in the subsequent and gradual enrichment activated by what is seen. The player's story and the complex reality of his emotional life always discover the autonomous meaning implicit in them, even though, in the act of playing, it is unknown to the player himself and to the analyst.

In going back over slides of scenes built years earlier, the gap between the emotional recollection of those moments and what is seen at present is felt by both patient and analyst. In reviewing, images are re-presented in the perspective of a spatiotemporal discrepancy. The text represented by the process of

[67] The term, "hermeneutical circle," borrowed from Schleiermacher, expresses that movement which, in interpreting a text, links the parts to the whole and the whole to the parts, in a mutual and increasing enrichment. The procedure is useful for understanding analytical work, both in the "here and now" of a session (horizontal view) and at the time it took place (vertical view).

scenes built over the years, after having been experienced, now lies there before the "reader." And with each new reading he reopens and completes it, as if to "understand above all the discourse as well as, and then better than, the author himself."[68]

Reviewing activates an emotional field in which the observer, the patient as well as the analyst, assume a new attitude: "experienced" and "seen" no longer coincide as they did at the time of playing, but are distinct. At that moment, the patient is, as it were, both inside and outside the scene, recognizes its belonging and at the same time feels its otherness. We know that the slides also alter and distort the spaces, carry the signature of the photographer, even if he regularly uses the same positions. What changes instead is the experiencing of space, from when the player conquers it in building the scene to when it is seen as a whole in the slide.

The experiencing of time also changes drastically: it shrinks in a transversal and longitudinal sense. Scene building implies a series of actions, whereas in the slide everything is fixed in a sort of simultaneity. By the same token, the scene-building process that unfolded in years of analytical work shrinks to only a limited number of encounters. The gap in perspective is the result of this shrinking process. A surprising sense of otherness forces its way into what is remembered and recognized as one's own.

I believe that this gap provokes a stimulus, sometimes an uneasiness, in the person reviewing the scenes but at the same time makes it possible to discern relationships between the parts, which, during construction, were seen and experienced from a different angle. Between the "experienced" of then and the "seen" of now an utterly new field of experience and reflection opens up. What the former means is the immediacy which brings to the fore the perception of objects and feelings in a significant, but also irrational correspondence, separating it from all the rest. "Reviewing," instead, is an experience that presents the

[68] I give a special meaning to Schleiermacher's paradoxical remark, quoted in Fornero (1993), which prepared the way to hermeneutics. By "author" I refer here not only to the patient, but also to the patient-analyst relationship itself as a creative unit of the text, of that never-ending narration that is fathomed with time.

representation as a whole. What leaps to the fore is the structure of the scene, gains the upper hand, is a principle of consistency between its various aspects. From this new angle of participation both analyst and patient are led to associate the recollections and emotional experiences shared during analysis with the relationships perceived between the individual elements. The forms which were partly or completely forgotten often come as a surprise, precisely because they are now charged with meaning. Their structure, as well as their relationship to the whole, activates new associations with the analytical experience stored in the memory of both participants.

In my experience with Enrico, I realized that the revisited scenes had provided both his and my consciousness unwonted room for thought. I think this new angle made the independence of the experienced event clearer to both of us. The emotion had passed from the experience of us both to sharing through the play-images and lastly to an unexpected state of independency during the review. It was as if my companion in years of analysis had realized that an "other-than-self" event had taken place in his innermost reaches.

For me, a whole new chapter of investigation opened up. It was not so much a recapitulation of the course of our analysis and its related memories, as I thought it would be at first, but of a here-and-now experience. The associations often-unforeseen, the dreams of the moment, the shared emotional dynamics, proved that, even after a period of years, I was experiencing the vitality of a symbolic event. The slides revealed the complexity of a thinking by images and a resonance of feelings that took us both by surprise.

## 2 From Images to Words: The Mobilizing of Energy

My encounter with Enrico, which I have used here to describe the events that reviewing brought about, was for me particularly fortunate. Only later did I realize that this impact with the concrete visibility of sand scenes could lead to energic changes in the analytical field that are not always easy to control. Discovering the effect that the representation of the scenes had on Enrico and me certainly offered me unexpected elements for exploring and reading the "text" of our analytical relationship anew. The truth is, however, that, in this case, as in other subsequent reviewing experiences, the particular relationship with the play scenes permitted me to show emotional phenomena that were unexpectedly charged with energy. In other cases, the hoped-for elaboration did not take place or ran into obstacles of various kinds, ending up with the relationship being broken off. These failures enabled me to understand that to approach and comment on scenes, with a direct impact of consciousness on the feelings represented, can trigger an energic explosion.

For the moment, with my limited personal experience (only a few dozen reviews), I can give only a few general suggestions. I believe that in certain cases, failure was due to the negative influence of my seeking confirmation. Carried away by "scientific" interests, I realized only later that during the review I was looking for a logical line of development in the observed process instead of paying attention to the signs coming from the interpersonal field. I still remember with dismay the moment when, after over a year of analytical work with a patient and excited by what she had expressed in a most interesting sequence of play scenes, I showed the series of slides to her. The picture that emerged included the story it told, the probable meaning of each individual objects, their relationship to the feelings shared in the analytical field, and highlighted, as well, the organization of the process experienced through sandplay. To my great regret and surprise, the patient, who until then had eagerly participated in the analysis, left me. I have thought a great deal about this experience and about what must have happened. My enthusiasm, which led me to anticipate the reviewing, was certainly the symptom of something that had gone unnoticed in my countertransference. What I said might have been right, but it did not take into account the other person's needs and the signs coming in from the field. I did not pay enough attention to my emotional impulse, which was only expressed and not reflected. Nor, evidently, did I listen to other warnings that were undoubtedly present in the woman's attitude, in her words and contemporaneous dreams: I did not wait for what was genuine in what we had sowed to germinate. Because of my emotional need, not recognized and acted upon, I had unwittingly interrupted a symbolic experience and harmed the protagonist in the process.

This mistake, and other similar ones, taught me how destructive words can be if they do not succeed in corresponding to the ongoing symbolic experience and unconsciously serve the interests or needs of the analyst. Using words during play and during a review of the scenes can be damaging when they are impulsive and not determined by the signs emerging from the field. In the next chapter, I will try to describe how and when the analyst's words can intervene in the analytical field as an essential moment in the ongoing symbolic process, in this way releasing its maximum transforming potential. In fact, I am more and more convinced that emotions can develop all their energy and bring about a permanent change in the ego's capacities of response, when they attain the verbal level of symbolic expression.

This research, only just begun, makes it possible to understand how the visualization of a representation allows us to approach the phenomenon of "taking stock" which is always the fruit of a confrontation with emotions that is not easy. When a review of play scenes achieves its goal, it makes contact with the relativity of the ego's ascendancy, opening it up to the symbolic dimension. Awareness of personal limits and the possibility of acting and sharing with others go hand in hand. Actually, the most significant contribution of this experience for me was understanding that the possibility of reaching a more integrated level of consciousness means passing through an intermediate zone of great emotional turbulence: in the process of this integration, the individual runs the risk of losing a sense of self. When the scene is shown again on a slide, what had been experienced in a partial and fragmentary way finds a unity of its own on a new level of integration.

The player can realize that his body has been the vehicle of an articulated symbolic communication: hands and eyesight already expressed something that was still severed from conscious verbal thinking. One can quite agree with Jung when he says (1942/1954, par. 391): "It is not I who create myself, rather I happen to myself" in describing the experience of the patient who sees the difference between "experienced" and "seen" and is surprised by what has happened to him.

The rational presumptuousness of an adult consciousness, with which it usually defends its achievements, must give way to a new attitude. A new dimension of the ego, a relativity of its own, emerges which does not mean losing, but broadening what has been previously acquired. The expression of consciousness, formerly bound to the "here and now," to a single prevailing point of view, can become authentically symbolic and focus on a multitude of possible relationships in a whole of which only fragments were previously seen. The horizon widens and the individual point of view, now relative and no longer absolute, discovers the dimension of an exchange with others and with reality.

Observing with patients a sequence of scenes created years before not only enhances the consciousness of both parties, but also makes it possible to perceive in the present the hidden stage direction of that unfolding.[69] A sharing takes place on a new level of consciousness, a symbolic experience which goes beyond what has hitherto been understood, opening up new horizons. These are the moments when the transpersonal dimension of the psychic event can become perceptible to both and change the perspective of what has been experienced in analysis.

[69] In Chapter XVII, I will try to further investigate this aspect according to the Jungian experience of Self.

# XV The Whens and Hows of Transformation: Play as Compared to Dialogue

*The secret of metaphor is to be found in the paradox of a substitution where the thing substituted is still present.* G. Agamben (1977) p.176

The psyche is known to have a capacity for self-healing, succeeds, that is, in independently undertaking actions that not only maintain its balance in coping with the necessities imposed by life's demands, but sometimes transform, even drastically, the possibilities of response and creativity in the individual.[70]

Analytical psychotherapy, whose aim is to cure through psychic transformation, should be seen in a two-fold perspective: on the one hand it seeks to activate an interpersonal field where the potentialities of psychic self-healing can be awakened, on the other it uses its chosen instrument, namely interpretation. These two therapeutic actions are integrated together. The former is maternal in essence, tends towards containment, emotional resonance in the sharing, and tries to distinguish and affect inter-subjective field conditions that foster new responses to the invasive action of emotions. The latter is paternal in essence, a complex action which, as we shall see shortly, finds expression on various lev-

[70] By "self-healing" I mean that complex group of actions aimed at maintaining the balance, which the psyche spontaneously calls into play, not unlike the way biological defenses do. The emotional field between individual and environment are all-important for the full success or failure of this still little-known process. From this viewpoint, I imagine psychosis to be the psychic equivalent of autoimmune diseases, a defense that has become pathological and self-destructive. The various psychopathological conditions can therefore be considered attempts at self-healing which have failed or only partially succeeded.

els. It is to be found in the spatiotemporal organization of play scenes as well as in their words that interpret; from metaphor to concept. Its purpose is to recognize and describe emotional dynamics, distinguish them and merge what was first fragmentary into an overall view.

What I want above all to emphasize in this chapter is how sandplay taught me to see and distinguish more clearly the emotional factors in the field that foster the spontaneous symbolic process of self-healing.[71]

## 1 Analytical Field and Self-healing

The analyst must succeed in singling out the potentialities and limits of the self-treating event of the psyche. As we know, in particular field situations, in collective rituals, for example, phenomena of psychic transformations can take place that are brilliantly successful, but also difficult to control. Emotions can be set free which determine a therapeutic or, on the contrary, a catastrophic effect. The positive or negative influence, the contagion of health or sickness, is a mysterious process of the collective unconscious which still escapes our understanding.

In the psychotherapeutic sphere, as well, particular field situations can provoke similar phenomena, in both a positive and negative sense. Charismatic personalities, who have deep rapport with the theory they profess, because his rapport is rooted in a personal experience of transformation, may activate a psychic field that is open to the symbolic experience. Their belief can have a deeply healing effect, as the transformation of the symptoms of the individual patient, and the transpersonal symbolic level of the dreams or scenes produced in the interpersonal field, both go to show.[72] In these situations, however, there is also a risk that the omnipotent narcissistic aspects of the personality of who-

[71] Winnicott's teachings were fundamental for understanding the importance of entering into relationship with objects and of using objects for psychic transformation.
[72] See the magnificent process described by Dora Kalff (Montecchi, 1984).

ever plays the part of analyst, may prevail. The figure of the therapist tends to hold a central place in the psyche of the analysand, and create a situation of dependency that can also be long-lasting. In such cases, it is difficult to be able to tell the difference between a genuine transforming symbolic process and a shared emotional over-emphasis. The consequences of this psychological condition can be known only later. In the above situations, words are indicative because they often assume an assertive tone based on the therapist's beliefs: they are stated as facts leaving no room for doubt, much less for a differentiated personal opinion.

These premises must lead the analyst to ask with greater responsibility what the emotional factors are that facilitate the possibility of self-healing in the analytical field. I was orientated towards the importance of this question by my clinical experience. When I started using sandplay I was surprised to discover that a sequence of play scenes could, in particularly intense situations in the field, lead to a transformation of feelings, with even remarkable changes in the symptomatological picture, as well. On these occasions, words were absent or at the most limited to a restraining commentary, devoid of verbal interpretation, which at that moment lay outside my possibilities. The appearance of a symbolic representation in the tray was the only thing that could lead to a radical change of feelings in the analytical field.[73]

In Chapter III, when I described Anna's sequence of play scenes, I gave an example of "self-healing" exclusively through sandplay. On that lucky occasion, I also tried to understand what the emotional conditions were that helped bring about the symbolic process between us. The clinical change in the protagonist took place, in fact, in strict relationship with the way the sandplay representations and her dreams developed, whereas our dialogue played a role of careful containment. The symbolic integration though play scenes was the motive of that change. For me the clearest factor of transformation was Anna's ability to distinguish and represent the contradictory aspects of the conflict that

[73] Dora Kalff has effectively taught us the importance of that "free and protected" interpersonal psychic space in which the transpersonal symbolic process of healing takes place. See Montecchi (1984) and Navone (1984).

dominated her, and with time to create a series of representations that indicated the transformation of the relationship between consciousness and the autonomous complexes. In that sequence of sand scenes, emotions that were still confused and experienced with the sense of otherness that is peculiar to impersonal experience, reached a personal level of expression, leading to manifest changes in the feeling-tone of the relationship. I believe that on that occasion my participation, aiming at the empathic and protective containment of her playing, had also played a fundamental role, as I learned from Dora Kalff. With time I understood the crucial importance of other emotional aspects, as well, in triggering the activation of the symbolic process. Not by a deliberate choice but by necessity, I remember that I had gone through a long period with Anna in which a sense of loss and disorientation prevailed. I believe that only when the playing started did my curiosity about what was happening (a curiosity that gradually turned into a deep interest) also serve a catalyzing function.

Today, I consider the experience of losing pre-existing convictions, shared by patient and analyst, to be essential for activating the possibility of a spontaneous and successful symbolic process. Patients who do not know what to do in the presence of that smooth empty surface of sand, but even so succeed in yielding to the perception of the moment, is the most precise metaphor of the loss of reference points and the possibility of overcoming that loss. Like the analyst who is listening, the player must first of all be able to open up to different levels of perception.[74] The sand, the limited space, the objects offer him a wide range of stimuli, just as different aspects of communication appear to the analyst's perception. This melting pot of stimuli includes those that seem already familiar as well as the still indefinite and unsettling ones that create an almost unbearable atmosphere of bewilderment and confusion. Feelings sometimes also appear on the scene through unexpected physical sensations.

So the presupposition of a successful symbolic process, on both a verbal and imaginal level, means encountering one's limits. By experiencing the tension this condition creates, both analyst and patient are obliged to look beyond what

[74] See Montecchi (1997) p. 60.

is already known. This brings about a need for completion which opens inner sight to the emerging representations. From an attitude that seeks similarities and pays attention to often already known details, the subject, be it patient or analyst, goes beyond the usual boundaries of his perception and responds with a need for consistency which then and there may seem accidental to the consciousness of the observer. Instead, with time the sudden fantasy that has appeared to the analyst while listening, or to the patient while organizing a sand scene, can reveal an inner consistency and an overdetermination charged with meaning. So the limits themselves stimulate the never-ending search for the most suitable expression of emotional experience.

We know that a network of meanings acquired through experience sustains the stability of consciousness. But like all things, the attribution of verbal meaning, valid for a certain period of life, tends to age: it contains only a few possible responses which in the course of time prove to be inadequate. In the analytical field, there is a constant vital transition from the verbal to the preverbal level in the symbolic process. Words which with time age and lose their symbolic power must start drawing again on the images offered by fantasies, dreams or play scenes. In this constant exchange from words to images and from images to words, analytical listening also takes place, until a significant narrative structure offering the possibility of subsequent verbal interventions is established. Likewise, the images that appear in the organization of a representation need to reach the level of shared speech in order to develop in the interests of the ego all the potential energy contained in the emotions. These are the moments when the capacity of consciousness for reflecting is activated. From level to level, from isolated images to the creation of representations and lastly to words, the symbolic process can succeed in releasing all its energy or, on the contrary, fail to develop.

This mental capacity to perceive what appears on different levels, from the known to the unknown, from the rational to the irrational, is only apparently axiomatic and

> demands an even greater effort, calls for an even lengthier apprenticeship, needs an even finer exactness than is typical of any true profession. But it is necessary to know how to wait, as the peasant does, for the seed to grow and reach maturity.

What Martin Heidegger says (1959b, p. 53) captures the essence of the ability of both the patient and the analyst to yield to the perception of the moment, but also to know how to wait so as not to lay what is already known, hence reassuring, over what is happening. Heidegger's words make it possible to understand the underlying task, the training needed in order to reach that form of thinking which he called "meditant" as against "calculant" thinking which aims at only preordained results (*ibid.*, p. 53):

> Meditative thinking demands of us not to cling one-sidedly to a single idea, nor to run down a one-track course of ideas.

The basic difficulty of this particular tendency to "pit meditative thinking decisively against merely calculative thinking" (*ibid.* p. 53) lies in abandoning one's usual defenses and risking the experience of having no responses, with the sense of loss this may entail.[75]

Heidegger helps us understand "what" the appropriate goal is, but we must also ask "how" this capacity for attention and waiting can be aroused in the analytical field: a psychic attitude that is only partly the fruit of a deliberate decision. When this happens, a particular level of consciousness is activated, different from the consciousness that aims at a set purpose. "Calculant thinking," like direct verbal thinking, can be described as a linear approach to a goal, whereas "meditant thinking," with its typical "waitingness," passes over the same points and at a pace which seems rhythmic and circular.

The playing involved in building a significant scene follows the same course. What is striking is the silence and concentration of the patient, the delicacy and at the same time the rhythm of his gestures, while he seems to be looking for a suggestion from in the material itself he is touching. The silence

[75] On this subject, see Aite (1998).

and waiting of the analyst are superimposable on these moments: what takes place is comparable to the playing field, and just as the sand is ready to receive every stimulus, every movement, without changing its nature, so the analyst must attempt to perceive the quality of that silence and of the patient's movements while building the scene, in terms of the impact they have on him. Though we usually pay greater attention to our own train of thoughts, we must try to widen the range of our perception. Training consists in following the circularity, the rhythm, as it were, of the responses we perceive at the edges of lucidity, on a physical level or in the emotional atmosphere of the encounter.

The words spoken involuntarily, which can interrupt that apparent immobility, are, I feel, the equivalent of those carefully considered gestures: they too have slowed down, are more subdued. I am convinced that the rhythm of words and gestures indicates a willingness to perceive the different-from-self, an opening to "meditant" thinking which, in Heidegger's words, knows how "to wait, like the peasant, for the seed to grow and reach maturity". So the capacity you want is not so much to set a direction as to "trust" and wait.[76]

In the end, if the analyst is not prepared to renounce what is known to him, and to live with the discomfort of having no responses, in order to perceive the still obscure fluctuation of thoughts, emotions and sensations which sometimes invade the analytical field, he risks seeing nothing but what he already knows. By no accident, interpretation capable of opening up new perspectives of thinking originates in a field dominated by the lack of (or by discomfort so intense as to oblige abandoning) the usual responses: vital necessity leads in an unknown direction only when adequate responses for confronting uncontrollable emotions no longer exist.

[76] Dora Kalff's notion of "free and protected space" catches an essential aspect of this psychic field that fosters symbolization. On this subject, see Navone (1984).

## 2 The Transpersonal Aspect of the "Self-healing" Event

From the point of view sustained in these pages, psychic pathology is the expression of the failure of the capacity to represent the emotions activated by contact with the world. Nor is it to be excluded that, just as happens with the body when it is taken sick, the failed symbolic organization of experience in a mental representation can also cause sometimes-irreversible damage in the relationships between deep emotional charges and the ego complex. It is possible to theorize that the analogies between body and psyche are greater than we think, and have yet to be made fundamentally clear. The psyche's capacity to transform emotions, or its possible failure to do so in particular field conditions, seem to be the psychical equivalent of physical metabolism, which can absorb into its structure whatever is needed for developing or falling ill.

As is well-known, Jung in his research conceived the existence of a superpersonal, collective level of the unconscious, supported by archetypal models of behavior where recurring and involuntary responses are constructed for adapting and developing in the face of life's demands. Human history provides countless examples of this spontaneous symbolic activity, of which myths and religious systems are the most apparent. These first seeds of research have had a subsequent development. The present-day "transpersonal psychology"[77] is an attempt to inquire further in this direction.

Of this theoretical model I would like to mention here only the evolutionary pattern of the psyche, where importance is given to the successive levels of integration in the relationship between consciousness and emotions. So-called "pre-personal," "personal," and "transpersonal" stages have several points in common with my experience with sandplay in recent years. Above all, I learned that the transpersonal dimension of the psychic event shared with patients is the result of delving into the analytical relationship at length. This dimension of sharing is reached and perceived, I would say, when analyst and

[77] Regarding "transpersonal psychology" see Wilbe (1981).

patient become aware of their conscious and unconscious coparticipation in an autonomous process that has involved and changed them both.

In particular, reviewing sand scenes, an experience discussed in the previous chapter, put me in touch with the transpersonal dimension of the symbolic event. In the analytical field, sharing and reconstructing the scene-building process after a period of time make it possible to see how most of the process had been unexpectedly autonomous and escaped the control of the ego of the two participants. For the analyst and the patient, this "other," experienced heir innermost reaches, shows that the transpersonal dimension of the event was always present and operative, even if not perceived at the moment. Only in rare clinical situations have I chanced to share moments of transpersonal experience in the analytical field. On those occasions it is as if the experience had changed, taking on, for example, an almost tangible intensity in the concentrated silence accompanying the building of a play scene, due to the emotional atmosphere created in the relationship. In Chapter XVII, discussing self-experience as seen through sandplay, I try to describe an experience of this sort that I had during the building of a scene. In the review that took place years later, the transpersonal event was shared with the protagonist on a more conscious level, one easier to put into words, and by virtue of the tone and intensity of the dialogue and of the changes that had come about in her life, resulted in considerable alterations in the analytical field.[78] Reviewing sand scenes after a period of time, an experience I have gone into more thoroughly in recent years, has proved more and more clearly that words are not always synonymous with a rational interpretative act, but can, with the infinite variety of its expressive levels, bring transformation about in the analytical field.

The transpersonal dimension of the psychic experience shared in the analytical field, as a symbolic phenomenon of change, is, in my opinion, always the fruit of a long and difficult process in which, however, shared speech plays an important role. What the analyst says is known to have an inhibiting effect

[78] Regarding the process of healing through self-healing see Mancini Carducci (1997).

on the symbolic process activated by sandplay and determine a rational organization, a virtual colonization of the other's freedom, but it is equally true that it can create room for symbolization. It brings to bear a complex action which contains and meets the need halfway, acting as a bridge in a slow progressive transition to the words of interpretation. For human beings, verbal expression is a symbolic necessity whose coming-to-be should be carefully studied because it constitutes the full symbolic transformation of emotions and feelings that can be overwhelming.

## 3 Words That Further Self-healing and Prepare for Interpretation

Shared speech in the form of dialogue furthers the symbolic self-healing process. In its circular rhythm, this use of words plays an essential role of containment that stimulates and facilitates what the interlocutor seeks to express. Understanding this aspect of dialogue makes it possible to understand its importance in opening the field to spontaneous self-healing and to the whens and hows of interpretation.

Dialogue inspired by this purpose is different from improvised dialogue at the service of the ego, which is typical of support therapy. The possibility of an analytical dimension is not achieved by an outward approach (constant silence at all costs, words used exclusively for pointing out defenses or for interpreting); it is rather the result of a theoretical stance that contemplates different tempos and levels in the use of the speaking voice.

The attention the analyst pays to the difference between the needs and the wishes[79] invading the analytical field offers useful information regarding the

[79] The capacity to wish is based on a previously acquired distinction between oneself and the other; need indicates a primary lack that must be made good in order for the process of self-distinction to be reactivated.

different stages required for bringing the interpretative act to maturity. Winnicott stresses this point (1958, p. 288):

> If a regressed patient *needs* quiet, then without it nothing can be done at all. If the need is not met the result is not anger but only a reproduction of the environmental failure situation which has stopped the processes of self growth. The individual's capacity to "wish" has become interfered with, and we witness the reappearance of the original cause of a sense of futility.

Being able to recognize and confront a primary need with patients makes it possible to understand how necessary waiting can be. A dialogue that is aware of what is going on is better than a premature interpretation.

In sandplay, the element of *need* is clear, especially in the relationship with the materials. Handling the sand, using water or colors without objects, describe this primary regressive necessity. The emotional tone of the relationship and the words accompanying the scene building clearly show when it is a question of resistance or when there is a need which, as Masud Khan says (1977, p. 25), has to be "managed":

> Managing actually means offering that adaptation to environment within and outside the clinical situation, which the patient has not experienced in childhood, and without which all he can do is to exist through the reactive utilization of his defense mechanisms and the force of his id. Only when the management has been successful can the work of interpretation have clinical value. Management and interpretation often go hand-in-hand, mutually sustaining and facilitating each other in the patient's whole life experience.

In the first case, the patient handles nothing but the material repeatedly in a series of sandplays. His gestures are particularly intense and rhythmic, almost as if to evoke the sensuousness of that contact, but the same expressive level is maintained; using objects and scene-building are avoided. In such cases, what the analyst has to say can be important in an attempt to break down the patient's resistances and give access to change in the field by pointing out the defensive repetitiousness of that way of establishing contact with the sand tray.

In other situations, the same way of handling the material takes on different characteristics: it is a constructive phase which, after a while, paves the way to a careful use of objects in the scene as well. In such cases, words can accompany the imaginal event, sometimes in the form of exclamations or witticisms, at others of recounting some sudden recollection.[80] In the above sequence, contacting and handling the material, using water and color, would seem to be the way of "managing" a need that triggers a subsequent phase in the patient's expressive capacities.

## 4 Words As a Vital Necessity

In my experience, I have had the impression that an unbroken thread holds different levels of expression in both play and words together. The communication of the feelings active in the relationship transpires in the way the patient goes over to the playing field. There is a transition between different levels of expression, from using the sand by itself or together with objects, to the natural inanimate forms and personifications which often precede involuntary exclamations or recollections. Likewise, what the patient says in the analytical field, even when he is not playing, may provide a glimpse of a similar process. With time, defensive, repetitive, humdrum words assume the pace of a smoother-flowing dialogue that leads to sharing, and which, in particular moments, may take the form of an exclamation which establishes a direct contact with feelings.

It is like seeing the integration of successive phases of expression into a continuum of images and words. Verbal or imaginal communication implements the need to express feelings, to share emotions and lend substance to thinking.

The famous episode of the child described by Freud in *Beyond the Pleasure Principle* (1920, p. 15) offers valuable proof, I feel, of the moment in which

[80] In Chapter X, I describe this moment in the construction of a scene by a woman.

words emerge spontaneously from playing to give full expression to, and understand, the real experience:

> The child had a wooden reel with a piece of string tied round it. It never occurred to him to pull it along the floor behind him, for instance, and play at its being a carriage. What he did was to hold the reel by the string and very skilfully throw it over the edge of his curtained cot, so that it disappeared into it, at the same time uttering his expressive "o-o-o-o." He then pulled the reel out of the cot again by the string and hailed its reappearance with a joyful "da" [there]. This, then, was the complete game - disappearance and return. As a rule one only witnessed its first act, which was repeated untiringly as a game in itself, though there is no doubt that the greater pleasure was attached to the second act.

I would like to point out how in the above episode playing with the reel and string the more exciting moments of disappearance and reappearance were always accompanied by an exclamation. Both gestures involved repetition: a way of giving form to emotions on two levels. The perfectly distinct utterance of sound commenting the two moments of the scene stresses the management of loss with the "o-o-o-o" of disappointment and the "da" of contentment at the reappearance. Using an object in playing seems to open the way to the utterance of a very distinct sound. What we have here is a spontaneous integration of gesture and sound which distinguish even more the two moments of the game. New words in a highly personal idiom are created as a necessary development in the expression of ongoing feelings. Freud's footnote confirms this interpretation:

> One day the child's mother had been away for several hours and on her return was met with the words "Baby o-o-o-o!" which was at first incomprehensible. It soon turned out, however, that during this long period of solitude the child had found a method of making *himself* disappear. He had discovered his reflection in a full-length mirror which did not quite reach to the ground, so that by crouching down he could make his mirror-image "gone."

The “o-o-o-o” of disappearance and loss had become a word, a still private word, that the child connected with the word, “baby,” that he copied and learned from the grown-ups. So what we have here is a further transition, an even more complex integration: the child has passed from managing his feelings through play to a meaningful exclamation, a bridge to shared speech, which involves an even sharper distinction of feelings and self with regard to others.

I have returned to this well-known episode to show how, in the development of the symbolic process, words, or the use of verbal representation, are necessary for the transformation of feelings. In adults, where shared speech is already an existing structure, we come upon the same process when new emotions are under way. Words that surface while a scene is being built assume the pace of a dialogue whose tone is different than usual, or of an exclamation of surprise, sometimes to the point of offering a full-flown interpretation of what is going on.

Thinking over the scenes that have been presented so far, I remember a student who, during the session described in Chapter IX, exclaimed that the ditch he had dug between the riders and the mountaintop was like a wound, or when he finished the scene, calmly telling me the story of his childhood friend, the dinosaur, who kept him company and quieted his fears when he went to bed at night.

# XVI Interpretation Through Images and Words: From Subjectivity to Sharing

*When speaking of interpretation, we should not be concerned with images but with consciousness: to open it, to dispose it and to let it define itself in relation to the unconscious dynamics represented in images.* E.G. Humbert (1979) p. 22

For me, building a sand scene means interpreting in space and time the tissue of sensations, perceptions, emotions and feelings the patient is experiencing. Present in his movements is a confrontation, a giving shape to subjective experience and the adventure of both intrapyschic (between consciousness and the unconscious) and interpersonal communication begins. The representation taking shape in the analytical field speaks to the patient and at the same time to the other person present: the analyst himself. In recent years I have become more and more convinced that playing and shared speech are more closely related than is commonly believed. The similarities between the two levels of expression, apparently poles apart, have always struck me as being greater than the differences.

In the analytical field, words in the form of "dialogue" or of "interpretation" deeply resemble playing where first an object is chosen from among others and then a scene is built. If we observe a player intent on building his sand picture, we notice how, after moment of embarrassment, he breaks free and makes the moves his perceptions suggest. I have already mentioned the interchange, the "give-and-take," that is created between the individual and the playing field.[81] His actions take a circular course that is very similar to a dialogue between two

[81] See Chapter II.

people. The moments of silence, as if pausing to think, or the quick sequences, like those of somebody following the thread of an indication or of a discourse underway, are clearly visible in his movements. As in playing, the characteristic words of a dialogue open a field of agreement, explore and at the same time contain in the sharing.

The moves the player makes, choosing one of many objects and placing it in the scene in order to build an organized whole which gradually takes on a consistent meaning for him, seems to be the metaphor of words which first designate a feeling and then relate it to a situation. Playing is also very similar to interpretation. In both, the subject takes a content that is to his taste and relates it to other contents with a view to creating a consistent whole. Underlying play and words there seems to be a psychic act with similar structural features.

In the transition from choosing an object to organizing it into the finished whole of the representation, something takes place that is like a dialogue between two people, where at a certain point interpretation emerges that connects different aspects of a shared experience. Just as a sand scene is built amidst endless trials and errors until something relatively equivalent to the experience is created, I see the same thing happening in an interpretation which achieves integration only gradually. I believe that in order to permanently change its relationship with split or repressed complexes, consciousness must go through this same gradual process of integration.

## 1 Language and Myth

The deep similarity, confirmed in my experience, between emerging images and words, between the narrative structure of a scene and the story it tells, is confirmed by something Cassirer says (1946, p. 88):

> Language and myth stand in an original and indissoluble correlation with one another, from which they both emerge but gradually as indipendent elements. They are two diverse shoots from the same parent stem, the same impulse of

symbolic formulation, springing from the same basic mental activity, a concentration and heightening of simple sensory experience. In the vocables of speech and in primitive mythic figurations, the same inner process finds its consummation: they are both resolutions of an inner tension, the representation of subjective impulses and excitations in definite objective forms and figures.

Words and myths, the latter viewed as the capacity to represent through images, express, for Cassirer as well, the same substantial energy that gives form to human emotions and elaborates them symbolically. Cassirer goes on to remark (*ibid:* p, 56, p. 90):

> [Language and myth... tend] toward concentration, telescoping, separate characterization.... The mental view is not widened, but compressed: it is, so to speak, distilled into a single point.

In this Cassirer sees the genesis of denomination, the first word that designates, as well as of the mythic figure, the god that appears. In sandplay, each single choice of object, each form that takes shape, recalls that intuition "focused on a single point." At the moment of playing, the player chooses out of the flow of perceptions what turns out to lie closest to his emotional experience, to the charge of feelings that dwells in the depths.

Apart from the theory that links the words that designate to the choice of objects, there is in what Cassirer says the possibility of understanding certain particular clinical moments; he observes (*ibid*: p. 97, p. 26):

> Language does not belong exclusively to the realm of myth; it bears within itself, from its very beginning, another power, the power of logic.

> This synthesis cannot be achieved immediately and at a single stroke; it has to be worked out step by step, by a progressive activity of relating separate notions or sense impressions with each other, and then gathering up the resultant wholes into greater complexes, until finally the union of all these separate complexes yields the coherent picture of the totality of things.

Described here is a psychic act that is the exact equivalent of building a play scene, where the individual elements chosen find their place in relation to the others. Meaning is achieved through the mutual relationships of the individual elements in space as well as the temporal sequence in which they are placed, in other words, through the totality of the representation taking place. The player looks beyond the limit of intuitions focused on a single form and carries out a new mental act whose basic element is the relationship between the parts.

From thinking in terms of individual images to representation, from the name-giving vocal gesture to the possibility of linking words together in a new interpretation. Cassirer sees in this process the force of the *logos*. It is a psychic presence that culminates in verbal thinking, but is already active on the level of representation, as well (*ibid.,* p. 27).

> All the concepts of physics have no other aim than to transform the "rhapsody of perceptions," by which the world of the sense is actually presented to us, into a system, a coherent epitome of laws.

What Cassirer says here is what I go on seeing in my clinical experience. Words and symbolization through images continually interrelate and "stage" two levels of a single integrating process of feelings. During the building of a scene, when an image appears that shatters the preordained sequence, spontaneous speech immediately feels the after-effect. The moment an experience is evinced on the play level, verbal expressions different in their pace and color get activated and memories from the distant past may also find a way of emerging.

To be sure, the emotional event Cassirer has described for primitive linguistic concepts helps to catch the moment when an image extracted through sandplay starts to assess emotions and transform them into ideas. When images organize themselves into representation, a new "peripeteia of consciousness" begins which the analyst tries to evoke, at the moment he deems most suitable, by going back and associating it with what has been experienced in the relationship.

## 2 The Whens and Hows of Words That Interpret

Just as in the process of building a play scene where the form is gradually defined on intermediate levels before a finished structure is reached, so with the whens and hows of words. The analyst's interpretation takes place in basically two stages: a single detail is extracted, and then placed into a significant whole. These two stages in the usage of words, first the choosing and then the building, involve the totality of the communication taking place in the relationship. In the analytical space described here, the "text" that is gradually being assembled in order to be read and understood, involves both the playing and the ongoing dialogue. In an interpretation, details are first chosen and placed in the field of encounter, then when the time is ripe, a whole story can take shape.

The first stage is interpreting through metaphorical images, an "unsaturated" act from a purely descriptive, cognitive point of view. The second is the form in which the various cognitive, emotional and sensory levels of an experience are organized and interrelated.

Repressed or split emotions, imprisoned in the secondary complexes, go through a gradual process of integration from part-images to the organization of a representation, on the playing and verbal level. It is often necessary, in the presence of unspeakable emotions, to return to the initial way of confronting emotions, to physical experience in order to activate a symbolic process that releases the energies confined to the repetitive circuits of pathology. As happens with patients in front of the empty field of sand, so the analyst must for first be able, as far as possible, to do away with attributions of already established meaning, in order to address the inimitable phenomenon of encountering the other.

When discussing the question of listening, I described the attitude, the manner and the levels of perception most suited for preparing oneself for experiencing an interpersonal event. The first signs that an emotion is about to make its appearance and is perceived in the analytical field appertain to a pre-visual level of expression, which leaves a deep mark on both analyst and patient. The analyst can say and do things he never imagined and which are not a part of his character. They are sudden, apparently unwarranted acts, like when a player chooses an object or creates a figure of any kind in the sand. His being absorbed by the scene that is being built corresponds to that coming into contact with emotions I propose to describe. To represent these moments, analytical research resorts to the mechanisms of projection, of identification and projective identification.

When the analyst realizes he has been carried away by an emotion still free in the field a "third" party makes its way between him and the other and demands to be represented in order to be known. The choice and the use of objects in sandplay define this moment, which testifies to a mutual involvement, sometimes triggering unexpected emotions and sudden regressions, which an alert analyst can detect and distinguish in himself and the other.

Verbal interpretation, whether by means of metaphorical images that seek to sever the preexisting connections of meaning, or of well-constructed stories that connect a body of information into a new perspective, proves its effectiveness or insufficiency in the responses it gives rise to in the analytical field. When words succeed in their intent, they change the feelings expressed in the relationship, and the element of surprise offers the best and most compelling proof that the change has been detected. The direct experience of dialogue indicates emotional acceptance in the form of new associations, sudden memories or in subsequent dreams or fantasies. An amazing tissue of emotions and feelings is revealed in this "give-and-take" between the interpreting of, and the listening to, emerging signs. In fact, interpretation first of all constructs the transition from a "pre-personal" to a "personal" level of relating to emotions. From the disconcerting intrusiveness of the first level, the individual's experience takes on the hues and forms of his particular story, as happens with dreaming and playing. A symbolic change, this, which, in an analytical field such as the above, can make it possible for the powerful, at times destructive, energy of emotions to be absorbed. Only subsequently does that further change we call the transpersonal dimension become possible. The emphasis immediately given to the spiritual aspects of the psychic event shared in therapy often conceals a defensive short-circuiting. The therapist who acts simply as the transpersonal go-between, and loses touch with what the sharing experience has inspired in him, sometimes to the point of giving him a feeling of complete helplessness, has failed his task, but most of all can cause damage to the other. Which is why it is necessary in himself and the other to take the long path of observing, of understanding, without forgetting the basic value of the act of interpretation. If the hows and whens of this are carried out, at what is considered the right and useful moment, carefully measuring the responses of the field, transformation is possible.[82]

## 3 Interpretation Through Images: The Use of Metaphors Extracted From the Sand Scene

From my experience with sandplay I have learned that the time it takes for the moment of interpretation to mature must be respected. It must take a path that begins with an initial recovery of metaphors through images and ends with a well-constructed mental act. Only by going through what is, cognitively speaking, an unsaturated level of interpretation, can knowledge be acquired that relates thinking in images to thinking in words. So in the beginning the analyst tries to formulate the metaphor extracted from the context of the patient's involuntary discourse or from a careful analysis of repetitious behavior noticed in the analytical field.

In my experience, metaphors taken from the play scenes possess a degree of vitality and a disruptive capacity that are wholly unexpected in the dominating circuits of defensive thinking. The first scenes of a sequence especially can afford surprising metaphorical images which become "denominations" of shared feelings. In these first stages of interpretation, the analyst extracts from the patient's play scene only individual aspects of the representation, not yet an or-

[82] For a critical survey of the concept of interpretation and the corresponding ways this verbal act can be carried out in the analytical field, see Jervis (1989).

ganized and coherent discourse. These verbal acts, in my opinion, correspond to the choosing and using of objects that precedes the final integration of the whole scenes. The analyst's goal is to siphon off the feeling underlying that aspect of the representation which has appeared in the sand tray in order to "dissolve" it into shared speech. According to this hypothesis, the objects and the forms built in the sand convey a mental blueprint that is not yet acceptable to the reflective consciousness identified with speech.

It should be pointed out that these unsaturated verbal and cognitive interventions come about through a listening that aims at catching similarities and differences on an emotional level with what is happening in the "here and now" of the relationship. Speaking of listening, I have already explained this mental attitude which I might also call yielding to the preconscious, like "dreaming with eyes wide open."[83] It often happens that only much later does the analyst get an inkling of the emotion that has led to the choice of a given object or a given form in the play scene. By yielding to his listening, he revisits the scene, inhabits it as it were, explores it virtually piece by piece. An object, a sign that seemed significant ever since the session in which the scene was created, is used to comment upon an emotional atmosphere, an attitude or an argument existing at that moment in the communication.

The analyst's words, as metaphorical as the objects the patient uses, are the psychological equivalent of placing a figure in the scene, inserting what has already happened on the level of play into the interpersonal space. The analyst may verbalize the metaphorical interpretation through images in different ways. In my experience, a metaphor extracted from a scene can be offered directly as a comment upon an interpersonal emotional state.

I remember Enrico's reaction when I mentioned his defense based on an obedient and repetitive acquiescence in his relationship to me.[84] This is a simple example of how the verbal use of a metaphor extracted from a scene, even an old scene built long before, may be more capable of causing a rupture than a

[83] See Chapter VI above.
[84] I describe this scene in Chapter XIII.

mere description of behavior in the analytical field. The "lichen" object Enrico chose in his first sand picture all of a sudden struck me as the most appropriate metaphor for expressing his passive compliance and at the same time his soaking up all my energy like a parasite. Then and there Enrico listened to what I said in silence, with no apparent emotion, but the next night he had a dream:

> I phoned my father, but Aite answered instead. I apologized. The analyst replied: "Did you let the magistracy know about the phone call?"

In our later reconstruction, the lichen in that scene seemed more and more like the passive dependency with which he defensively warded off the harassing verticality of a sadistic super-ego represented by the rigid tree-trunk placed on the upper left side of his first scene. The dream brought what was the experience between us to the fore. The "lichen" defense I took note of was actually inimical to that violent unidentified presence in Enrico's life which he projected onto me during the session and which I, without realizing it, let him do.

In actual fact, by conveying a part image of a whole, an unsaturated interpretation touches a relationship. That day the connection between "lichen" and "tree trunk" most certainly dominated our analytical space. Interpretation through images acts as a probe sounding the depths, and from the consequent reactions draws evidence of the deepest meaning of that detail of the scene.

What in the relationship is experienced as emotionally shared out merges into the organized unity of the representation. "Tree trunk" and "lichen," united in the scene along with other aspects, were differentiated and distinguished between Enrico and me. I lived without realizing it the emotional charge of the sadistic super-ego he projected, but I in turn projected onto him the parasitism of the lichen. The interplay of identifications and projections going on between us were unified into a single representation in the play scene, which could be very helpful for understanding the ongoing dynamics between us. My memory of this fragmentary moment of a session, which brings back the unsettling presence between us of the severely judging verticality of the tree trunk, proves to me that on the verbal level I was stressing an aspect that I found hard to bear.

The response aroused in the patient then and there, or subsequently, is the only one that decides whether what has been said has or has not opened a path for underlying feelings. Sometimes there is no immediate resonance, only subsequently, as was the case with Enrico. Sometimes, instead, it comes right away as a surprise and suddenly changes the predominant train of thinking in the relationship.

At other times the analyst's words do not describe for the patient the metaphor that has come to his mind while listening. His remarks, like his silences, are limited to references to some previous scene or a detail of it. In their pace and tone, what his words convey is the atmosphere of a scene that has already been shared with the patient, but without being specifically mentioned, a presentation of an image as with Enrico in the above example. I consider this way of introducing a metaphor preparatory the other, since the time it takes to pass from the subjective expression of playing to shared speech must be carefully assessed.[85] The undeniable effectiveness of unsaturated interpretation through images makes choosing the right moment very important, because of the emotional impact it can have on the analytical field.

With time I learned to provide patients with metaphors that represent emotional contents that lie closest to consciousness. Objects confined to primitive expressive levels are still out of reach of possible verbalization. In Enrico's case, it would have been wiser to associate the highly expressive mobility of the "clown and ballerina" figures (the sole representatives of the human world) in the top right-hand corner of the scene with his parasitic "lichen-like" immobility. This partial mistake was a clear indication of the transferential and countertransferential dynamics under way in our relationship at that moment. It is no accident that the above-mentioned dream had its source in the emotional charge we experienced between us, and which went nearly unnoticed by me.

[85] See in Chapter XIV the mistakes made by reviewing the play scenes with the patient too soon.

## 4 Interpretation That Constructs

Interpretation that organizes different levels of an individual experience into a coherent whole is "saturated" because sensations, perceptions, emotions and feelings that have been experienced and ideas that have gradually surfaced with time, find their place in the narrative structure of a story that seems to be complete, but which is actually never finished and always being revised.

A patient achieves this same integration when he organizes into the unity of the representation what has been chosen separately in the play scene. He first sorts out the individual aspects of an emotional experience, then, catching sight of ever-new connections, joins them together. Hillman, 1975, p. 31:

> Separation comes first. It is a way of gaining distance. This *separatio* (in the language of alchemy) offers internal detachment, as if there were now more interior space for movement and for placing events, where before there was a conglomerate adhesion of parts or a monolithic identification with each and all, a sense of being stuck in one's problem

A process of synthesis is present in constructing a play scene as well as in an interpretation which tends to connect various levels of an experience. I believe that a good analysis sets off a similar process, one that in itself is never-ending and lasts a lifetime. I often happen to remember certain dreams in my own personal history I have impressed in my memory, or sand scenes I made years ago, and I go on discovering new connections and new angles I had never seen before. Whereas unsaturated interpretation tends to sever the ties with previous attributions of meaning in order to activate a process of distinguishing and extracting new elements, saturated interpretation synthesizes the whole, and can reach a new concept that changes the way the entire experience is understood. It often happens that one takes what are merely rational explanations, usually in the terms of acquired meanings, for a conceptual and cognitive synthesis, which is instead the fruit of a long and often laborious elaboration of experience. Cassirer (1959, p, 25), speaking of mythical thinking, stresses precisely this moment:

> ... we can show that all the intellectual labor whereby the mind forms general concepts out of specific impressions is directed toward breaking the isolation of the datum, wresting it from the "here and now" of its actual occurrence, relating it to other things and gathering it and them into some inclusive order, into the unity of a "system."

It is significant that Cassirer describes the same transition from details to the universal in both representations and concepts, in both thinking by images and thinking by words. From this point of view, the part image that enters into the unity of the representation of a play scene is the first formulation of an emerging thought. Building a finished mental representation would seem, on the level of verbal thinking, to have its equivalent in the structuring of the individual parts into a concept. As we have already seen, Cassirer (*ibid,* p. 88) explained apropos of this:

> In the vocables of speech and in primitive mythic figurations, the same inner process finds its consummation: they are both resolutions of an inner tension, the representation of subjective impulses and excitations in definite objective forms and figures.

Sandplay, in its limited space and the use of materials it offers, activates the mysterious tension that leads particular perceptions to reunite in the unity of a system. This is the symbolic process which the peculiar situation of sandplay inspires, by eluding the control of the defenses that words often give expression to. Through play, emotional events become experience. Aspiring to unity in the representation and extracting new concepts that change the perspective of verbal thinking, are the two extremities of a single integrating process.

So, according to the basic theory of this book, the identical symbolic aspiring aims at reaching its goal. It first seeks the new word that can designate the emerging image in order to tell a story that is capable of expressing more and more completely the narrative structure of a life.

# 5 The Long Journey of Words That Interpret

Representations appearing in the playing field can, as we have seen with regard to self-healing, lead to the synthesis of a living symbol which very soon transforms the individual's feelings and his way of relating to the world. This spontaneous result is not accidental, but is nurtured in a soil, some of whose basic emotional elements of which I have tried to single out in my discussion. When the symbolic experience of transformation through sandplay appears with all its force in a field where containment and silence are all-important, the analyst's personal qualities are, I believe, essential. His competence and experience go hand in hand with the depth of his humanity. The analyst knows that what he has experienced first hand in coping with his own conflicts is of fundamental importance. The narrative structure of his personal history bears the signs of a never-ending process. And it is precisely these weak points which, returned to time and again, have become precious signposts showing the path he and his patients must take. They assume and give symbolic meaning to our past story: but this is a value that must be rediscovered every time, since every time they can make us repeat the same mistaken attitudes that afflicted us in the past.

The long journey of words in the analytical field, from dialogue to interpretation, with the different stages sandplay has taught us, and which I have just attempted to describe, has two main reasons. The first, the positive one confirmed time and again, is that words that express feelings are necessary because they transform all the energy contained in them, making it available to life, and grasp their meaning, however laboriously. As I observed in the previous chapter, the child with the reel, described by Freud, makes us realize how, after having "interpreted" his emotions through the use of an object, he found it necessary, in order to express himself, to resort to a private word and then to a "grown-up" word. First through play then through words, the child found a way of telling his story of loss and rediscovery and thus assumes a new relationship with his emotions and the people around him (Maffei, 1996). The second reason, which may seem a limit but is actually a fascinating quest, is that a network of words and concepts needs to be created in order to approach the mystery around us, and which in itself we know to be inaccessible. Watching carefully seeing clearly (which has always struck me, etymologically, as the closest equivalent in meaning to the term religion [*re-ligio*]) is the path words allow us take, even with all the possible mistakes. I prefer this long difficult path of words that interpret to the path on the giddy heights where the spirit and the unspeakable reign. It is this path I feel must be taken with patients, in order to give them, after they leave, an instrument for continuing to walk on their own.

# XVIII Staging the Representation as Self-experience

*The self comprises infinitely more than a mere ego, as the symbolism has shown from the old. It is as much one's self, and all other selves, as the ego. Individuation does not shut out from the world, but gathers the world to oneself.* C.G. Jung (1947/1954) par. 432

The endeavor to integrate, to make what is divided whole and consistent, is a typical undertaking of the psyche, which, as we have seen, allows us to follow quite clearly the building of a scene. The patient's gestures, which at first seem accidental, eventually reveal a sort of behind-the-scene staging that guides what was initially fragmentary towards unity. I have always associated this coming-to-be, which seems to be supported by an unconscious overdetermined ground plan, with the amazing way organs are formed as we learn from embryology. The configuration under construction on the one hand defines the differences between the feelings that have been experienced and highlights the complexity of a narrative structure, and on the other expresses an organizational impulse towards uniting what in the beginning seemed separate. It is precisely with the unfolding of imaginal visibility in the human psychic economy, in personal and collective stories, that Jung hypothesized the presence of an integrating dynamism he called "Self." Self cannot be spoken of in terms of structure, but only by describing it as a complex dynamic presence which starting from an aggregate of elements aims at a unitary formation.[86]

[86] Today molecular biology is breaking the code of the formation of organisms around the genome and has succeeded in activating the biological process experimentally in which organs and complex systems are integrated by completely altering their function. The resemblance to the notion of self described here is perfectly clear (Boncinelli, 1999).

In clinical experience the psychic act that organizes and visualizes a mental representation, as is the case with dreams, fantasies or scene-building, is the chosen place where this process is disclosed. Sandplay, by rendering the coming-to-be of the representative act perceptible in space and time, makes a valuable contribution to the study of this process.

The quadrangular shape of the sand tray, in my opinion, helps get the distinction between contradictory emotional elements into focus. The spatiotemporal sequence of the building-gestures seems to depict a striving for unity, a circling around a virtual center in the making. The unfolding of the act of building a scene in the analytical field makes it possible to follow the above process and to perceive the related energic variations as shared feelings. The separation and the integration, the tendency to differentiate the separate parts, but also to unite them, strike me as visible metaphors of an ongoing psychic dynamism.

## 1 Towards the Center

The spontaneous organizational impulse typical of the psyche's integrating function, that impulse which as it evolves tends to construct a more and more integrated whole out of an initial fragmentariness, was acknowledged by Jung in the concept itself of feeling-toned complex even before his theory of self had been formulated. The dissociability of the psyche in the clash with emotions and the subsequent striving for unity, towards a center which blends the fragments of experience into a new representation, seem to be two constituent moments of a spontaneous process of psychic coming-to-be.

The organization of emotional experience into a feeling-toned unity is, in fact, a manifestation of the psyche's tendency to structure itself into centralized units that are split but which even so tend to integrate into new forms by coming into relationship with consciousness. As we have seen, every complex is the result of the integration of a body of sensory, emotional and ideational experiences that have a feeling-tone in common.

The ego taking shape as it develops is itself a complex distinguished by the intrapsychic experience of centrality. Its taking root is closely connected to the whole of our body image that stays with us throughout life with the feeling that we are always the same. Jung perceived this spontaneous undertaking of the psyche in both his personal experience of confronting the unconscious and in his study of patients' dreams and drawings (Jung, 1961, VI, par. 222):

> When I began drawing the mandalas, however, I saw that everything, all the paths I had been following, all the steps I had taken, were leading back to a single point – namely, to the mid-point. It became increasingly plain to me that the mandala is the centre. It is the exponent of all paths. It is the path of the centre, to the individuation (...) I knew that in finding the mandala as an expression of the self I had attained what was for me the ultimate. Perhaps someone else knows more, but not I.

In the history of both individuals and the species, spontaneous human graphic expressions offer a host of observations about this coming-to-be. Rectangular or square shapes, they too typically human, correspond to the possibility of differentiating a still indistinct whole into separate parts, whereas circular shapes stress the striving for unity, typical of the psychic totality, of the self. Proof that the spontaneous striving for centrality appears in the organizational impulse of mental representation comes from studying the "mandalas" of eastern and western origin. In fact, circular forms appear throughout human history, from primitive rock-paintings up to the most sophisticated religious iconography.

It is significant that experiencing the centrality of the emerging ego complex is to be found in the earliest scrawls of children and in myths. Studies of children's drawings show that a striving for the centrality of the figures and patterns involved is a constant feature. Jung found the same motifs in early alchemist writings. In *Psychology and Alchemy* he devoted a chapter to the "Symbolism of the mandala," where he relates the dreams of patients in which mandalas, and recurring circular forms, appear, which (Jung, 1944, par. 126) unless everything deceives us, (...) signify nothing less than a psychic centre of the personality not to be identified with the ego.

Erich Neumann (1949), who studied human imaginal projections as the expression of the self's organizational urge, sees in the Uroborus of Egyptian myths one of the oldest images of this striving for centrality. In his view, the snake swallowing its tail (the original dragon from time immemorial) corresponds to the borderline experience preceding and accompanying the embryonic ego prior to the process of distinguishing between the self and the world.

M. Fordham (1969, 1976) applied this point of view to children, carrying on further investigations. His concept of primary self, seen as "a constant state of integration," represents the totality of the psyche and the soma in a germinal, still undifferentiated state. The psychophysical development of children originates in this condition of initial unity through dynamic processes which he calls "deintegration-integration." What Fordham observed in childhood development and pathology exists throughout life in the dynamic processes that continually modulate the relationship between emotions and the ego complex.

Ernst Bernhard (1969, p. 20), in his comments on the subject, stresses the same basic concept by using the term "entelechy." In the phenomena of life, something operates which contains the goal within itself. The vital urge towards differentiation and subsequent integration "stages" the evolution towards complexity, with considerable emotional alterations in the single individual. The reflective recognition of the process experienced may be reached by altering the level of conscious participation in the phenomenon, and become self-experience.[87]

[87] In reviewing sandplay scenes at a later time (see Chapter XIV above) this level of the integration of feelings may be reached. A transformation comes about in the individual due to the awareness that a process beyond the control of consciousness has guided the building of the play scenes created at the time of the analysis. This is an experience which not only can change the overall view of our personal and analytical history, but also lead to a transformation of our behavior and our possibilities of taking action in life.

Eugenio Gaddini, taking a Freudian approach, maintains the same basic concept (1989, p. 562):

> When referring to the self, I prefer using the term organization, not so much in order to distinguish it formally from its structure (id, ego, superego), but because I believe that the self cannot be spoken of in structural terms. The self is a complex organization which gradually unfolds through elementary means. The mental function is differentiated in more and more complex ways as the organization unfolds.

## 2 Experiencing the Center in the Analytical Field

Once the defenses have been overcome or reduced, when a situation has been created in the analytical field that can encourage the contact between the ego complex and the underlying complex nuclei, a few recurring clinical signs appear. The first clear evidence for the observer is the change of pace in the player's movements. I would say that the emotional inquiry into a feeling the player has experienced is visible in the very sequence of the moves he makes.

The tempo of a player's moves in contact with the materials at hand mirrors the elaboration going on between the ego and the feelings. Normally, an individual's gestures and words are habitual and constant. A different tempo, at moments slower or faster, alternating with pauses, is the first signs of a new relationship with the emotional situation. The pauses and the recommencements of the action show that the patient is looking for a correspondence between the perception of the object and the material and the intuition of a tone or emotional color that is making its way in.

Variations in the pace of the player's movements are evidence of an attempt to single out and delineate similarities and differences. The gestures are much different when they are motivated more by the defenses than by the confrontation with feelings, because they seem repetitious, mechanical, without pauses or second thoughts. When, instead, the path leading to the center is taken other signs as well accompany those just described. Dreams immediately following a given scene often bear the imprint of what has happened through the building of that scene.

## 3 Laura Towards Her Center

When Laura came to me she was deeply depressed. She was 33 and a man she was very attached to had just left her. As a teacher she was highly thought of and though she succeeded in establishing good relationships with the children, she was reserved, of few words, sometimes even standoffish with adults. This attitude was more marked with men, especially if she was attracted to them emotionally. On those occasions it was almost completely impossible for her to express herself, she would withdraw into an excruciating mutism before turning away. It was probably for these reasons that the man she loved failed to understand her feelings. Beneath this rigid defense that appeared like a mask on her face, Laura concealed a particular delicacy and sensitivity that made it possible for her to listen to children.

In the story she told I was struck by the fits of anxiety she frequently experienced as a girl, overwhelming moments often dominated by the fear of being poisoned by eating away from home. Her delicacy, related to an "outside" felt to be dangerous, tinged her self-image with fantasies verging on delirium.

The structure of her beginning scenes, where she used only the sand, bears out the depth of her disturbance, which in the past had involved the very way she experienced her body image. As I remarked before,[88] the use of the play material offers significant indications of the entity and nature of the psychic disturbance in progress, as well as to what extent the ego complex has been compromised. We know, in fact, how closely related physical experience is to psychic self-experience.

Laura's stiffness of expression also immediately showed itself in our relationship: she was precise, punctual, said things in a low voice, placed her writ-

[88] See Chapter II above.

ten dreams on the desk and said nothing. She always chose the chair facing me, moving it as far away as possible. Silence very soon played a leading role between us, lay heavy on us like a cement block that created anxiety in the field. Only her clutched hands revealed the emotional difficulty, while her body was frozen stiff, almost immobile. The few words she uttered were cold, affected, almost as if to avoid any sort of emotional tone, or suddenly harsh, cutting, sometimes even violent. They expressed her self-doubt or the sense of futility for being there in that would-be encounter.

I was contaminated by the emotional tension in the field, felt so incapable of helping her and impotent that I was led to read her dreams and comment on them almost as if to find a foothold. As the months went by, I realized more and more how defensive and useless my talking about the possible meaning of dreams was, while the compulsion to repeat dominated us. The tension present in the analytical field drove me to ask her to have a try at sandplay.

*Contact with the sand releases images and words*. In my notes of the time I discover the series of moves she made. Avoiding contact with the surface, Laura sprinkled some water in the middle of the tray. Her gestures, at first absent-minded and mechanical, gradually became more careful, more thoughtful. At a certain point, she lifted the carafe and poured out a stream of water as if to make a hole in the sand, in a sort of give-and-take between the action of the water and the crumpling sand (Fig. 13, Images). She seemed to be carried away by what she was doing when she said, almost to herself and in a low voice: "It's like the surface of the moon." She suddenly seemed to get an idea, went quickly over to another neighboring tray, scooped all the sand up in the middle to make a hill, and went on pouring water in large quantities. Her gestures, at first slow and deliberate, became quick and mechanical, almost feverish (Fig. 14, Images).

After exclaiming that the surface was lunar, a distinct change in the way Laura worked and expressed herself took place in the field. She passed almost impulsively from the thoughtful and cautious gestures she had just shown to sinking her hands into the sand, dirtying them and pouring out all the water there was.

Today I see this scene again as the first indication that contact had been established with some still obscure emotion, but at the same time as a first significant beginning of a symbolic process. I might even say that that variation in pace and the two forms that appeared, the "lunar-cavity" and the "hill," had brought the emerging narrative structure of the self to the scene. It is as if perceiving the material had set free an organizational pressure that delineated two opposites. The two forms were still divided into two separate scenes, but were part of a single sequence of images that were linked by a narrative structure yet to be discovered.

It is as if the lunar-crater-cavity image Laura had suddenly caught sight of had led her to push beyond her usual confines. And I believe that the hill was not merely the contrary, formally speaking, of the lunar cavity that had appeared just before, but at that moment triggered in Laura an unwonted and contrary self-experience. Through sandplay, two metaphors had appeared in our relationship which, from my point of view, brought out, however obscurely, an experience that Laura was unable to communicate in words.

The analytical field had been enriched by level of expression that went beyond defensive repetition. Those forms could be used as images for understanding the emerging feelings. From my viewpoint, the symbolic activity induced by the materials tended to unite, in two successive scenes, feelings which in the analytical field were experienced as separate and unconsciously projected alternately by her or by me. At the time I only sensed what was happening, and I confined myself to noting with great surprise the emotional change perceived in the analytical field.

The careful notes I took right after the session, which are even easier to understand today, helped me inquire further into the meaning of those gestures. In those intense emotional contexts, Laura established a contact with others, like that untouched and untouchable surface of sand, and seemed to have no possibility of response. The set expression on her face, which could seem to be indifference, reflected her defense against emotions: she was cool and aloof like that moon which had appeared between us. And the following gesture of piling the island-hill up in the middle of the scene and impulsively soaking it with water, dirtying her hands in the process, I later associated with the rare moments when, with unmistakable anger tempered by keen pleasure, Laura sharply criticized our analytical work.

The crater of the moon is an effective metaphor for understanding how at certain moments she saw herself as a woman. In fact, in her relationships with men she often felt exposed and passive, like that surface of sand splashed with water. The hill, in addition, indicated her isolation, the impenetrable silence with which she defended herself to the point of becoming inaccessible to contacts of any kind.

The two separate parts she had created still today help me go back in my memory to the emotional dynamics that were shared in the analytical field. The "crater" and "hill" metaphors make it possible to understand both her painful passiveness and her excitability, both her trying to seem indifferent and the impenetrable force of her isolation. That inaccessible hill also nicely expressed what experiencing me could be like, my silence which she felt to be demanding and which at that time she could counter with only the painful self-emptiness in lack of an adequate response. My tendency to talk about dreams, instead of perceiving and sharing deeply the silence between us, was inspired by the emotional field I had experienced. I eventually realized that this was a way of reacting to my feeling like that extinct crater, under the pressure of invasive and at times agonizing emotions. What I was doing was to try and reach the stability of the "hill" instead of attempting to bring out the narrative structure present in her and between us.

An understanding of the transference and countertransference could begin to make use of the metaphors extracted through sandplay and recognize them as active and operative images between us. Her defenses had long prevailed on a verbal level, inhibiting feelings. So the moment of involuntary words, the voiced exclamation recognizing the moon as she played, was significant. Thinking it over today, that exclamation not only confirmed that an analogy was emerging, but expressed a resonance to the presence of an active image that deeply involved the patient. In fact, exclamations reflect a state of wonder that generally involves all levels of being, also making it possible for us to cry out. The "moon" came as a surprise, as happens when contact with the repressed is unexpectedly established, and ended up completely altering the context.

At that moment, with the image barely perceived, Laura had emerged from her silence and from the disappointing chilliness of that falling water which had dug a hole into the sand. She had pushed beyond the confines she defensively recognized as her own in order to accept the new in the unwonted and feverish act of creating the "hill."

*The hill: a significant metaphor*. Laura went back to the tray only one month later. Though this time she did not wet the sand she did pile it up again in the middle. She divided it carefully into four equal parts, of which only those on the right seemed to stand out against the background (Fig. 15, Images). In the silence that reigned for the entire session, she concentrated on building four bridges between the little hills.

I was struck by the fact that when she started playing again she repeated the form that had appeared the month before. Very intense feelings must have been condensed in the representation if it returned after so much time. It was further proof that that "hill" had been so significant that it returned to immediately force itself upon her imagination again even a month later.

The form in her last sand scene had been picked up again, but immediately transformed into an archipelago of connected islands. The carefully built bridges revealed a striving to reunite and to understand what had appeared to be separate. Her use of the materials had become aware, both in the division into parts and in the building of the bridges. By concentrating on the same image again, I would say that Laura felt the need to divide it up into parts, but at the same time she recomposed it differently. With the four bridges she seemed to be trying to "assess" that obscure presence by outflanking it.

The apparent simplicity of the scenes I have presented so far makes it easy to see the way the representation of feelings is organized. The self, as the hidden hand behind this unfolding which sandplay makes particularly clear, seems to direct the sequence of the scenes. I am not so much interested here in emphasizing that deep feelings seem to be condensed in the forms that have appeared, or in re-examining her particular story, as in pointing out two aspects of this organizing process already to be found in her first series of moves.

The patient's simple choices reveal an initial move which seemed to be seeking correspondences and differences. I would say that, in a still confused emotional context, forms were extracted from the scene that proved useful for knowing Laura better. Correspondences, reexamined today, are not only the result of a personal opinion and of the easy tendency we all have to choose things that correspond to our personal assumptions, but are sustained by the energic effect produced in the field. As we have already remarked, recognizing the "moon" not only released the "hill" metaphor, but also led to a change in the patient's emotional and physical participation. Her gestures themselves moved at a different pace that clearly revealed emotions which her defenses had kept at a safe distance.

A no less significant detail confirming the correspondence that was found is the enduring vitality of the "hill" shape a month after the previous scene. The metaphoric image seems to have become an acquired fact, almost as if it were a signifier that Laura could now dispose of to express what was still an unspeakable experience.

Her participation, like mine as the analyst at that moment, took place on only a superficial level of consciousness. The scene of the archipelagos indicated that, along with the moves aimed at discovering a correspondence, the need arose to coordinate what was taking shape around a virtual center. Formal evidence of this is the circularity suggested by the bridges.

*The center: the "perforated uterus," metaphor of a story.* Three days later, Laura returned to the sand tray, added some water to the dry sand, working it with her hands to find the right consistency. She piled it all up into a hill again, and this time, with smooth and harmonious gestures, ran her fingers over all parts of it, shaping it into a form that stretched diagonally across the tray (Fig. 16, Images).

I find in my notes her keen concentration, the buoyant pace of her contact with the sand. To my perception, her fingers moved skillfully, as if they were dancing. In the photograph, the work on that form shows this lightness of touch. The last thing she did in that session was to carefully and cautiously dig a hole through the top of the hill down to the blue floor of the tray. There was in her digging the attempt to make the hole perfectly round. She worked on it a long time and when she got what she wanted she stopped and looked at it a while as if seized by a sudden impression. "It's a uterus," she said with feeling, "a perforated uterus."

For her, whose defenses were so high, the emotional tone of what she said was unusual, as well as the reference to her intimate parts, to the femininity always excluded from her generally dry and terse manner of speaking. In my notes I find I make a point of the expressive flow of her talk. It was as if her words, along with her playing and her physical movements, gave proof of a more relaxed atmosphere in which she seemed more confident and centered on herself. A quite exceptional atmosphere of free and quiet sharing arose between us in the silence. I always remembered this particular experience as one of those moments when a symbolic or transpersonal perception is activated in the field due to the shared emotional atmosphere in the field.

*The revision nine years later.* I reviewed those scenes with Laura nine years after the end of the analysis. When we went to review the slides of her scenes, which we had both partly forgotten, I realized for the first time what the narrative structure was that linked them together. The above sequence of scenes, like others we reviewed on that occasion, struck us as being closely interrelated and more understandable in view of what had happened in her six years of analytical work. There were like a text which, by becoming more legible, revealed, to our great surprise, a well-constructed story.

The scenes had given rise to a hermeneutic process between us, where further meaning appeared that had escaped us while the scene was being built and which afforded an unexpected comprehension of emotions and feelings we had shared and experienced in the analytical field in those years of analysis. The impression I still get today from the above sequence of scenes, as from the notes I took at the time, is that a complex experience was condensed in the images which only years later could acquire greater legibility and the possibility of being translated into words.

In the act of playing, the patient realizes what is happening in a still vague or subconscious way, as a barely perceivable state dominated by a sense of necessity which, unrecognized, determines his choices and placements. Only the later reviewing made it possible for the underlying unitary narrative structure of that process, which characterizes the individual scene-building as well as the order of the scenes, to be discovered and recognized with surprise.

Self-experience in the act of playing is felt as a compositional need that for the most part escapes the consciousness of both. There are, at any rate, moments of particular emotional intensity in which a symbolic experience is perceived in the analytical field.

The "perforated uterus" described above was one of those transforming moments shared by patient and analyst alike. What emerged above all during the review was the logic of the sequence of scenes which created surprise and amazement in the player. In her innermost being, there where each of us was convinced we were the masters of our choices, something unexpected had happened. Anyone who has had the experience senses that something other has moved and operated in obedience to some unknown command.

I would like to point out one aspect of the review which shows the difference in the level of participation I have tried to explain. In reviewing the "lunar crater," the "hill," and the "archipelago" together, a significant correspondence with the narrative structure of feelings experienced and recognized in analysis was rediscovered in those choices. In the review those forms struck us as anticipations, as metaphors laden with shared emotional dynamics, which then and there were still indefinite for our consciousness. What had already been represented allusively in the play scene only later could begin to be recognized and distinguished in words.

In reviewing the "perforated uterus," instead, communication between us took on a different tone. Laura's attention was first focused on the round hole which she had forgotten. Here are the associations she made, according to my notes:

> It's like a piercing eye that forces you to stay fixed, that exercises a power of its own...

and:

> It's like a spiral leading inside or a black hole that shatters the unity of the whole, a tension... each of us has a black hole.

These words showed her intense emotional participation in the presence of that image. The tone of her words and the pauses in what she said were different from her associations in the previous scenes. I remember that then and there I was struck by her referring to feelings shared and lost, like the suicide of a friend who spoke to her of his "black hole," without her being able to foresee what would happen a little later. It was as if during review many painful themes of her story had coagulated around that hole, which was unexpected and forgotten, strangely enough, considering the intensity that had accompanied its making.

As I listened in silence, certain significant moments in our analytic relationship came to mind. I remembered when she succeeded in sharing the sense of contrition and abandon she felt while masturbating, moments of pleasure and at the same time of anger towards herself. I recalled her irrational fear of being poisoned by food eaten away from home, the incoercible dependency on her parents as well as the almost uncontrollable hatred.

As we watched the slide of that scene, Laura's words and my memories circled around that hole just as she had done in her careful digging years earlier. Only after that did she turn her attention to the rest of the scene, to that uterus which she had molded with her light rhythmic touch, signs of which are still visible in the photograph.

What she said at that moment regarded basic issues that had emerged in analysis. Dominating them all was the memory of her mother, of her emotional solitude as a woman, which had made a deep impression on her. The family myth of how disappointing her birth had been because she was the second girl reappeared, as well as her violent jealousy of the brother who was born later and loved more. That at the sight of the photograph a tissue of such old and deep feelings had been reactivated in the field also seemed to be proved by a dream she had the next day:

> I saw myself stretched out on the bed I slept in as a girl with two obscure female figures hovering over me. My throat was clamped in a vice, I wanted to but could not speak. I realized the analyst was present, but further away. I could only move my hands to try and make myself be seen and catch his attention.

I immediately thought that it was precisely her hands which, through sand-play, had eventually opened my eyes to her nearly inaccessible world. The dream introduced something else into the field, proving the effect that our re-viewing had had: words felt to be impossible, referring to a specific period of her life, now reemerged in the dream, whereas reviewing that scene had re-leased feelings which had never been expressed. The hole in the scene from so long ago had probably coagulated a sense of impotence that was now "repre-sented" in the dream as a choked scream.

In my notes of the time I found a trace of something she said at the end of the session:

> Sometimes you touch with your hand [see with your own eyes] and believe.

I remember that then and there this seemed paradoxical to me, being over-emphatic, exaggerated, but at the same time plausible. In fact, it corresponded to an atmosphere of complete emotional sharing.

The perception I remember distinctly having had during the session, and which now reappeared between us, though involving us less, was of a particu-lar charged psychic event, apparently neither hers nor mine, but "third," trans-personal, between us. It was one of the experiences in which I believe I shared that particular emotional dimension Jung called "numinous"[89] (Jung, 1938/ 1940, par. 6):

> The *numinosum* is either a quality belonging to a visible object or the influence of an invisible presence that causes a peculiar alteration of consciousness.

I believe that on that occasion a very special condition of consciousness had been activated which, when it is genuine and not the result of psychic inflation, can have a transforming effect on the personality. The over-emphatic words of the time were confirmed again while reviewing the scene years later.

In the days following the review, Laura recounted an incidental episode. She had gotten into a quarrel with someone who had unfairly criticized her on the job. Thinking about it with deep feeling, she had a fantasy of threatening that person with an object:

> It was the perforated uterus – she said in amazement – as if it were an ostentorium held up against someone who was out to hurt you.

What struck me was that in the fantasy the image of the scene we had just reviewed was replaced by a living Christian symbol, namely the consecrated host. After a period of years, an event similar in its emotional intensity and in the tone of Laura's conscious participation had reappeared. A single thread, an identical character which I might describe as an "overtone," connected different levels of emotional experience. The flowing pace of her gestures, which I had noticed while she was building the scene, the form itself of the image in which two very distinct opposites in the above-mentioned process were joined together, and lastly the emotional experiences her words brought back to the reviewing: all these expressions, on more and more integrated levels of consciousness, revealed an experience that was like rediscovering a center of force that created balance. The "self as other" seems to be the best way to describe this experience.

[89] Jung borrowed the term "numinous" from Rudolf Otto (1917).

Laura's consciousness began to perceive the autonomous movement of her psyche towards a new center of balance in a unified way, though experiencing firsthand even intense emotional variations. One last thing she said made me see this aspect. Looking at the slide, she realized that her attention moved back and forth between the body of the uterus and the hole; it was as if her consciousness was given to canceling out one or the other in turn, whereas the scene showed their coming together. She could find no associations for the form that joined them together. If you think of it, that symbolic form we had shared, and which had already revealed great vitality at the time it was built and again years later during the review, suggested a blueprint of integration that had yet to be carried out.

# XVIII New Paths, New Goals

*In the same way that the body needs food, and not just any kind of food, but only what suits it, the psyche needs to know the meaning of its existence – not just any meaning, but the meaning of those images and ideas which reflect its nature and which originate in the unconscious.* C.G. Jung (1945/1954) par. 476

At the end of this survey of the landscapes the psyche succeeds in building through sandplay, I have the feeling I still have a great deal to see and understand.

In the beginning, I emphasized how useful an instrument this method had been for opening new and unusual perspectives of communication in the analytical field. Shared speech and playing, in their relationships and differences, offered me a new possibility for perceiving psychic phenomena. My clinical experience was therefore enriched by a further occasion to reflect on events shared with patients and on my participation: using sandplay allowed me to observe from a different angle the patient's inner world, and the emotions and feelings that emerge in the analytical field and can involve both the patient and the analyst.

Looking back now on the landscapes of the psyche I have visited with companions in analytical work, some of which I have described in the present text, I realize how much this experience helped me to take a closer look at many aspects of the theoretical principles that guide me in the analytical field. Chapter by chapter, my point of reference has constantly been Jung's research and theoretical approach. His way of seeing things is complex and I do not always share it, but it is full of valuable insights that have yet to be investigated and verified in clinical experience.

In our intriguing work we know we must never stop asking "how" we observe what is happening in the analytical field, together with describing and delimiting "what" we think we recognize, until in the end we succeed in hypothesizing a "why." The psychic event that involves both participants and which, in itself, in its constitutional complexity, is never fully definable, requires a constant revision of the theoretical frame of reference our approach in the analytical field is based on.

I have tried to show how sandplay is a natural outgrowth of certain basic concepts of Jungian research. Using it in the analysis of adults represents an important development because of the epistemological implications it involves but, upon closer examination, it is another product of the same theoretical approach.

For the kind of experience it proposes in the analytical situation, sandplay arouses curiosity and interest in therapists, together with legitimate doubts and sometimes inexplicable rejections. There are persistent mental stereotypes which in this case are activated primarily by the "concreteness" of the play situation and the relationship with objects belonging to the analyst. With adults especially greater is the fear of an impulsive "acting out" or the suspicion that the regression will have negative repercussions on the interpersonal communication. All this still makes it impossible to understand when, how, and in which psychic field, the physical experience of playing can, on the contrary, be a symbolic vehicle of deep emotions which words often fail to convey.

The matter must be approached with enthusiasm and intellectual honesty in order for the problems raised to be examined with a critical eye.[90] As I said, the main obstacle for an objective judgment would seem to be related most of all to the fact that sandplay involves a physical participation: it is feared that this level of experience may evoke the phantasms that are always lurking in every analysis. Primary emotions connected with life-and-death impulses may be experienced in a particular and intense way when the body becomes the vehicle of communication, but it is also true that, precisely on this level, unexpected channels can be found for reaching symbolic representation.

[90] Pignatelli (1994, p. 157) clearly expresses the legitimate doubts of the analyst who has had no direct experience with sandplay.

## 1 An Instrument for Research

I am convinced that using concrete play activities with adults may widen our view and let us see, in a new perspective, the role mental representation has in the psychic economy. In fact, adults, who have at their disposal a more highly differentiated capacity for introspection and communication than children, represent a very promising experimental field of research.

The perspective the relationship between shared speech and playing provides has allowed me to see more clearly the emotional variations that accompany the phenomenon and to investigate more thoroughly the interpersonal conditions of the field that encourage it. It is a way of reactivating and provoking in the analytical situation the transforming event which can come about when a representation takes shape through the act of playing. Experiencing the imaginal process on a bodily level and carrying it to the concrete visibility of the scene make it possible to study the effects it has, at that particular moment, on the intrapsychic and interpersonal level. When the representation becomes visible in dreams, fantasies or playing, we are in the presence of a significant moment in the process of the symbolization of feelings, whose importance as a transforming force is still underrated.

Playing was immediately placed in the category of desires, as it certainly should be, but I believe it is also right to include it in the category of vital needs. I am convinced that representations that give expression to feelings, in both the previsual and visual stage, come about as a need, in all ages of life, at moments when new responses have to be found. As human beings have always testified (and continue to testify), both ontogenetically and phylogenetically. It is a need which has always figured in human experience: from rock-drawings in prehistoric caves to the intuition of modern-day man that a solution must be found to a vitally important problem.[91]

[91] Apropos of this, Carotenuto (1998, p. 117) writes: "It is precisely by virtue of the marvels that men began to admire creation and the first questions arose about nature and life. We may consider it a primary, essential emotion which merges inquiry and doubt, an ecstatic stupor that does not give way to mystery but is indeed tempted to unveil it."

Crucial to analytical research was understanding that such a need takes a creative turn when the individual is forced to face up to his limitations and the pain of losing preexistent certainties. It is easy, in fact, to lapse defensively into the grandiloquence of creativity, overlooking the other side of an experience that intimates an elusive dimension, often terrifying in its strangeness.

A no less important step was realizing that for this typically human need to come to bear a concrete area of experience is required where perceptive reality and imagination meet in order to conceive and give shape to feelings. In the end it is out of this melting-pot that the emotions and ideas emerge which we succeed in expressing in words, the concepts which inspire thinking, new ways of seeing and working.[92] An artist friend of mine expressed this relationship very lucidly (Lai, 2000):

> Man needs to put together the visible and the invisible, so he makes up fables, myths, legends, festivities, songs, art.

I think Jung (1937, par. 241) suggested a way for better understanding the phenomenon when he introduced the theory of "reflective instinct" or "reflective impulse"[93]:

> Ordinarily we do not think of "reflection" as ever having been instinctive, but associate it with a conscious state of mind. *Reflexio* means bending back and, used psychologically, would denote the fact that the reflex which carries the stimulus over into its instinctive discharge is interfered with by psychization (...) *Reflexio* is turning inwards, with the result that, instead of an instinctive action, there ensues a succession of derivative contents or state which may be termed reflection or deliberation. Thus in place of the compulsive act there appears a

[92] Winnicott was the first to conceive the transforming importance of this intermediary or potential area. The function of illusion (*in-ludus*) is fundamental in Winnicott's theory and analytical practice. See Winnicott (1971) and Chapter VI above.
[93] I have already considered this aspect in Chapter VI.

certain degree of freedom, and in place of predictability a relative unpredictability as to the effect of the impulse.

After being "taken" by the experience of what Jung calls "reflective instinct," patients often defend themselves: they abandon the field where they have chanced upon feelings, memories and still obscure sensations through their organization into a scene, as if they needed to hold what has happened at a focal distance, sometimes even forgetting it, because it is not always something that consciousness finds easy to bear.

But as we have seen from the examples given in the present volume, the vitality of this experience can emerge spontaneously in any case. As is already born out during the playing by words that are different in tone or by sudden memories. The phenomenon can also make its presence felt in dreams that appear after coming into contact with sandplay. In the course of analysis, what has taken shape in the play scene can become, for the patient and the analyst himself, a meaningful metaphor, sometimes a constant point of reference, for understanding the feelings shared in the relationship.

A specific characteristic of sandplay, compared with other methods that use the body as the vehicle of symbolization, is precisely the variety of interconnected levels of expression: from the tactile and proprioceptive sensations engendered by contact with the sand, to their relationship with the visual perceptions of the forms and chosen objects, and finally to the direct confrontation with the concrete space of the field in the way they are placed. It is a complex organization that relates previsual aspects of the emotional experience up until they are integrated visually.

Sandplay provides a multilevel network of stimuli, in which primitive ways of feeling combine with differentiated perceptions, up to the final unitary organization of a representation that encapsulates them. Using sand, where touch and kinesthesis prevail, evokes the oldest level of relationship with emotions experienced in the period of growth. It can activate an emotional experience that is archetypal in character and intensity. Using different objects in the play space is in itself a perception that paves the way to a multilevel confrontation and dialogue with feelings.

I maintain, therefore, that in sandplay the physical rapport with emotions and feelings in the relationship is given two channels of symbolic expression; it is structured according to archetypal procedures and intensities in the handling of the materials and the choosing of objects, whereas, by creating spatiotemporal relationships between them, it implements levels of reflective experience corresponding to the ego complex and levels of partial consciousness.

Consequently, these two channels of symbolization facilitate the activation of often troubling or invasive feeling-toned complexes. Which is why, when the path of bodily experience is taken, the different levels of activation must be kept in mind if an analytical attitude is to be reached that is aware of the forces involved. Sandplay can, in fact, stimulate a direct confrontation with feelings that can upset the sometimes unstable balance of consciousness.

As we know, the great communicative potentiality of imaginal experiences through the body is often not accompanied by corresponding possibilities of elaboration. I believe sandplay, in the antinomic prospect I have set forth in these pages, opens a field of investigation full of possible developments for studying the influence of bodily experience with respect to feelings, with the consequent effect on the time an analysis will take.

For me, the flexibility of sandplay, as well as its capacity to encourage elaboration in patients, lies precisely in the way its levels of expression are organized through images that reveal a close correspondence to verbal language. In fact, the basic assumption of this book is that this particular form of preverbal symbolization shows a deep similarity to verbal language. The spatiotemporal organization of a scene is like a language structure that connects subjects and objects consecutively. In the act of playing, objects are chosen and interrelated just like language denominates the feelings expressed and lastly indicates with verbs the relationship between the subject and one's experience. From this standpoint, the individual elements of a scene play the same important role that words do when they are organized into a unified story. It is this feature that distinguishes sandplay from other present-day methods of bodily symbolization, which makes it particularly suited to analysis and least exposed to the risks of other forms that use the body to activate the imagination.[94]

There is another aspect I would like to emphasize: sandplay's flexibility, the result of the differentiated perceptive levels it offers, runs up against a constitutional limit. Every prefabricated object can satisfy the patient's requests and building intentions only to a certain extent and therefore demands adaptation. I believe that, paradoxically, this disadvantage provokes a need for an even greater definition, which finds a specific means of expression by carefully pondering the way every object is chosen and placed and the way the space of the scene is used. The constitutional limit of sandplay, with respect to the player's looking, has the same effect as the shift from private to shared speech. It is a limit that makes us sense the inadequacy of our means of communication, both verbal and imaginal, and which consequently inspires a fruitful need for further defining.

## 2 Suggestions for Clinical Research

I would like to end by indicating several areas of future research in which sandplay can make an important contribution to our understanding. I am convinced that through sandplay certain essential aspects always present in the confrontation with the psyche can find important and useful suggestions for further investigation.

*Transference-countertransference in play scenes.* When players succeed in entering into the spirit of sandplay and in trusting the perceptions the sand and the objects in that space give them, imagination can start guiding their moves. A

[94] A comparative research is still lacking between the various forms of bodily symbolization of feelings, such as drawing, dance-therapy or the various techniques used today in art-therapy. I believe it is necessary to establish their differences with respect to sandplay in order to begin to start discussing what each method has to offer, its advantages and risks and its possible use in analytical practice.

kind of emotional relationship with the event is created which Jung, borrowing the term from Levy-Bruhl, called "mystic participation" (1921, par. 781):

> It consists in the fact that the subject cannot clearly distinguish himself from the object but is bound to it by a direct relationship which amounts to partial identity. This identity results from an *a priori* oneness of subject and object. *Participation mystique* is a vestige of this primitive condition (...) Among civilized peoples it usually occurs between persons, seldom between a person and a thing. In the first case it is a transference relationship, in which the object (as a rule) obtains a sort of magical – i.e. absolute – influence over the subject. In the second case there is a similar influence on the part of the thing, or else an *identification* with a thing or the idea of a thing.

This observation, dating from 1921, foretells later developments in analytical research[95] and provides a theoretical framework for something which, over recent years, has become increasingly clearer to me. In the situation described above, it is as if the relationship with the object conveyed feelings which up to that moment were subconscious or unconscious. The participation patients experience as they organize the building of a scene is not only endopsychic or intrapersonal, but reveals an effect on the field; at certain moments it becomes distinctly interpersonal and can also involve the analyst.

That "thing," the object or the form made out of sand, apparently the patient's very own, has such a deep effect on the field as to induce emotions and feelings that cannot always be controlled consciously. I realized this when I found certain scenes so unbearable I was forced to put them aside and refuse to photograph them as I usually do. Fortunately, my professional sense of duty and my customary courtesy always prevailed, because later those same scenes would turn out to convey overwhelming emotional charges and lead me to understand the ongoing emotions and my consequent defense.[96] In other words, I

[95] I am thinking in particular of the phenomenon of projective identification brought out by Melanie Klein.

[96] In the previous chapter, I describe the sequence of Laura's first sand scenes, which by no coincidence I had forgotten for years until she returned for other reasons and we began the revision together.

contend that a close relationship exists between the forms that appear in the scene and the transference and countertransference dynamics that are active in the relationship. The choice of objects and their placings in the space of the scene seem to be connected to the forms of participation via identification and projection Jung spoke of.

I believe that the spatiotemporal structure of a scene can help us approach and understand invasive emotional experiences that we find hard to acknowledge by creating a new viewpoint of the narrative tissue of identifications and cross-projections that are part of the transference process. Only with time did I realize that the most deeply involving emotional dynamics in the analytical field were connected with objects or forms that had appeared in the scene. What opened my eyes, in particular, was reviewing the process through the images in the sand scenes.

I remember that in the beginning I started my research by dividing the play-area into zones in order to verify in which zone the objects that seemed to induce less controllable feelings in the analytical field appeared most frequently.[97] I later realized that the complexity of the process could not be understood by taking only the space into account, but that both the moment of representation, hence the temporal sequence, and the object's level of expression (natural, abstract, imaginary or realistic) had to be considered. There appeared behind every sandplay form emotionally "active" in the field of encounter with patients, a more complex tissue of determinants. As I mentioned in previous chapters, I was sometimes able to approach the phenomenon only years later. What is certain, however, is that the awareness some objects more than others were able to inspire in me had a positive effect on my attitude.

Asking questions and paying attention to the details of every play-choice, always keeping the feelings present in mind, allowed me to see how some ob-

[97] I have dealt with this question elsewhere (Aite, 1976) on the basis of clinical experience, and advanced several hypotheses about the image-producing value of specific zones of the playing field, which had been shown by French researchers working with the "Imaginary Village Test" (Macchielli, 1960, pp. 223 ff.). The same subject has recently been taken up again by Joel Ryce-Menuhin (1992).

jects, in certain situations of the field, were metaphors charged with emotional experiences shared in analysis, to be reintroduced at the right moment, also through interpretation. I believe this opens a path for exploring the whens and hows of an effective interpretation.

When I think back now on some of the objects that were the carriers of "active fantasies" and triggered emotions in the analytical field, I see again some of the play scenes described in previous chapters. I recall, for example, the sudden invasion of color in Eva's scene, in which the "statue with the broken legs" appeared (Chapter XII, Figs. 11 and 11a, Images). Only gradually did I realize how much the transferential dynamics which had long immobilized me, turned me, as it were, into a statue, face-to-face with feelings which had been over-invasive for both of us, had already been expressed in that metaphor. The association of this metaphor with feelings shared in the analytical field, and the interpretation through images that subsequently took place in the analysis, changed the feeling-tone between us, opening the way to new possibilities of communication.

Equally unexpected in the young man's scene described in Chapter IX (Figs. 10 and 10a, Images) was the "bleeding wound" that suddenly burst onto the playing field, preventing the riders from reaching the peak. That red slash not only revealed in the patient's first sandplay the castration anxiety he had not yet mentioned, but was also the metaphor of a division between us, of his keeping me at a distance, inducing in the field an idealization of the relationship I secretly complied with in order to hold off emotional charges I found hard to contain.

I then noticed how in the relationship between shared feelings and play scenes the emotional dynamics in the analytical field changed as the objects used changed: from impersonal forms to more and more personalized forms that lay close to the domain of the ego. The more invasive and capable feelings were of arousing distinct countertransferential reactions, the more the materials or colors rather than objects were the vehicles of expression. In a series of sandplay scenes built over a period of time I was able to see this difference quite clearly.[98] In other words the change in the level of expression in the playing field can bring about evident energic transformations in the analytical field.

These first observations suggest a possibility for research that has yet to be investigated. They offer the analyst a new viewpoint of the emotional processes and their transformations in the analytical field.

*The structure of scenes and psychopathological cases.* Observing the relationship between the structure of scenes in their spatiotemporal unfolding and various psychopathological disorders has opened up new perspectives. Further indicative lines of investigation have emerged that will be better understood as sandplay is gradually put to greater clinical use.

In the forms of deepest psychic suffering, the sand and the colors are, in my experience, often the most effective symbolic conveyors of split or repressed feeling-toned complexes. This possibility of expression is often preceded by a defensive phase in which play-actions devoid of rhythm, almost mechanical, make use of objects but avoid contact with the sand.

I would like to point out something else: when a symbolic process is set into motion in which anxiety-laden complex-nuclei attain representation, the forms that gradually emerge often assume partial aspects of a whole. For example, only one part of a body will appear in the form of an object or a shape made out of the sand: a head, a limb, instead of a whole figure. I have always been very struck by this sort of choice because it touches on the dread of disintegration, with the painful fragmentation of a vital whole. What appears can be seen as a "part object" but from my point of view I prefer the term "part personal-

[98] The Anna series described in Chapter III shows the same development. At first, the impersonal use of sand and color found a correspondence in the more violent emotional dynamics existent between us, whereas the gradual personalization of the imagery went hand in hand with a deep change in our shared feelings. Sometimes also during the building of a scene, the relationship induced between the transition from personal to impersonal and vice versa in the representation, and the emotional charges shared in the analytical field, can be distinguished. See the building sequence in Eva's scene described in Chapter XII.

ity."[99] This term in fact presupposes the idea of a transforming process of feeling that tends towards a harmonious whole, which can be represented by personification, and at the same time expresses the failure of this undertaking because of a dissociation experienced as an irreparable loss.[100]

The type of objects used in the course of events opens other perspectives: stones, plants, abstract or imaginary forms collective in character, at first distinctly prevail over miniature objects of human figures from various facets of real life. These choices are highly indicative, in that they differ from the human personifications that lie closest to everyday experience. It is symptomatic that during a process of symbolization, when the relationship with feelings is stabilized and

[99] For a clearer understanding of this, see Anna's play scenes as described in Chapter III. By observing them now one after the other, a double process of differentiation in the symbolization can be noticed. At first, the sand and color are used to produce a "monster" head, like a two-dimensional drawing (Fig. 1, Images) which eventually develops into evermore clearly defined three-dimensional forms, like the bust of the "African witch-doctor" (Fig. 3, Images) and ultimately the "dragon" that speaks to the little girl (Fig. 8, Images). Out of the representation of part objects that suggest a wholeness without representing it, a first whole figure – the "dragon" – gradually emerges. The forms that appear, aside from being partial, assume a primarily archetypal, transpersonal, imaginal character, as in fairy-tales. But from the very first sand scene a process of symbolization also appears that tends more and more towards a personification that lies close to the ego dimension. The character of these images, at first imaginary and still vague, like the "woman that isn't," the reflection of a woman's face in the water (Fig, 2, Images), becomes more concrete and realistic, like the representation of the little girl (Fig, 8, Images) who succeeds in talking to the "dragon." Besides these two levels of symbolization I would like to point out the changes that take place in their reciprocal relationship. In the beginning, when what still prevailed in Anna was the archetypal character of the representation, with respect to forms related to the experience of the ego, the emotions and feelings in the analytical field were undefined and intense and involved us both deeply. Looking at the entire sequence today I notice that as the differentiation process gradually took shape and ended up defining whole figures, the intensity of the feelings in the relationship also changed. The struggle to transform the representation of separate parts into a whole figure endowed with meaning is a process which, in Anna's case, is expressed on both levels. Symbolization that is archetypal and personal in character, but most of all the relationship between these two levels of representation, have changed with time, distinctly so in symptomatological terms.

[100] See the clinical experience described at the end of Chapter XII.

the dialogue becomes more fluent and richer in personal contents, this second type of personified choices tends to prevail over the initial collective forms.

The scene Enrico commented on in Chapter XIII (Fig. 12, Images) shows the fragmentation as well as the impersonal choice of objects. I recall the two pieces of bark representing lovers in the middle of the scene, the standing tree trunk, the lichen. The plantlike nature of these objects was offset by the only personifications present: clowns and ballerinas.

Does this way of representing mean anything? Does the combining of partial, impersonal forms and differentiated personifications offer a perspective for understanding the organization of borderline personalities? By following these first indications can we see the difference between these scenes and those scenes where the representation assumes the character of a neurotic structure, as appears, quite distinctly, I feel, in the student's scene described in Chapter IX (Fig. 10, Images). Here the objects are set into a harmonious whole where the personifications are complete and consistent.

*Confronting the psychotic experience.* The recent introduction of sandplay into public mental health institutions has led to research on a larger scale than what has been so far possible privately. Experiments are being carried out with psychotic adults in individual and group psychotherapy.[101]

I believe that the characteristics of sandplay are well suited to further research into psychotic disturbances, which can either invade and completely overwhelm an individual or occupy only certain areas of his personality without apparently endangering its unity. Approaching and sharing the experiences of the psychotic is at once difficult and deeply involving. Psychotic anxiety tends to contaminate anyone approaching it, triggering emotions that are hard to contain. It is, in fact, a psychic condition that, in more serious cases, is distinguished by the loss of a boundary line between subject and object, between

[101] See in this respect the section of the 3rd National AIPA Conference devoted to "Serious mental disorders and sandplay in public and private institutions," in *Studi Junghiani*, Vol. 3, N. 5/6 (1997). See in particular Bona Pompei (1997), Fersurella (1997), Porseo (1997). Sandplay has recently been used with groups of psychotic patients; see Malinconico (1999).

inside and outside, between intrapsychic and interpersonal, between emotions and the surrounding world.

From a psychodynamic point of view, in the psychotic experience invasive emotional tensions with an extreme need for nearness alternate with phases of untold distance: in certain stark moments, the need for others alternates with panic due to their very presence (Maffei, 1977, pp. 13-53). In this fluctuation between total isolation and a contact that seeks symbiosis, creating an intermediate space between inside and outside, between oneself and the other, is difficult.

Psychotics seem to be blocked, as if imprisoned in dominant, repetitive images that come out in their behavior, in their gestures and facial expressions, as well as in their words and the figures that appear in their drawings or sandplay scenes. In psychotic or prepsychotic states aspects of the collective unconscious emerge that produce basic ontological life-and-death conditions. It is precisely these experiences that gave the young Jung his first insights into the collective unconscious: the fantasy material seems to be organized according to recurring narrative structures typical of myths, also in different individuals. In each one of them, the forms of imagination recall the same motifs to be found in religious iconography, in myths and folk tales. Their presence in this sort of pathology offers further indirect proof that the differentiation of an individual whose evolution has been blocked is replaced by deep collective determinants.

In the attempt to understand this mysterious continent of psychotic experience, ways must be found for entering the zone of total isolation and non-communication present in the interpersonal field, and at the same time for recognizing and controlling any possible contagion by very powerful emotional charges. We know, in fact, that by confusing inside with outside, oneself with the world, the psychotic is able to experience what is intrapsychic as extrapsychic, and vice versus. In child and adult therapy, the aim of sandplay is to provide a space in which the capacity to represent experience may be activated, be given a form.

As I mentioned earlier, typical of the psychotic state are the highly invasive psychic charges which often have a ruinous effect on the therapist's ability to perceive and participate emotionally. One might say that the patient's gestures and words, whether coherent or not, tend to occupy every corner of the relationship, bring about a symbiotic approachment or an apparently autonomous distancing so intense as to absorb or exclude the relationship. The therapist contaminated by the ongoing emotions can become the object of the patient's disorder and no longer the observer only.

Without question the psychotic state activates the most archaic nuclei of the analyst's unconscious that leads to the loss of that distancing which enables him to listen to and distinguish field-induced emotions so as to be able to picture them. Consequently, the psychotic charge also induces the participating observer to confuse inside with outside, deprives him, in other words, of that intermediate or potential space in which intrapsychic and interpersonal, perception and representation, enter into relationship.[102] Feelings of listless withdrawal to the point of unconquerable boredom, a sense of sterility due to the glaciation of all emotions, alternate with moments of apprehension and anxiety, at times experienced on a physical level.

At first, when patients go on ignoring the sand tray, the therapist must carry out a containment, even resort to physical contact and, if necessary, to the use of drugs which, by weakening the psychotic core that has taken possession of the patient's entire personality, can make it easier to establish when he should intervene. It is very important that the therapist has around him a team that helps him reflect and understand the deep activation produced by the psychotic nuclei.

To succeed in using sandplay and stimulating the disposition to represent means creating a point of reference and of anchorage for both participants. It is along this line of thinking that I will try to answer one question in particular: does the return to a process of symbolization, that comes about through playing with sand and objects, release some possibility of symbolic transformation and hence of communication, even in someone afflicted by this severe disorder?

Gaetano Benedetti calls the therapeutic approach stemming from his research "configurating psychotherapy" (Benedetti, 1997, p. 223):

[102] These terms are mediated by Winnicott's research (1971).

> In psychotherapy the effect of images can be deduced from the fact that the defense structures in the character of certain patients are founded on a psychic layer between language and emotional life. These defense structures are circumvented thanks to the direct access to the images, whose libidinal investment or explanatory dynamics break down the defenses, as it were, from "below" without any direct verbal confrontation with the conceptual issues (...) The regression of patients who paint or draw may be compared to the rapt concentration of children as they play, of children who, defending themselves against the pressing needs of the outside world, discover the path of the inner *imagines* that are devised as transitional objects between past and future. Contained in the blueprint of an image, as in playing, is a "trial and error" action in which involuntary gestures measure and, by configurating, interpret the degree and demands of the phantasmic reality itself.

I agree with Benedetti and feel that what he says applies equally to sandplay, which also aims at configurating. The reference to children and their playing by no accident includes the relationship with objects, as a physiological way of coping with emotions during growth.

What is still missing, however, is the idea that is central to this book, namely that the use of materials and objects in a concrete space is a path that can also taken by adults. By offering a way of relating to emotions and feelings which also in childhood precedes the capacity to draw, another path has opened up for research. I believe that the therapist who uses sandplay with both children and adults, with the concrete play area as his referent, has an additional possibility for studying psychotic phenomena encountered in the relationship. I recall in this regard therapeutic experiments carried out with psychotic children (Gabbriellini and Nissim, 1989). At first the children had no contact with their interlocutor or with the play area; they simply charged into the room or annihilated the entire space. They were imprisoned in their stereotypes, would explode into sudden gesticulations or shouts, as if reacting to images or hallucinations seen in a total confusion between inside and outside. While sharing these experiences in supervision, I was struck first of all by the way the space was used. The initial chaos filled every corner of the room indiscriminately and then converged gradually onto the sand tray. It was most of all the therapist's psychic capacity for self-restraint, the attention he paid to his emotional reactions, that made this transition possible. At a certain moment, the playing field, at first rejected, then set upon and swept clean, was "discovered" in its "perceptive responses." When the space was accepted and recognized, using the material began to serve the imagination. The changes in the surface of the sand and the objects used were like interlocutors in an imaginary exchange between the child and that field. In other words, the playing space, at first ignored and then attacked, eventually became a protagonist which, resistant and indestructible to attacks of any kind, gradually imposed its concrete presence. As we know, sand is sensitive to the slightest gesture, the slightest touch, interacting with the player in a fascinating way. Children, like adults, approach the sand with interest; it enables that exchange between body and matter which, in my opinion, is one of the oldest mainsprings of the capacity to think.

This possibility implicit in sandplay is greater than the possibility offered by drawing, which presumes the ability to copy structured forms. Sand is significant in itself for it succeeds in activating not only visual, but tactile kinesthetic perceptions which facilitate the appearance of psychic situations very early on (Gabbriellini and Nissim, 1989, p, 48):

> Sand, which is malleable and indestructible and can be shaped, moistened and touched in endless ways, appears to be an "object-forerunner" in the sense that it provides and withstands tactile sensations which form the basis of the previsual mental material.[103]

It is important to observe the gestural or verbal changes in patients, whether adult or children, with respect to the way the various expressive possibilities of sand are used: from simply taking note of the marks left when the surface is touched, to seeing how the suggestion is taken to finish off a form that is still barely intelligible. Contacting the sand opens up a series of expressive levels that bear a relationship to previsual emotional material. The way the sand is used can also be seen as a true metaphor of the relationship established with the

[103] "Object-forerunner" and "previsual mental material" are terms taken from Balint (1968).

analyst. In the initial stage, the analyst is treated exactly like the sand which has the great virtue of being at once malleable and indestructible. With training, the therapist can also become “malleable” and let deep emotions affect him in a sharing that are sometimes very hard to handle. Just as touching the sand leaves a mark, so the analyst who has succeeded in assuming the right attitude must let emotions sink into him while retaining at the same time the possibility of recognizing them, of defining them, also with the assistance of a control group to help him maintain the necessary focal distance for perceiving. A guiding principle of great importance is the possibility of checking whether what is happening in the environment and in the playing field is the expression of an emotional contagion that is infecting the analyst’s personality. He can from time to time compare what he is experiencing to the way patients are using the sand and the objects. I believe that the therapist who has firmly established his position in the field, also visually speaking, has greater possibilities of understanding and confronting psychotic dynamics.

Paying attention to what is happening visually in the way the space and the materials are used takes on even greater importance when one follows the evolution of verbal sounds: from stifled cries to words hurled like objects, along with the stories that dramatize what is happening in the tray. It is a different way of listening to and viewing the same emotional event in the analytical field: from the confusion of words upon momentary contact to words that give meaning.

Sandplay provides a valuable perspective of the complex expressive intertwining, constantly stressed in these pages, between play and verbal levels, of representation and words. When patients establish contact with the sand tray and accept the experience, the effect on their verbalization is immediate. A consulting room that includes sandplay always offers this prospect. Verbalizing seems to be constant in psychotic patients, as well. In other words, when an emotion finds a perceptual foothold and becomes visible in a representation an emotional and energic variation takes place in the analytical field that touches both participants.

My experience with pychoses is still too limited, but I believe that future inquiry will make it possible to detect different phases or levels of relationship with images. In some cases, I was struck by how the use of objects, in the midst of an outpouring of words, brought about changes in the pace and tone of the words, as is the case with neurotics, but also sudden witty remarks as unexpected as some weird object. In later stages, words are coordinated with gestures and comment upon them. The convergence of playing and words alters the relational field. In these situations, it has always seemed to me that I had left behind the initial chaos and started to think and feel again. The coordination of playing and words often brings out new associations, memories or significant dreams in patients. In the field, recognizable countertransferential feelings become perceptible to the analyst's listening. It is the moment when the possibility arises of giving verbal form to metaphors that have previously appeared in the playing field, and of attempting a metaphorical interpretation through images.

*Mind-body and sandplay.* Another path yet to be explored concerns the mysterious relationship between feeling-toned complexes and the body. In Jung's theoretical approach, repressed or split feelings are thought to continue exerting a subconscious or unconscious influence on an organic level. Body memory, which has been fixed in the complex that has been removed from consciousness and kept at a distance by the defenses, would seem, under favorable field conditions, to continue bringing energic action to bear on the body and cause variations both in the kinesthesis in general and in individual organs or organic systems. According to this point of view, feelings that are repressed for purposes of adaptation as we develop, or emotions that are split and never expressed because incompatible with the environment, can all at once find a psychic field suitable for breaking into the ego complex and the body framework that is its organic substrate.

When the affective charge of a repressed complex is reactivated by an emotional field or emotions are released that have never established contact with the ego, the reaction of this central complex (seen as a conscious or unconscious feeling-toned unit) would be at once psychological and somatic. One may assume that the ongoing charge can possibly be what determines on a physical level the choice of organs and perhaps even the characteristic forms of psychosomatic or organic disorders. This assumption, which seeks to discover what the dynamics are between the ego complex and other complexes also on a body level, opens a still unexplored territory for research in which sandplay can play an important role.

The goal is to try and stimulate a disposition to represent in patients with definite organic pathological syndromes. Today a relationship is believed to exist between a personality-structure and a predisposition for particular physical ailments. It would be very useful in this research to bring out the unconscious imaginal dimension in patients suffering from different organic or psychosomatic disorders. The two levels of symbolization typical of sandplay, as I mentioned earlier, may suggest a way for recurring differences and similarities to be grasped. It would be equally important to be able to show how the imaginal processes set going in sandplay take shape with regard to the way individual cases progress.

I believe that this research, as yet to be undertaken, into the relationships between mind and body can open up a perspective on other basic aspects connected with the visualization of emotions anchored in the somatic substratum. Again I am reminded of the assumption that is central to my research in the present volume.

Giving emotions a visual representation changes the energic relationship between the ego complex and the secondary complexes: does this transformation also have an effect on the somatic substratum of the complex-structure and therefore exert an influence on organic functioning? Can the visualization of deep emotional tensions change the organic responses to pathological disorders?

The possibility of carrying out large-scale research could lead to some interesting surprises. In child therapy, where sandplay has long been in use, in hospitals, as well, the first reports have already come in, regarding both psychosomatic disorders such as loss of hair and dermatitus, and organic disorders such as diabetes or neoplasia. In children suffering from cancer, for example, a significant difference has been noticed. It would seem that some of them, who "staged" in sandplay the representation of violent clashes with archaic personifications, apparently had greater prospects of recovery and responded better to pharmacological and surgical treatment. It is as if representing the vital struggle taking place in their organism reflected a potentiality and a more favorable progress. In other children, whose scenes seemed to be stereotyped and aimed at covering up the organic drama taking place, the tumor metastasis progress was faster and more violent. Aside from any possible explanation of the emotional dynamics to be found in these cases, the fact remains that, as appears in the way the play scene is organized, the visualization of deep emotional charges seems to correspond to a different progress of the disease.[104] This first data would seem to confirm that this is indeed a highly promising field of research. Sandplay gives a perspective on the mysterious world of body-mind relationships and on the meaning that the unfolding of a transforming symbolic representation can have in the psychic and physical economy.

## 3 Children Continue to Show the Way

To succeed in understanding the origins of emotional conflicts and to indicate the guiding principles of the theory of technique in psychotherapeutic practice and in theoretical formulation, children and their world have always been the point of reference. This same metaphor seemed to be the most suited to represent and express the mysterious world of drives, of the invasive emotions that are their prime subjective expression, all the way to the ultimate possibility of controlling, in an increasingly thoughtful and conscious fashion, their at once creative and destructive force.

The data acquired over years of research has opened up new horizons through the direct observation of children and babies, which has taught, and is still teaching, us much about the metabolism of feelings and about the role

[104] In pediatric hospitals like the "Bambino Gesù" in Rome, research of this kind through sandplay has been underway for some time. See Marinucci (1989, 1977).

emotional responses to the environment play in the long and difficult journey we take to define ourselves and to be.

Sandplay in adult analytical psychotherapy has gone further. Understanding and treating feelings through body experience means regaining the capacity to perceive, regaining the levels of consciousness and of elaboration which were once ours in childhood, whereas the defenses of the ego tend to wall all feeling into repetitive pathological circuits. So, by offering access to communication through images, sandplay makes it possible for vitality to be restored to the experienced event, which is often only partially conveyed by words.

In conclusion, I would like to give my poet friend, Luciano De Giovanni (1996, p. 109), the last word, as he addresses the mystery of playing with the same fullness of heart I feel at the end of my journey through the landscapes of the psyche:

*After so many sounds*
*and images*
*and jumbled words*

*a return to earth,*
*to the roots*
*to the fading of memories*

*to the silent prayer,*
*to the unscathed faith*
*of the happy times long past.*

# Acknowledgements

I would like to thank everyone who has let me to see and understand the landscapes of the psyche by sharing conflicts, sorrows and moments of joyful surprise in analysis. I should also like to thank my wife, Livia and Luciana Baldaccini, Gianni and Silvia Grassi, and the many other friends who with their affectionate presence and assistance have accompanied me in the slow evolution of this book. I would especially like to thank my colleagues at the Analytical Laboratory of Images who, by continuing down the same path, are opening up new horizons in the clinical use of sandplay as well as in research. I should also like to thank my translator, Robert W. Mann, for his sensitive and skillful rendering of the original Italian text, broadening his horizons beyond the linguistic barrier. Last, I would like to thank Daniela Iorio, my longtime friend and fellow analyst, for her precious help and constructive suggestions during the course of the English translation.

# Bibliography

Citations to the work of Agamben, Artaud, Bertolucci, Calvino, Durand refer to the Italian editions, and the interested reader is referred to:

Agamben, Giorgio (1993), *Stanzas:Word and Phantasm in Western Culture*, Minneapolis: University of Minnesota Press
Artaud, Antonin (1994): The *Theater and Its Double,* New York: Grove Press
Bertolucci, Attilio (1994): *Selected Poems*, Northumberland: Bloodaxe Books
Calvino, Italo (1996), *Six Memos for the Next Millennium*, New York: Vintage
Durand, Gilbert (1999), *The Anthropological Structures of the Imaginary*, Mt Nebo, Australia: Boombana Publications

AA.VV. (1998), *Affetti e pensiero*, Bergamo: Moretti & Vitali
AA.VV. (1982), *Il pensiero di D.W.Winnicott*, Rome: Armando
Abbagnano, N. (1993), *Storia della filosofia*, Vol.4, Turin: Utet
Agamben, Giorgio (1977), *Stanze. La parola e il fantasma nella cultura occidentale,* Turin: Einaudi
Aite, Paolo:
– (1970), "La tecnica della sabbia nella psicologia di C.G.Jung," *Rivista di psicologia analitica*, Vol. 1, No. 2
– (1976), "Immaginazione come comunicazione," *Rivista di psicologia analitica*, Vol. 7, No. 1
– (1978), "Ego and Image," *Journal of Analitycal Psychology*, Vol. 23, No. 4
– (1989), "Percorsi dell'immagine. Il Gioco della Sabbia nella terapia e nella ricerca," *Rivista di psicologia analitica*, No. 39
– (1994), "Sognando con le mani. Il Gioco della Sabbia nella terapia analitica dell'adulto," *Rivista di psicologia analitica*, No. 50
– (1998), "Vitalità del negativo: creatività e distruttività in analisi," *Rivista di psicologia analitica*, No. 5
Aite, Paolo, Carotenuto, Aldo (1989), *Itinerari del pensiero junghiano*, Milan: Cortina

Ammann, Ruth (1991), *Healing and Transformation in Sandplay: Creative Processes Become Visible*, Chicago: Open Court Publishing Company
Anzieu, Didier (1989), *The Skin Ego,* New Haven: Yale University Press
Artaud, Antonin (1938), *Il teatro e il suo doppio*, Turin: Einaudi
Arthus, H. (1947), "Le test du village," *Psyche*, Vol.19
Aversa, L.:
- (1995), a cura di, *Fondamenti di psicologia analitica*, Rome: Laterza
- (1999), a cura di, *Psicologia analitica: la teoria della clinica*, Turin: Bollati Boringhieri

Bachelard, Gaston (1943), *Psicoanalisi dell'aria,* Como: Red 1997
Balint, Michael:
- (1959), *Thrills and Regressions*, Madison: International Universities Press
- (1968), *The Basic Fault: Therapeutic Aspects of Regression*, London: Tavistock Publications

Baranger, W., Baranger, M. (1990), *La situazione psicoanalitica come campo bipersonale*, Milan: Cortina
Benedetti, G.:
- (1980), *Alienazione e personazione nella psicoterapia della malattia mentale*, Milan: Cortina
- (1991), *Paziente e terapeuta nell'esperienza psicotica*, Turin: Bollati Boringhieri
- (1997), *La psicoterapia come sfida esistenziale*, Milan: Cortina

Bernhard, E. (1969), *Mitobiografia*, Milan: Adelphi
Berry, P. (1974), *An Approach to the Dream*, Putnam: Spring Publication
Bertolucci, Attilio (1990), *Sirio*, Milan: Garzanti
Blumenberg, Hans (1979), *Work on Myth*, Translation by R. Wallace, Cambridge: The MIT Press, 1988
Bolgar, H., Fischer, L.K. (1940), "The Toy Test: a Psychodiagnostic Method," *Psychology Bulletin*, Vol. 34
Bona Pompei, A. (1997), "Domina il silenzio dove non è mai stato suono," *Studi junghiani*, Vol. 3, No. 5-6
Boncinelli, Edoardo (1999), Il cervello, la mente e l'anima, Milan: Mondadori
Borges, Jorge Luis (2000), "The Maker" (Kenneth Krabbenhoft, Trans.) in Alexander Coleman (Ed.) *Selected Poems*, London/New York: The Penguin Books

Bühler, C., Kelley, G. (1941), *The World Test. A Measurement of Emotional Disturbance. Manual of Direction*, New York: Psychic Corp.

Calvino, Italo (1988), Lezioni americane: sei proposte per il prossimo millennio, Milan: Garzanti

Carotenuto, Aldo (1992), *Trattato di psicologia analitica*, Turin: Utet

Cassirer, Ernst (1946), *Language and Myth,* Translated by Susanne K. Langer, Mineola: Dover Publications

Castellana, Franco, Malinconico, Angelo (2002), *Giochi antichi e parole nuove. Il Gioco della Sabbia in campo analitico*, Milan: Vivarium

Chianese, Domenico (1998), *Costruzioni e campo analitico*, Rome: Borla

Colli, Giorgio (1969), *Filosofia dell'espressione*, Milan: Adelphi

Coppola Pignatelli, P. (1982), *Spazio e immaginario: maschile e femminile in architettura*, Rome: Officina

De Giovanni, Luciano (1996), *Con te prigioniero*, Rome: Anterem

Di Benedetto, Antonio (1991), "L'ascolto del pre-verbale come principio degli affetti," *Rivista di Psicoanalisi*, Vol. 37, No. 2

Durand, Gilbert (1963), *Le strutture antropologiche dell'immaginario*, Bari: Dedalo, 1972

Eagle, Morris N. (1984), *Recent Developments in Psychoanalysis: A Critical Evaluation*, Cambridge: Harvard University Press

Erikson, E.H. (1987), *Way of Looking at Things: Selected Papers 1930-1980*, Editor: S.P. Schlien, New York: W.W. Norton & Co.

Fersurella, Sandra (1997), "Quel che diventa il tocco misterioso," *Studi junghiani*, Vol. 3, No. 5-6

Fordham, Michael:

- (1956), "Active Imagination and Imaginative Activity," *Journal of Analytical Psychology*, Vol. 1, No. 3
- (1967), "Active Imagination, Deintegration or Disintegration?" *Journal of Analytical Psychology*, Vol. 12, No. 1
- (1976), *The Self and Autism*, London: Karnac Books
- (1996), *Children As Individuals*, London: Free Association Books

Franz von, Marie-Luise:

- (1958), "Aktive Imagination in der Psychologie von C.G. Jung", in *Religion und Psychotherapie*, Stuttgart: Klett
- (1978), *Alchemical Active Imagination*, New York: Spring

- (1999), *Archetypal Dimensions of the Psyche*, Boston: Shambhala
Friedman, Harrie (1994), *Sandplay: Past, Present and Future*, Oxford: Routledge
Freud, Sigmund (1953), *The Standard Edition of the Complete Psychological Works of Sigmund Freud*, London: The Hogarth Press:
- *Extracts From the Fliess Papers* (1950 [1892-1899]), Vol. I
- *The Interpretation of Dreams* (1900), Vol. IV
- *On Dreams* (1900), Vol. V
- *The Psychopathology of Everyday Life* (1901), Vol. VI
- *Analysis of a Phobia in a Five-Year-Old Boy* (1909), Vol. X
- *Beyond the Pleasure Principle* (1920), Vol. XVIII
- *New Introductory Lectures on Psycho-Analysis* (1933 [1932]), Vol. XXII
- *Findings, Ideas, Problems* (1938), Vol. XXIII
Gabbriellini, G., Nissim S.:
- (1988), *Sandplay with a psicotic child*, in Sidoli M., Davies M., *Jungian Child Psychoterapy: Individuation in childhood*, London: Karnac Books
- (1989), "Spazio, corpo, immagini: il gioco della sabbia nell'autismo e nella psicosi infantile," in Aite (1989)
Gaburri, Eugenio (1997), *Emozione e interpretazione. Psicoanalisi del campo emotivo*, Turin: Bollati Boringhieri
Gadamer, H.G. (1960), *Truth and Method*, First Published 1975, Trans. J. Weinsheimer and D.G.Marshall, London: Sheed and Ward, 1988
Gaddini, Eugenio:
- (1992), "Fantasie difensive precoci e processo psicoanalitico", *Rivista di Psicoanalisi*, Vol. 28
- (1989), *Scritti 1953-1985*, Milan: Cortina
Galimberti, Umberto:
- (1983), *Il corpo,* Milan: Feltrinelli
- (1999), *Psiche e techne. L'uomo nell'età della tecnica*, Milan: Feltrinelli
Garzonio, Marco (1997), "Da una costola di Jung. Il processo di individuazione nella Sandplay", in Montecchi, 1997
Grassi, Ernesto (1989), *Potenza dell'immagine: rivalutazione della retorica*, Milan: Guerini
Hannah, Barbara:
- (1953), *Some Remarks on Active Imagination*, New York: Spring

- (1981), *Encounters with the Soul: Active Imagination, as Developed by C.G. Jung*, Santa Monica: Sigo Press

Heidegger, Martin:
- (1959a), *On the Way to Language*, Translation by P. Herz, San Francisco: HarperOne, 1982
- (1959b), *Discourse on Thinking*, Translation by J. Anderson and E.H. Freund, New York: Harper Perennial, 1966/1969

Hillman, James (1978), *Re-Visioning Psychology*, New York: HarperCollins

Humbert, E.G.:
- (1979), "Il ruolo dell'immagine nella psicologia analitica," *Rivista di Psicologia Analitica*, No. 20
- (1988), *C. G. Jung: The Fundamentals of Theory and Practice*, New York: Chiron Publications

Jervis, Giovanni (1989), *La psicoanalisi come esercizio critico*, Milan: Garzanti

Jung, Carl Gustav (1973), *The Collected Works of C.G. Jung*, Translating by R.F.C. Hull, Editors Herbert Read, Michael Fordham, Gerhard Adler, London: Routledge & Kegan Paul:
- (1912/1952), *Symbols of Transformation*, Vol. 5
- (1919), *Instinct and the Unconscious*, Vol.8
- (1920/1948), *The Psychological Foundations of Belief in Spirits*, Vol. 8
- (1921), *Psychological Types*, Vol. 6
- (1928/1931), *Analytic Psychology and Weltanschauung*, Vol. 8
- (1929), *Problems of Modern Psychotherapy*, Vol. 16
- (1929/1957), *Commentary on "The Secret of the Golden Flower,"* Vol. 13
- (1931), *The Aims of Psychotherapy*, Vol. 16
- (1934), *A Review of the Complex Theory*, Vol. 8
- (1935a), *Principles of Practical Psychotherapy*, Vol. 16
- (1935b), *The Tavistock Lectures*, Vol. 18
- (1937), *Psychological Factors Determining Human Behaviour*, Vol. 8
- (1938/1940), *Psychology and Religion*, Vol. 11
- (1939), *Foreword to Suzuki's "Introduction to Zen Buddhism,"* Vol. 11
- (1940), *The Psychology of the Child Archetype*, Vol. 9/I
- (1942/1954), *Transformation Symbolism in the Mass*, Vol. 11
- (1944), *Psychology and Alchemy*, Vol. 12
- (1945), *Medicine and Psychotherapy*, Vol. 16

- (1945/1954), *The Philosophical Tree*, Vol. 13
- (1946), *The Psychology of the Transference*, Vol. 16
- (1947/1954), *On the Nature of the Psyche*, Vol. 8
- (1955/1956), *Mysterium Coniunctionis*, Vol. 14/II
- (1957/1958), *The Transcendent Function*, Vol. 8

Jung, C.G. (1961), *Memories, Dreams and Reflections*, Edited by Aniela Jaffé, Transl. by R. and C. Winston, London: Collins The Fontana Library, 1967

Kalff, Dora:

- (1966), *Sandplay: A Psychotherapeutic Approach to the Psyche*, Santa Monica, Ca.: Sigo Press, 1980
- (1988), "Beyond the Shadow," *Archives of Sandplay Therapy*, No. 1
- (1991), "Introduction to Sandplay Therapy," *Journal of Sandplay Therapy*, Vol. 1, p. 9-15

Khan, Masud M.R.:

- (1974), *The Privacy of the Self: Papers on Psychoanalytic Theory and Technique*, London: Hogarth Press
- (1975), Winnicott, D.W., *Through Pediatrics to Psychoanalysis*, Introduction by M.Masud R. Khan, New York: Basic Books
- (1977), Introduzione, in AA.VV., *Il pensiero di D.W. Winnicott*, Rome: Armando, 1982

Klein, Melanie:

- (1923), *Contributions to Psycho-Analysis 1921-1945*, London: Hogarth Press, 1965
- (1927), "Symposium on Child Analysis," *International Journal of Psycho-Analysis*, Vol.8, pp. 377-380

La Forgia, M., Marozza, M. Ilena (2000), *L'altro e la sua mente*, Rome: Fioriti

Lai, Maria (2000), *Lo scialle della luna*, Sassari: Edizioni A.D.

Leowald, Hans (1979), "Reflections on Psychoanalytic Process and Its Therapeutic Potential," *Psychoanalytical Study of Child*, Vol. 34, p. 155-167

Lowenfeld, Margaret (1939), "The World Pictures of Children," *British Journal of Medicine and Psychology*, Vol.18, p. 65-101

Mabille, P. (1950), *La technique du test du village*, Paris: Presses Universitaires de France

Màdera, Romano (1998), *Carl Gustav Jung: biografia e teoria*, Milan: Bruno Mondadori

Maffei, Giuseppe:
- (1977), Il mestiere di uomo. Ricerca sulla psicosi, Venice: Marsilio
- (1986), I linguaggi della psiche, Milan: Bompiani

Mahler, S.M.:
- (1968), *On Human Symbiosis and the Vicissitudes of Individuation Volume 1 Infantile Psychosis*, Madison: International University Press
- (1979), *The selected papers of Margaret S. Mahler, M.D. Volume I. Infantile Psychosis and Early Contributions*, New York: J. Aronson

Martini, Giuseppe (1998), *Ermeneutica e narrazione*, Turin: Bollati Boringhieri

Matte Blanco, Ignacio (1998), *The Unconscious as Infinite Sets: An Essay in Bi-logic*, London: Karnac Books

Montecchi, Francesco:
- (1984), *La psicoterapia infantile junghiana*, Rome: Il Pensiero Scientifico
- (1999), "Hands that Talk and Analytic Listening," *Journal of Sandplay Therapy*, VIII (1), 25-68
- (2004), "Transference, Counter-transference, Resistance: From Relationship to Representation," *Journal of Sandplay Therapy*, XIII, (2), 54-71

Moretti, G. (1979), "Schzofrenia: antropologia dell'incontro psicoterapeutico," *Giornale Studi di Psicologia Dinamica*, Vol. 3, No. 5, pp. 94-115

Mucchielli, Roger (1960), *Le "jeu du monde" et le test du village imaginaire*, Paris: Presses Universitaires de France

Navone, A. (1998), "The Double Birth: The Clinical Story of Emmanuel," *Journal of Sandplay Therapy*, VII, (1), pp. 27-60

Neumann, Erich (1995), *The Origins and History of Consciousness*, Princeton: Princeton University Press

Nietzsche, Friedrich (1879), *Human, All Too Human: A Book for Free Spirits,* R.J. Hollingdale (Ed. and Trans.), Cambridge: University Press

Otto, Rudolf (1917), *The Idea of the Holy*, Translation by John W. Harvey, New York: Oxford University Press, 1958

Pezzarossa, Bianca, Zanasi, Marco (1999), *Psicologia analitica e psicologia dei gruppi*, Rome: Borla

Plato:
- *Phaedrus*, http://classics.mit.edu/ Plato/phaedrus.html

Resnik, Salomon (1994), *Mental Space*, London: Karnac Books

Ricoeur, Paul:
- (1988), "La componente narrativa della psicoanalisi," *Metaxù*, No. 5, p. 7-19
- (1990), *Oneself as Another*, Trans. Kathleen Blamey, Chicago: University Of Chicago Press

Rilke, Rainer Maria (1993), *Letters to a Young Poet*, Transl. By M. D. Herter Norton, London/New York: W.W. Norton & Co. First Edition: 1934

Ryce-Menuhin, Joel (1992), *Junghian Sandplay: The Wonderful Therapy*, London/New York: Routledge

Sami Ali (1974), *L'espace imaginaire*, Paris: Gallimard

Segal, Hanna (1988), *Introduction to the Work of Melanie Klein*, London: Karnac Books

Starobinski, Jeanne (1984), *Ritratto dell'artista da saltimbanco*, Turin: Bollati Boringhieri

Tagliagambe, Silvano (1997), *Epistemologia del confine*, Milan: Il Saggiatore

Tarantini, Lidia (1996), *Lo sguardo che ascolta: immagine e parola nell'interpretazione analitica*, Rome: SEP Adversal

Trevi, Mario (1986), *Metafora del simbolo*, Milan: Cortina

Trinci, Manuela (1993), *Il bambino che gioca*, Turin: Bollati Boringhieri

Wilbe, K (1981), *Oltre i confini*, Assisi: La Cittadella, 1985

Winnicott, D.W.:
- (1958), *Through Pediatrics to Psychoanalysis: Collected Papers*, London: Routledge 1992
- (1965), *The Family and Individual Development*, London: Tavistock Publications
- (1971), *Playing and Reality* , New York: Routledge, 2005

Woolf, Virginia (1950), *The Waves* http://etext.library.adelaide.edu.au/w/woolf/virginia/w91w/complete.html

# Index

Printed in the United States
91380LV00004B/145-147/A

9 788895 145136